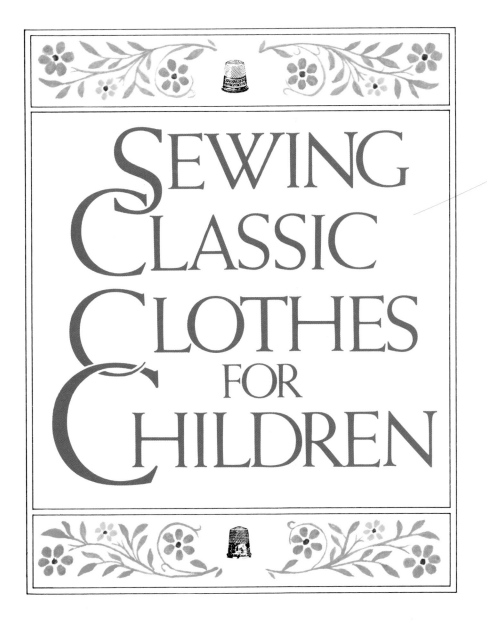

SEWING CLASSIC CLOTHES FOR CHILDREN

SEWING CLASSIC CLOTHES FOR CHILDREN

KITTY BENTON

HEARST BOOKS
NEW YORK

To Nick,
Francie, Kate, Emily, and Louisa,
and
to the wisdom of the snail

Acknowledgments

I never met a librarian I didn't like, and I gratefully thank the following staffs for sharing their knowledge so eagerly and for their frequent bursts of inspiration: New York Public Library; Library of Congress, Washington, D.C.; Frick Art Reference Library, New York; Irene Lewisohn Costume Reference Library, Metropolitan Museum of Art, New York; Donnell Children's Room, New York Public Library, New York; Pierpont Morgan Library, New York; Corcoran Gallery of Art Curatorial Library, Washington, D.C. The same is true for the staffs of the National Gallery of Art, Washington, D.C.; The Brooklyn Museum, costume collection, Brooklyn, New York; Metropolitan Museum of Art, costume collection, New York; Smithsonian Institution, costume collection, Washington, D.C.; Winterthur Museum, Wilmington, Delaware; The Boston Museum of Fine Arts.

Thanks also to practically everybody at the Fashion Institute of Technology, New York, but most of all to Marjorie Miller and the staff of the Institute's Library Media Services.

I have frequently raised an eyebrow at other authors' excessive personal acknowledgments, but this book could not be published without thanking (in alphabetical order) each and every one of the following; some for endless and continuing support and some for seemingly small but crucial favors: Ira Bartfield, Nicholas Benton, Louisa Biddle, Allen Bragdon, Sylvia Bigelow, Lily Bourne, Jane Boykin, Sara Callender, Becky Cleveland, Ann Marie Czaykowski, Stella Delacorte (for teaching me to smock on a New York City park bench twenty years ago), Hermine Dreyfuss, Daniel Albert Edge, Axie Gibbons, David Godine, Fitzhugh Green, Barbara Hultman, Marian King, Joan Kirk, and Carlotta Miles.

Special thanks to Sonja Douglas, the art director of this book, for making visions in an author's eye a reality and, if permitted, to Wendy Rieder, my editor, for her faith, persistence, and patience with this paranoid author. Thanks also to all my students at Ruffles and Flourishes, Arlington, Virginia, for their enthusiastic response to many of the special sewing techniques, and for teaching me, in turn.

For their help in contributing fabric for the projects, I also wish to thank the following: Ruffles and Flourishes, Arlington, Virginia; Laura Ashley Inc., New York; G Street Fabric Shop, Washington, D.C.; Wright's Bias Fold Tape Co., New York. Toys in the color photographs, courtesy of Childcraft Education Corp., New York City; red satin quilt (page 4), courtesy of The Posh Postman, Inc., New York City.

Copyright © 1981 by The Hearst Corporation

Picture credits

All photographs of projects © Michael S. Weinberg. 18—Courtesy Library of Congress. 20—"The Cradle" by Claude Monet, National Gallery of Art, Washington, D.C., Collection of Mr. and Mrs. Paul Mellon. 53—Courtesy Earnshaw Publications. 68—The Bettmann Archive. 83—Courtesy the author's family. 84—Illustration reproduced from *The Subject Was Children* by permission of the publishers, E. P. Dutton, New York. 87—*The Delineator,* Butterick Publishing Company Ltd., courtesy of Library/Media Services, Fashion Institute of Technology. 98—"The Daughters of Edward D. Boit" by John S. Sargent, courtesy Museum of Fine Arts, Boston. Gift of Mary Louisa Boit, Florence D. Boit, Jane Hibbard Boit, and Julia Overling Boit. 101—*The Delineator,* see credit above. 116—"Henry L. Wells" (artist unknown), courtesy National Gallery of Art, Washington, D.C. Gift of Edgar William and Bernice Chrysler Garbisch. 138—"Little Girl with Flower Basket" (artist unknown), courtesy National Gallery of Art, Washington, D.C. Gift of Edgar William and Bernice Chrysler Garbisch. 158—Courtesy Library of Congress. 174—Illustration reproduced by permission of the McCall Pattern Company; *The Delineator,* see credit above. Spot engravings on other pages from facsimile edition of an 1895 issue of the Montgomery Ward & Co. catalogue, copyright 1969 by Dover Publications Inc., New York City.

Contents

Introduction

ashion in dress would head most lists of things that are forever changing. But some fashions seem never to change; they become classics instead, varying little over the decades and even the centuries. For example, while it's immediately apparent that the photograph reproduced here is from another era—with the adults' clothing, the mother's hairdo, and the children's shoes all giveaways—the children's clothes, perfect examples of the classic style, are hardly different from those that young children wear today when they dress for formal occasions. As smocked dresses and sailor suits have been classics for a hundred years, so will they doubtless remain classics for another hundred.

While there are dozens of classic styles of children's clothing, all share certain characteristics: simplicity, durability, and timelessness—characteristics also shared by all of the projects in this book. The projects can be made from the original patterns furnished here, or by adapting commercial patterns now on the market. And, most importantly, they are all potential heirlooms. Long after the original wearer has outgrown these clothes, they can be passed on to brothers and sisters, their children, and even grandchildren.

Until about the 1920s, all clothing, especially children's, was either made at home or by a professional dressmaker. One of the most well-known specialists in children's clothing was Madame Lanvin, the

great couturière. A widow, she began supporting herself by making hats, and later diversified into making dresses for her clients and then for their children. Today, perfume bottles that carry the Lanvin name bear a reminder of those earlier times: a small image of a mother bending over her child.

Today, for reasons of cost, the demand for children's couturier clothing has diminished considerably; but it is still possible to produce custom-made, classic clothes for children, as this book amply demonstrates.

Many old natural-fiber fabrics, with such quaint names as nainsook, dimity, and mull, have given way to test-tube wonders—nylon, polyester, and acrylic. But survivors from earlier times, such as cotton calico, gingham and broadcloth, real linen, wool plaids, and fine velvet, are all manufactured today. And something else survives: sewing books from as long ago as 1770 show that the basics of construction and hand sewing have remained remarkably constant from country to country for more than 200 years. With sewing machines now doing much of the work, we may no longer devote twelve pages to teaching the running stitch, as Wilhelmina Hutchins did in 1914, but handwork has certainly not been excluded. Now it is saved for the fun part: smocking, embroidery, appliqué, and quilting.

In addition to the clothes and accessories projects offered here, a section on dressmaking skills explains and demonstrates all the sewing techniques required for making each of the projects. Also included are a list of mail-order sources for patterns, fabrics, and notions, as well as a section describing the care and cleaning of children's clothes. A few quick projects that are pure joy to make and to give as gifts have also been included, in the hope that sewing the classics will bring you pleasure, not only in the making, but in the enjoyment of the children who wear them.

———————— • ————————

This portrait of Theodore Roosevelt, Jr. (the president's son) and his family, made around 1919, is a lesson in how some fashions change and others endure. Eleanor Roosevelt's hairdo, her husband's uniform, and the children's shoes look dated, indeed, but the smocked dress worn by the daughter, the sailor suits on the boys, and the teddy bear are all timeless favorites.

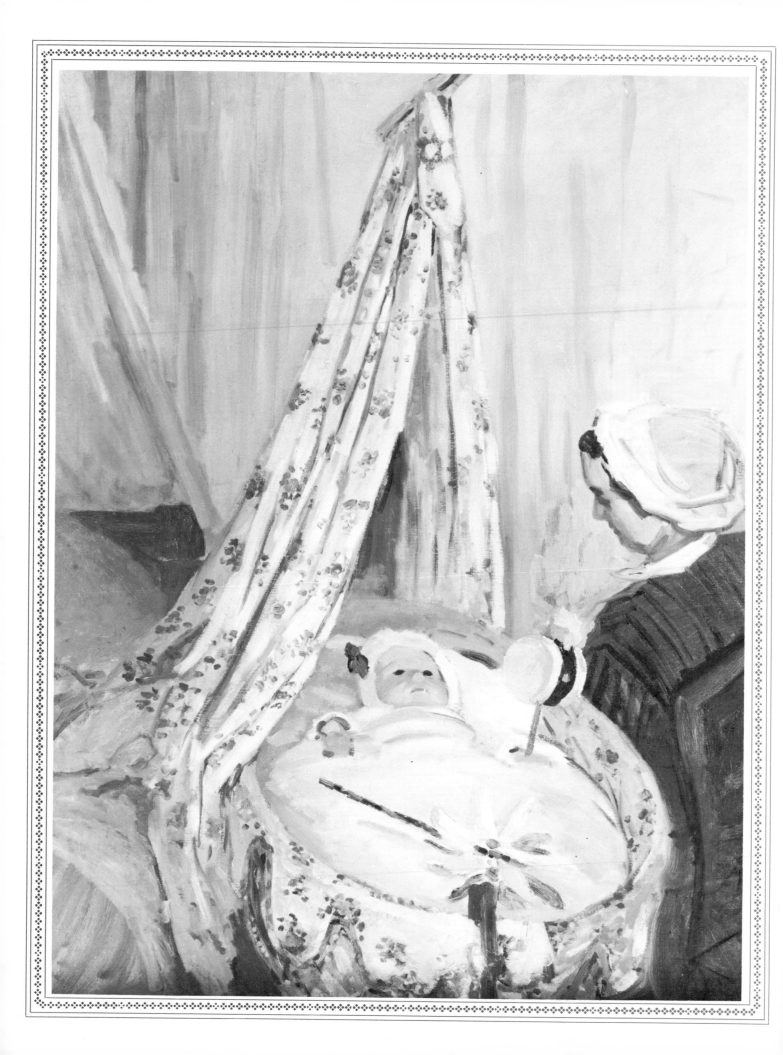

Timeless Gifts

Welcome, little stranger! A baby is born and suddenly we find a stranger in our midst. We welcome the new one with smiles and affection, as we become mother, father, sister, brother, grandparent, or proud friend. It matters not whether we have said hello to many babies, or are overcome with joy at a new experience; our response is invariably the same—to shower the little person with love and gifts. Such generosity is as old as recorded history, and so is the problem it raises: just what gifts shall we give the young child? For a new baby is a tiny enigma. Will he laugh or scowl? Will he bring us pride or sorrow? Will he wander the earth or stay among us? What gift shall we give the unknown?

Even if a baby's personality remains shrouded for a time in mystery, every child cries out at first for warmth, comfort, and love. All of these needs can be fulfilled in lovely ways by giving a young child any of the projects included in this chapter—all baby gifts that have changed little over the years, all gifts that will become treasured possessions.

"Welcome, little stranger!" These words themselves go back 200 years. They were found spelled out on a baby's pincushion from 1779, and they remind us that many types of baby gifts have been with us for centuries. But on the other hand, it takes only one generation for a gift to become an heirloom, a prized family possession that can be given and given again. Who has not heard as a child, "Your grandmother made this for your uncle when *he* was a baby." Thus the links between the generations are forged, and the pleasure grows with each repetition of the giving, especially when the gift is handmade.

You will find many types of projects to make in this chapter. Some are so easy that they can be completed in just a few hours; the frothy, delicate little lace cap is one of these. Others, such as the quilt, are a good deal more challenging. There are also two bibs, two different kinds of caps, a blanket, bunting, pillow, pincushion, and even a teddy bear—enough gifts to fill any baby's needs and to please anyone who sews. The introduction to each project will give you historical details and suggestions so that any project you make will be sewn in a true heirloom tradition.

In his 1867 painting "The Cradle," the French Impressionist Claude Monet portrayed not only his wife, Camille, and their son, Jean, but also a few of those special accessories that loving parents have given babies for generations: a frilly cap, a carefully worked blanket, and a pillow.

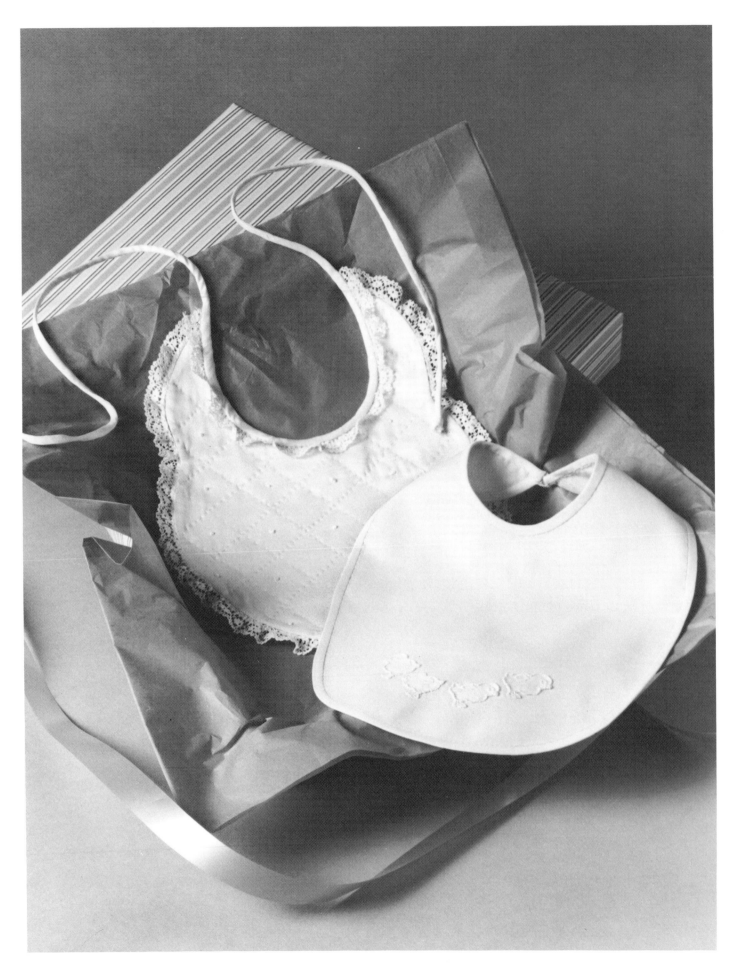

Quilted Bib

Bibs will be in style as long as babies drool. This quilted bib is adapted from heirlooms of silk in the archives of the Costume Institute of the Metropolitan Museum of Art in New York. Fortunately, we now have synthetic substitutes for silk that are certainly more practical, and, if well chosen, they can be just as lovely in the form of a dress-up bib. This is an ideal gift project because it looks so beautiful and only requires a few hours and minimal supplies to make. As a first project in quilting, the bib is unbeatable; it would even be a suitable undertaking for a child.

Materials

½ yard (.5 m) synthetic satin or twill, or any lustrous fabric with a tight weave

⅜ yard (.35 m) backing fabric

1¼ yards (1.2 m) of ⅞″-wide (22-mm) pregathered lace edging

A 9″ × 12″ (22.9 × 30.5-cm) piece of polyester batting

Quilting thread

1 skein white 6-strand embroidery floss

Making the pattern and cutting the fabric

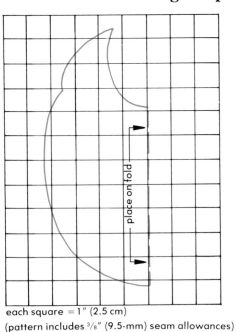

each square = 1″ (2.5 cm)
(pattern includes ⅜″ (9.5-mm) seam allowances)

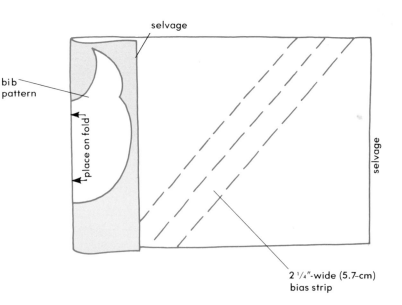

1. Cutting the fabric. Enlarge the pattern to the scale indicated and cut it out following the directions on page 175. One at a time, cut the pattern from the folded bib fabric, the backing, and the batting.

From the remaining bib fabric, cut enough 2¼″-wide (5.7-cm) bias strips to measure 41″ (104 cm) when pieced together for the neck binding and ties.

Sewing the bib

1. Assembling the bib. Baste the ⅞″-wide (22-mm) pregathered lace around the outside edge of the bib, right sides together, aligning the seam lines of the lace and the bib.

Lay the backing right side down over the right side of the lace-trimmed bib fabric.

The batting. Place the batting on top of the backing, aligning the edges, and baste all three layers together ⅜″ (9.5 mm) from the outside edges.

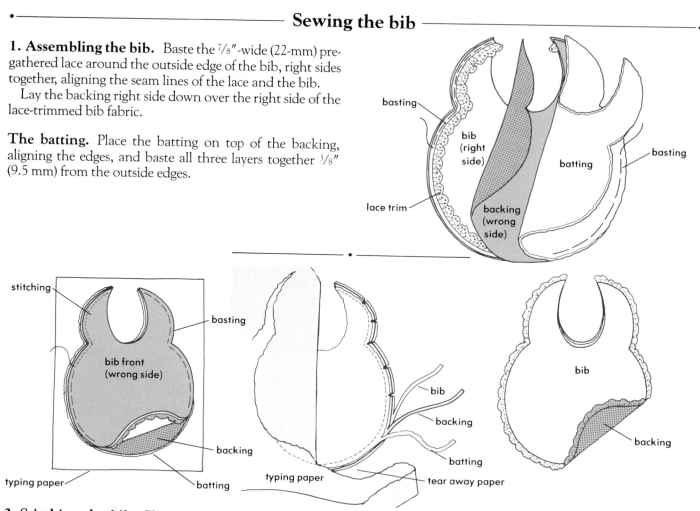

2. Stitching the bib. Place the bib, batting side down, on a piece of typing paper to keep the batting from snagging in the feed dog of the machine. Stitch ⅜″ (9.5 mm) from the edge, using the basting stitches as a seam guide, and taking one stitch across the corner as shown. Do not stitch around the neck edge.

Tear away the paper, and trim the seam allowances one by one, each to a different width. Notch the seam allowances along the outer curves, and clip them into the corners. Turn the bib right side out through the neck edge, and press the edges lightly.

3. Marking and basting the bib for quilting. Baste the neck edges of the bib together. Using a transparent or regular ruler and an embroidery marking pen with water-soluble ink, draw a line on the front of the bib that bisects it vertically. Then draw a line that bisects the bib horizontally between the lowest part of the neck edge and the bottom. Measure and mark a point ¾″ (19 mm) away from the center in each direction on the vertical and horizontal lines. Draw four crossing diagonal lines each connecting two of the dots on one side of the center point, as shown. Baste the layers of fabric and the batting together along the two center and four diagonal lines. Draw additional lines parallel to the first diagonals at 1″ (2.5-cm) intervals across the entire bib.

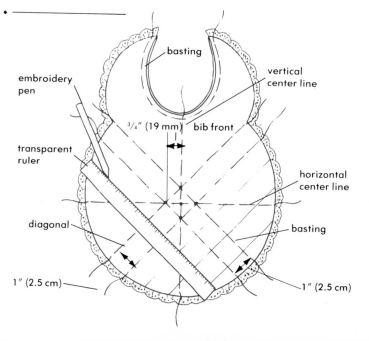

4. The quilting. Using quilting thread and starting at the center, sew rows of small running stitches along the marked diagonal lines. (Although special quilting needles are available that are shorter than regular sharps, they are not really necessary for quilting small projects such as this.) Do not attempt to pick up too many stitches at once, and be sure that the stitches go through all the layers: bib front, batting, and backing. Remove the basting.

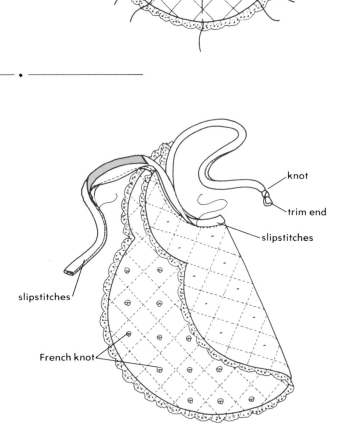

5. Finishing the bib. Pin the lace edging right side up to the right side of the bib, along the neckline, aligning the seam lines. Baste ³/₈″ (9.5 mm) from the edge.

The neck binding. Fold the pieced bias binding strip in half lengthwise, right side out, and press without stretching. Notch the center of one edge, as shown, then align that edge along the right side of the bib neckline, matching the notch to the bib center, and pin it in place. Stitch down the entire length and both ends of the bias strip, ³/₈″ (9.5 mm) from the edge. Do not stretch the binding or trim the seam allowances.

Turn the binding to the back of the bib, over the seam allowances, turn the raw edge under ³/₈″ (9.5 mm), and slipstitch it to the bib. Fold in the raw edges of each tie, hiding the stitching made earlier, and slipstitch the folded edges together. Knot the ends of the ties and trim away the excess fabric.

The embroidery. Using three strands of white embroidery floss, make a French knot in the center of every square across the center row, horizontally. Make similar rows of French knots in alternate rows of squares across the bib.

Appliquéd Bib

Gifts for baby boys are hard to find. Hence, this bib, which can be made in a couple of hours, is a quick, easy, and attractive solution to the problem. The appliqué pictured in the photograph was purchased, but if you prefer to design your own, use a crisp organdy or lawn, and follow the instructions in the "Dressmaking Skills" section of this book, making sure that the proportions of your design match the delicacy of the fabric and binding. Other unfamiliar stitches and techniques are also explained in "Dressmaking Skills."

Materials

Two ¹/₂ yards (.5 m) lawn, batiste, or cotton in contrasting colors

Sewing thread to match the fabrics

Appliqué, ready-made or original

A ¹/₄″-diameter (6-mm) white button

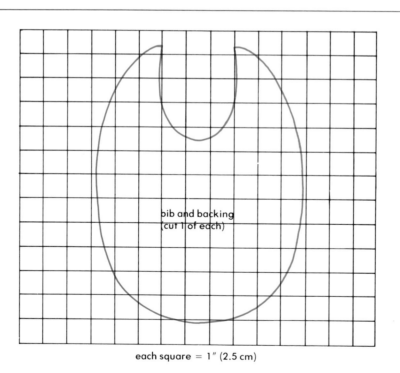

bib and backing
(cut 1 of each)

each square = 1″ (2.5 cm)

1. Cutting the fabric. Enlarge the bib pattern according to the scale indicated and cut it out, following the instructions on page 175. Lay one piece of fabric on top of the other, wrong sides together, and pin the pattern to the fabric pieces, making sure to place it in one corner of the fabric to minimize waste. Cut the bib pieces and choose one for the front and the constrasting one for the backing.

From the backing fabric, cut two bias strips 1¹/₈″ wide (2.9 cm) for French binding. One strip should be the length of the outside edge of the bib plus 1″ (2.5 cm), the other strip the length of the neck edge, plus ¹/₂″ (13 mm). The binding will look best if each strip is continuous and does not have to be pieced.

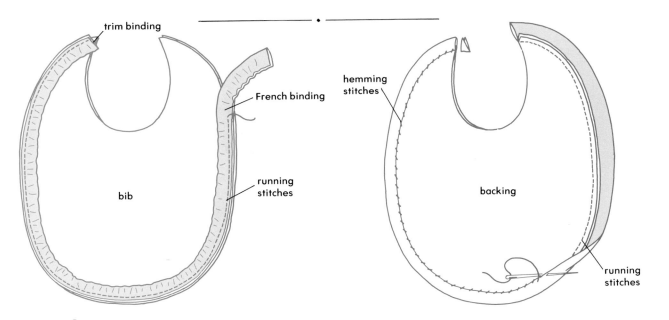

2. Assembling the bib. Pin the bib to the backing fabric, wrong sides together.

The outer binding. Pin the binding for the outside edge of the bib in place, aligning the cut edges and easing the binding slightly against the edge of the bib as you work, so that the folded edge of the binding will lie smooth when finished. This will cause both edges of the binding to ripple slightly.

Using small machine or hand running stitches, sew the binding to the bib $3/16''$ (5 mm) from the edge. Starting at the bottom of the bib and working up one side at a time, turn the folded edge of the binding over the unfinished edge of the bib, encasing the seam allowances, and pin it in place at the back of the bib. Hem the binding by catching it to the stitches visible on the underside of the bib. Trim the ends of the binding even with the neck edge of the bib.

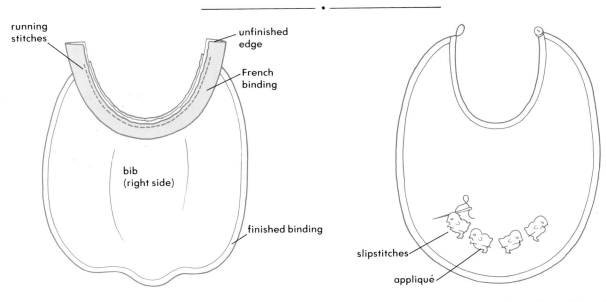

The neck binding. Center the second bias strip on the neck edge and pin, then attach it as you did the binding for the outer edge of the bib, working from the center outward and covering the cut ends of the outer binding. Turn the ends in even with the outer edge of the bib, and slipstitch them closed.

Attaching the button. Make a thread loop buttonhole for the button on one corner of the neck edge, and sew the button to the other corner.

The appliqué. Pin the appliqué in place, and secure it around the edges with tiny slipstitches.

Lace Cap

This cap is so easy to make that it requires no pattern and takes only a couple of hours to complete. It is also very inexpensive, though it looks costly, and makes a perfect companion to the christening dress on page 68. You may either draw the pattern directly on the fabric with a dressmaker's chalk pencil or first make a paper pattern, if you feel safer with that. Unfamiliar stitches and techniques are explained in the "Dressmaking Skills" section of this book.

Materials

½ yard (.5 m) white lawn, batiste, or similar lightweight fabric

White sewing thread

1 yard (.95 m) of ½"-wide (13-mm) white lace beading

½ yard (.5 m) of 3"-wide (7.6-cm) white lace, scalloped on one edge

2 yards (1.9 m) of ¼"-wide (6-mm) double-faced white satin ribbon

2½ yards (2.3 m) of ⅝"-wide (16-mm) double-faced white satin ribbon

Embroidery floss: white and pale green

Clear nail polish

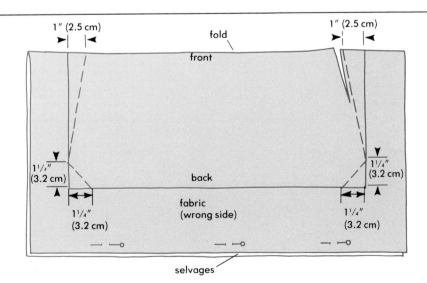

1. Cutting the fabric. Fold the fabric in half lengthwise, wrong side out, and pin the edges together.

Using the folded edge as one of the long sides, mark a rectangle that measures 15¾" × 7¼" (40 × 18.4 cm) with dressmaker's chalk. The folded edge will be the front, and the opposite cut side the back. (If you are making a paper pattern, draw the rectangle on paper and mark one long side the front and the other the back.)

Now measure and mark 1¼" (3.2 cm) from the back corners along the sides and along the back. On the front edge, measure and mark 1" (2.5 cm) from both corners.

Connect the three marks at each end of the pattern with dotted lines, and cut the fabric just inside the lines and inside the back edge. (If you made a paper pattern, follow the same directions; then lay the cut-out pattern on the folded fabric, with the front edge along the fold. Pin the pattern in place, and cut the fabric to the shape of the pattern.)

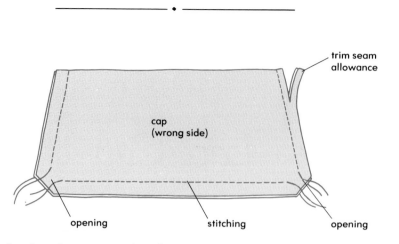

2. Stitching the cap. Stitch the three long open sides of the cap together, leaving ⅝″ (16-mm) seam allowances and stopping ½″ (13 mm) from the corners, as shown. Trim the seam allowances to ¼″ (6 mm).

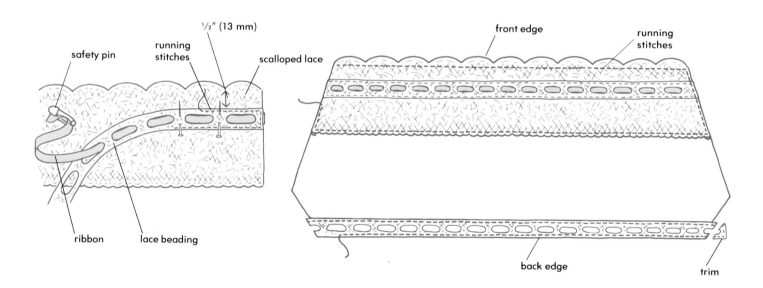

3. The lace trimming. Cut a 15″ (38.1-cm) length of the lace beading. Fasten a small safety pin to one end of the ¼″-wide (6-mm) ribbon, and use it to weave the ribbon in and out of the holes in the lace beading. Trim off the excess ribbon.

Cut a 15″ (38.1-cm) length of the scalloped lace. Pin the beading right side up to the right side of the scalloped lace ½″ (13 mm) in from the inner corners of the scallops. Stitch the beading to the scalloped lace around all four sides with fine running stitches.

Attaching the lace to the cap. Turn the cap right side out through one of the diagonal openings, and press it flat.

Center the beaded lace along the folded front edge of the cap, aligning the inner corners of the scallops with the fold so the tips of the scallops extend beyond it, and pin the lace in place. Trim the ends of the lace so they extend only ¼″ (6 mm) beyond the sides of the cap. Then turn the ends of the lace under, even with the edge of the cap. Attach the lace to the cap with fine running stitches around all four edges of the lace, hiding the stitches in the lace as much as possible.

Cut a 14″ (35.6-cm) strip of the lace beading, center it along the back edge of the cap, and pin it in place. Trim the ends ¼″ (6 mm) beyond the edge of the cap. Attach the long edges of the beading to the cap with fine running stitches.

4. Finishing the cap. Align the diagonal, open edges of the cap right sides together, and join them with a ¹/₄″ (6-mm) French seam.

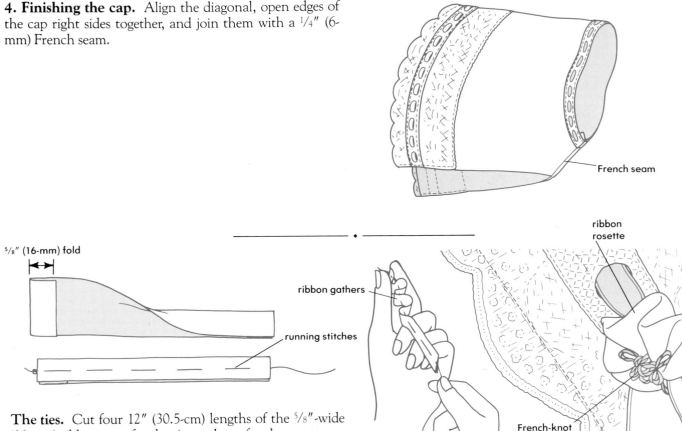

French seam

ribbon rosette

ribbon gathers

running stitches

French-knot flowers

⁵/₈″ (16-mm) fold

The ties. Cut four 12″ (30.5-cm) lengths of the ⁵/₈″-wide (16-mm) ribbon, two for the ties and two for the rosettes.

The rosettes. Fold up the end of one piece of ribbon ⁵/₈″ (16 mm), then fold the ribbon in half lengthwise, covering the end, and stitch the long edges together with five ³/₈″-long (9.5-mm) running stitches, spaced ³/₈″ (9.5 mm) apart.

Pull the ribbon up tightly into folds along the thread to form the rosette, and secure the folds with two or three fastening stitches. Repeat to make the second rosette.

Attach the ties and rosettes to the cap by placing a rosette over one end of each tie at each of the front corners of the cap, and make several tiny stitches through the center of the rosette to secure all three layers together. With three-strand lengths of embroidery floss, make a cluster of four or five white and four or five pale-green French knots through the center of each rosette to hide the earlier stitches and to fasten the folds tightly. Trim the ends of the ties on the diagonal.

The back tie. Make a bow at the back of the cap by threading a 27″ (68.6-cm) length of ¹/₄″-wide (6-mm) satin ribbon through the beading around the back opening, starting and ending at the seam. Draw it tight and make a bow with 12″-long (30.5-cm) streamers. Trim the ends of the streamers on a diagonal, dab them with a tiny amount of nail polish to keep them from raveling, and knot each one.

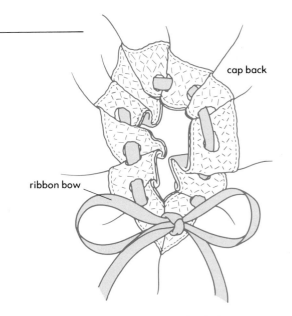

cap back

ribbon bow

Smocked Bonnet

This little bonnet is reminiscent of the "poke" bonnet of the past with its generous brim to shade a child's delicate skin from the sun. The smocking is an attractive modern touch. Because the construction of the bonnet is relatively easy and the smocking design uses two or three basic stitches, it makes a nice project for beginners. The hand smocking makes the bonnet a very special baby gift as well. Depending on your experience, the bonnet will take a day to a day and a half to make.

Refer to the "Dressmaking Skills" section for smocking basics and any other unfamiliar techniques mentioned in the following instructions.

—————————————————— **Materials** ——————————————————

¾ yard (.70 m) broadcloth, gingham, calico, or any other firmly woven lightweight fabric

Embroidery floss: 1 skein each peach, coral, and light green

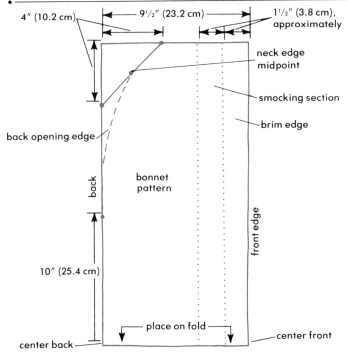

1. Making the pattern. This pattern is based on using the full width of 42"- to 48"-wide (107- to 122-cm) fabric.

Cut a strip of ordinary shelf paper, half the width of the fabric and 9½" (24.1 cm) wide. For example, if the fabric is 45" (1.2 m) wide, cut a piece of paper that is 22½" (57 cm) long and 9½" (24.1 cm) wide, making sure that the corners are at right angles. Measure 4" (10.2 cm) in each direction from the lower left corner and mark each point with a dot. Connect the dots with a straight line.

Mark the midpoint of the line, and label the upper half the "back." Mark the opposite long edge the "front," the opposite corner the "center front," the adjacent end the "neck edge," and the adjacent long edge the "back opening."

Measure and mark a point 10" (25.4 cm) from the center back corner of the pattern along the back edge. Join this mark and the midpoint of the diagonal line drawn previously with a curved line. Trim along the line.

2. Cutting the fabric. Fold the fabric in half lengthwise, wrong side out. Place the center front of the pattern along the fold, pin the pattern in place, and cut the fabric using the pattern as a guide.

Cut two 5"-wide (12.7-cm) ties, the length of half the fabric width. Cut a bias strip that is 2½" (6.4 cm) wide and 10" (25.4 cm) long.

33

Sewing the bonnet

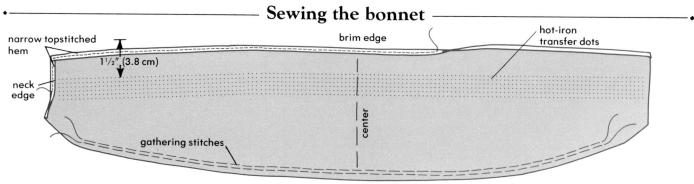

1. **Finishing the edges and the smocking preparation.** Make a narrow topstitched hem on both neck edges, and then across the brim edge of the bonnet.

Stitch two rows of gathering stitches along the back opening edge of the bonnet, the first row ¹/₄″ (6 mm) from the edge, the second ¹/₄″ (6 mm) inside the first.

The smocking preparation. By hand, using transfer dots, or with a pleating machine, make six rows of gathering stitches across the front of the bonnet, starting 1¹/₂″ (3.8 cm) from the brim edge and ¹/₂″ (13 mm) from each side and spacing the rows approximately ³/₈″ (9.5 mm) apart vertically. If you are working by hand, stamp the fabric with six rows of hot-iron smocking transfer dots, and sew them as shown in "Dressmaking Skills" section.

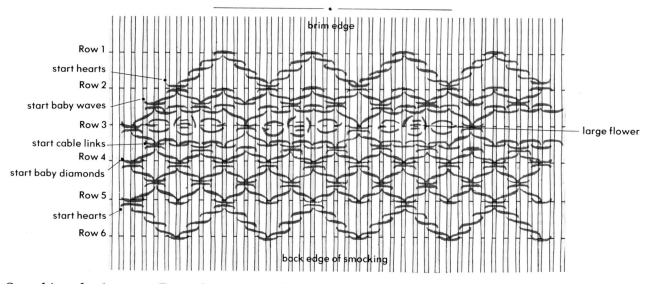

2. **Smocking the bonnet.** Draw the gathering threads until the pleats formed in the bonnet measure 1″ (2.5 cm) less than the child's head, measured from ear lobe to ear lobe across the top. Knot the threads in two groups of three.

Smocking. Begin smocking at the left end of the third row of gathering stitches, and work to the right side of the bonnet for all rows as instructed.

Cable links. Work one side of a baby wave down to halfway between Rows 3 and 4. Cable 7, starting with a down cable. Make a complete baby wave and cable 7 again. Continue this pattern across the row.

Starting at Row 3 again, make a similar row of baby waves and cables, but start by waving up to form cable links across the bonnet.

Baby waves. Midway between Rows 2 and 3, start a row of baby waves, beginning with a down cable back to back with the last cable in the cable links, and waving up. Complete the row of baby waves.

Hearts. Starting back to back with the last up cable in the previous row, work three-step hearts between Rows 1 and 2.

Baby diamonds. Work two rows of baby diamonds across Rows 4 and 5, as shown.

Hearts. Finish the design with three-step hearts, worked between Rows 5 and 6, starting back to back with the first down cable in the row above.

The flowers. Make a large flower at the center of each cable link following the directions in the "Dressmaking Skills" section.

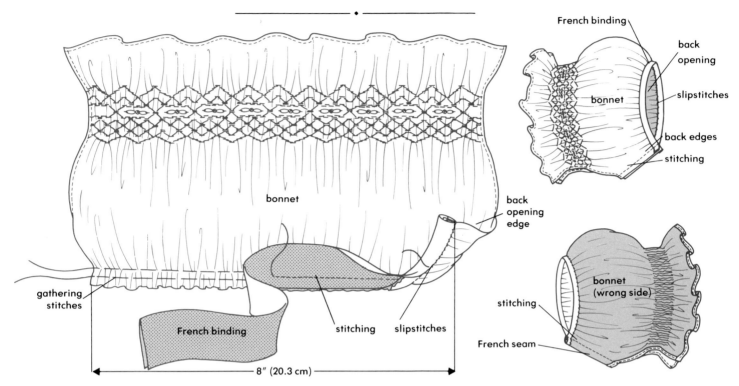

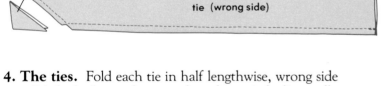

3. Finishing the back. Pull the fabric along the gathering threads at the back edge until it measures 8″ (20.3 cm) across. Make French binding with the strip of fabric cut earlier for that purpose, and center it along the back edge of the bonnet. Join the binding to the bonnet, leaving ³/₈″ (9.5-mm) seam allowances. Turn the binding over the seam allowances and secure it to the inside of the bonnet, catching the thread through the stitching of the seam that joins the binding to the bonnet.

The back seam. Fold the bonnet in half, right side out and neck edges together. Sew the back edges together with a French seam, concealing the cut ends of the binding in the seam.

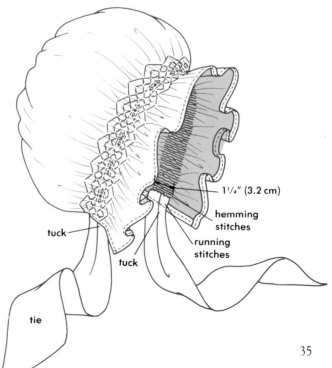

4. The ties. Fold each tie in half lengthwise, wrong side out. Stitch the long edges together, then stitch diagonally across one end, leaving ¹/₄″ (6-mm) seam allowances. Trim the seam allowances to ¹/₈″ (3 mm) outside the diagonal seam, and trim the corners. Turn the ties right side out, and press. Fold the unfinished edge under at the end of each tie, take a tuck along the edge, narrowing the end to a width of 1¹/₄″ (3.2 cm), and then stitch a tie to each front corner of the bonnet 1″ (2.5 cm) above the neck edge with a row of tiny hemming stitches along the fold. Secure the tie along the neck edge with a row of running stitches.

35

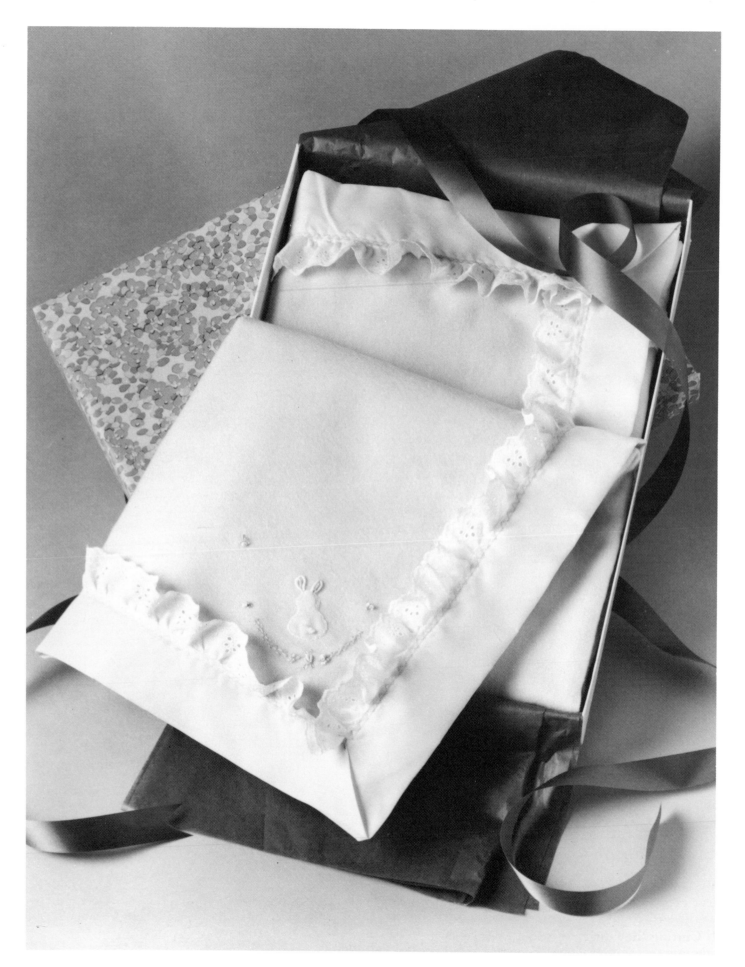

Eyelet-bound Carriage Blanket

Despite its delicate look, this carriage blanket will keep a baby warm in even the nippiest weather. The blanket, which measures 45 inches (114 cm) square, was cut from the same twin-bed blanket as the bunting pictured on page 52, and features similar delicate embroidery. However, the fabric can also be obtained by salvaging the best part of an old blanket. Blanketing can also be purchased by the yard, but the quality is usually inferior to that in ready-made blankets and the fabric is usually thinner. For a whimsical touch, add an appliquéd bunny with a fluffy "touch me" tail. Refer to the "Dressmaking Skills" section of the book for any unfamiliar sewing techniques not covered in the following instructions.

Materials

1¼ yards (1.2 m) of 45″-wide (114-cm) pastel blanket fabric

5 yards (4.6 m) blanket binding to match blanket fabric

5 yards (4.6 m) of 1½″-wide (3.8-cm) pregathered white eyelet edging

Sewing thread to match blanket fabric

A scrap of white flannel or velour

Embroidery floss: medium pink, pale green, and white

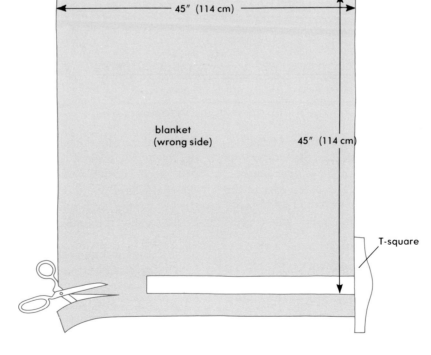

1. Cutting the fabric. Spread the blanket fabric wrong side up in a single layer. Using a T-square or other rigid ruler, mark off and cut a 45″ (114-cm) square of fabric.

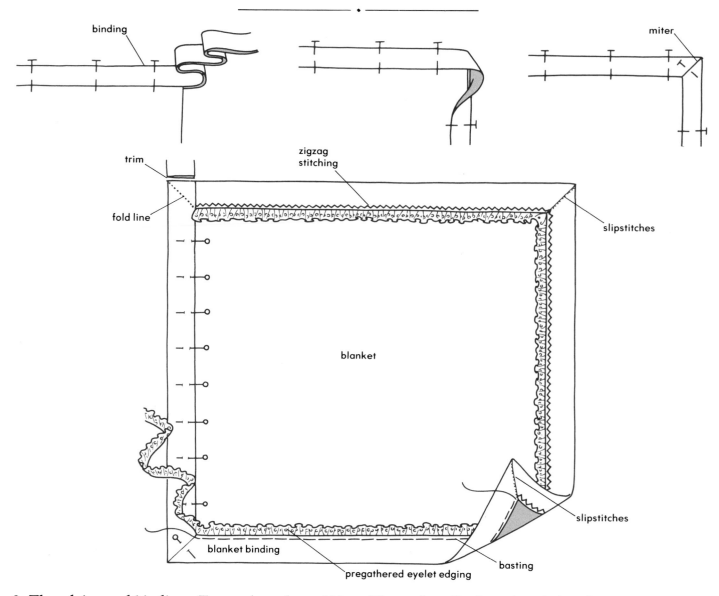

2. The edging and binding. Turn under and press ¼″ (6 mm) at the end of the blanket binding. Starting at one corner of the blanket fabric, slip the binding, right side out, over the edge of the blanket, so that the folded edge of the binding butts the edge of the blanket and the folded end is even with one side of the blanket. Pin the binding in place all the way to the next corner.

Mitering the corners. To form a miter on both sides of a corner, turn the binding around the corner in the direction in which you are attaching the binding, and pin it in place close to the corner, on the other side. Tuck the excess binding under at a diagonal to the corner on both sides of the blanket, and pin it in place. Repeat for each corner.

At the last corner, trim the binding ¼″ (6 mm) beyond the edge of the blanket and turn the excess fabric under even with the edge of the blanket. Then turn the folded corner of the binding under diagonally on both sides to form the last miter.

The eyelet. Slip the gathered edge of the eyelet, right side up, under the edge of the blanket binding, starting at the first mitered corner and covering ½″ (13 mm) of the end of the eyelet, and pin. Continue around the blanket, and at the last corner, turn under ½″ (13 mm) of the end of the eyelet so that the folded end aligns with the edge of the binding.

Baste the binding and eyelet in place through all layers, being sure to catch the edges of the binding on both the right and wrong sides of the blanket. Then, using the longest zigzag stitches possible on your machine, set ¼″ (6 mm) apart, topstitch the binding and eyelet in place. (If you wish, any appropriate decorative stitch—the feather-stitch, for example—can be used in place of the zigzag stitching.) Slipstitch the mitered edges of the binding at the corners of the blanket.

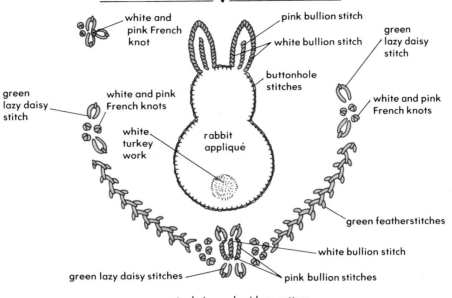

white and pink French knot

pink bullion stitch

white bullion stitch

buttonhole stitches

green lazy daisy stitch

white and pink French knots

green lazy daisy stitch

white and pink French knots

white turkey work

rabbit appliqué

green featherstitches

white bullion stitch

green lazy daisy stitches

pink bullion stitches

actual-size embroidery pattern

3. The rabbit appliqué and embroidery. Trace the actual-size rabbit design, not including the ears, to make a pattern, and use the pattern to cut the rabbit from white flannel. Pin the appliqué to the center of one corner of the blanket 2½" (6.4 cm) from the edge of the eyelet. Using two strands of white embroidery floss, sew the appliqué in place, around the outside edges of the rabbit, with tiny buttonhole stitches.

The tail. Make the tail about ¼" (6 mm) above the center bottom of the rabbit with Turkey work, as shown below.

The ears. Make each ear ½" (13 mm) long, with three side-by-side bullion stitches. Make a ⁵⁄₁₆"-long (8-mm) pink bullion stitch for the center of each ear, and outline it with two white bullion stitches, one at either side and meeting at the top end of the center stitch.

The flowers and branches. Embroider the rest of the design as follows: Make one pink and two white French knots side by side 1⅜" (3.5 cm) to each side of the rabbit at neck level. With green embroidery floss, make two lazy daisy stitches for leaves next to each cluster of French knots.

Starting about ⅝" (16 mm) below the rabbit and using an embroidery pen or dressmaker's chalk, draw an upward and outward curving 1¼"-long (3.2-cm) line to each side of the rabbit. Start the lines about 1" (2.5 cm) apart and end them about ½" (13 mm) from the clusters of flowers made earlier. Starting below the rabbit, sew a row of ⁵⁄₁₆"-long (8-mm) featherstitches along each line.

Make a cluster of French knots—two white, two pink, and one green—at the beginning of each line of featherstitches.

Directly between these flowers, make a third flower of vertical ¼"-long (6-mm) bullion stitches, one white bordered by two pink stitches. At each end of this flower, make two green lazy daisy stitches for leaves.

Add a last bouquet of two pink and one white French knots, with three lazy daisy leaves 1½" (3.8 cm) above and slightly to the left of the bouquet already stitched at the left of the rabbit.

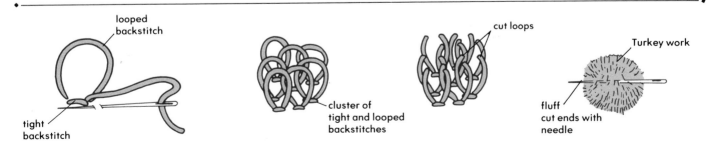

looped backstitch

tight backstitch

cluster of tight and looped backstitches

cut loops

Turkey work

fluff cut ends with needle

Turkey work. Make a small backstitch on the surface of the fabric. Then make another small backstitch, this time leaving a ¼" (6-mm) loop. Make another tight backstitch to secure the loop. Repeat, alternating looped and tight backstitches four or five times more within an area about ⅜" (9.5 cm) across to form a clump of loops. Cut through the tops of the loops. Using the embroidery needle, rub the cut floss firmly until the tail becomes tangled and fuzzy.

Smocked Pillow Sham

If you admire beautiful handwork, you'll love this smocked baby pillow. And if you happen to be a smocking enthusiast, you're in for a special treat. Actually, this lovely bit of luxury is a pillow sham, which means that you can whisk it off its pillow any time for laundering.

To make the pillow sham, you smock the center panel first (that's the fun part!) for ease of handling. Then you sew the sham together, a simple matter of adding some eyelet and stitching a seam and hem. Since this is such a popular item, you'll probably want to make several; try a different smocking design for each one, letting your imagination and experience be your guide.

Materials

¾ yard (.70 m) of 42″- to 45″-wide (107- to 114-cm) white broadcloth

1½ yards (1.4 m) of 1½″-wide (3.8-cm) eyelet beading

1½ yards (1.4 m) of ⅜″-wide (9.5-mm) light-blue double-faced satin ribbon

2 yards (1.9 m) of 2½″-wide (6.4-cm) pregathered eyelet edging

Six-strand embroidery floss: One skein each light blue, light yellow, medium yellow, dark yellow, and moss green

White sewing thread

Cutting the fabric

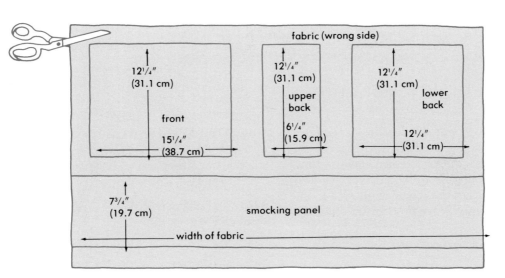

1. Measuring and cutting the fabric. Lay the broadcloth out, wrong side up, and mark and cut out the following pieces: one 12¼″ × 15¼″ (31.1 × 38.7-cm) front piece, one 12¼″ × 6¼″ (31.1 × 15.9-cm) upper back piece, one 12¼″ (31.1-cm) square for the lower back piece, and one 7¾″-wide (19.7-cm) panel the length of the entire fabric width for the smocking.

41

The smocking and embroidery

1. Preparing the smocking panel. Following the instructions for smocking on pages 183 through 189, make eighteen rows of gathering dots across the entire width of the fabric, making sure to center them. The inner sixteen rows are for the actual smocking, and the outer two auxiliary rows will stabilize the gathers at the top and bottom of the panel. (If you are using a pleating machine, omit the auxiliary rows, since the machine stitches a maximum of sixteen gathering rows.)

Gather the fabric, beginning and ending at the very edge on both sides. Pull up the gathering threads until the panel measures 10½″ (26.7 cm) across, and knot the threads for the inner sixteen gathering rows at the side edges in groups of four. Secure the ends of the auxiliary rows separately.

Count the total number of pleats and mark the "valley" between two center pleats with basting stitches. In the following instructions, the inner sixteen gathering rows will be identified by letters of the alphabet.

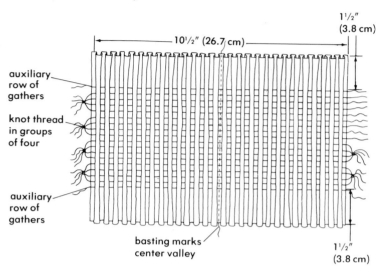

auxiliary row of gathers

knot thread in groups of four

auxiliary row of gathers

basting marks center valley

10½″ (26.7 cm)

1½″ (3.8 cm)

1½″ (3.8 cm)

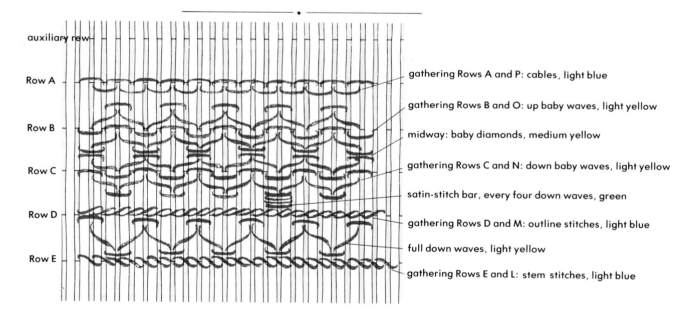

auxiliary row

Row A

Row B

Row C

Row D

Row E

gathering Rows A and P: cables, light blue

gathering Rows B and O: up baby waves, light yellow

midway: baby diamonds, medium yellow

gathering Rows C and N: down baby waves, light yellow

satin-stitch bar, every four down waves, green

gathering Rows D and M: outline stitches, light blue

full down waves, light yellow

gathering Rows E and L: stem stitches, light blue

2. Smocking the top and bottom borders. Work the top border, Rows A to E, as described below, then rotate the panel 180 degrees and work the same design between Rows P and L, starting at the outermost row and working from left to right and down toward the center of the pillow. Use three or four strands of embroidery floss for the smocking stitches.

Row A (P): Work in light-blue cables.

Row B (O): Using light yellow, work a row of up baby waves.

Row C (N): Using light yellow, work a row of down baby waves.

Midway between B and C (O and N): Using medium yellow, work a row of baby diamonds.

Rows D and E (M and L): Using light blue, work stem or outline stitches along each row. (See the description of this stitch below.) Turn the work 180 degrees at the end of Row D (M) and work across Row E (L) from left to right.

Midway between Rows D and E (M and L): Turn the work 180 degrees, then, using light yellow, work a row of full down waves.

Satin-stitch bars: Work green satin-stitch bars over two pleats between the baby waves on Row C (N) and the outline stitches on Row D (M), repeating a bar at the bottom of every fourth down wave. There should be a total of eleven bars at equal intervals across the pillow sham, top and bottom.

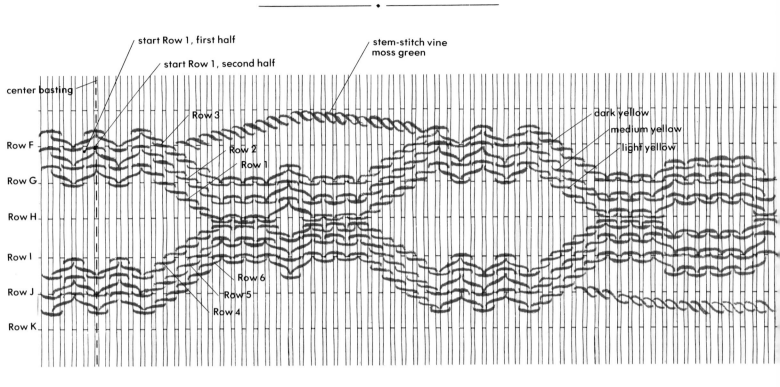

3. The center smocking design. The design at the center of the pillow sham is a combination of three large diamonds with baby waves on the top separated by cables on either side of a baby wave and finished at both sides with cable links.

Row 1, first half: Begin in the center and work to the right to space the diamonds evenly in the center of the panel. With light yellow, work an up cable over the center "valley" halfway between Rows F and G. Make a complete baby wave down to G and back, then wave 6 steps down to Row H. Stitch 5 cables along H, then make a baby wave halfway up to Row G and back. Stitch 5 cables along H, then wave 6 steps back up to halfway between rows G and H, ending with an up cable. Sew 2 complete baby waves down to G and back, then wave 6 steps down to Row H. Sew 5 cables, baby wave up halfway to Row G, cable 7, *baby wave down to H and back, and cable 7. Repeat from * to the end.

Row 1, second half: Turn the work around 180 degrees and bring the needle up in the center above the beginning cable stitch. Work this half of the row with the same order of stitches as the first, but in the reverse direction. (Turn the illustration 180 degrees as well so you can follow the pattern more easily.)

Row 2: Turn the work 180 degrees again to begin the second and all subsequent rows, and work across the entire length of each row from left to right, starting with whatever stitch the previous row started on. With medium yellow, work a row of stitches parallel to and in the same manner as Row 1, half a space above it.

Row 3: With dark yellow, work a row of stitches parallel to and in the same manner as Row 2, half a space above it.

Row 4: With light yellow, work the stitches to the right exactly as in Row 1, but in the opposite direction, as shown.

Row 5: With medium-yellow floss, work a row of stitches parallel to and in the same manner as Row 4, half a space below it.

Row 6: With dark yellow, work a row of stitches parallel to and in the same manner as Row 5, half a space below it.

The vine. Beginning at the left side of the panel about 1/4" (6 mm) below the end of the center design at Row 1, work a line of stem stitches that curves down to within 1/4" (6 mm) of the lower border and back up to the lower edge of the left diamond.

About 1/2" (13 mm) below the right top edge of the same diamond, continue the vine, making it curve up to within 1/4" (6 mm) of the top border and back down to the leftmost upper point of the center diamond. Continue the vine on the right side of the center diamond, working the same curves across the pillow sham in reverse.

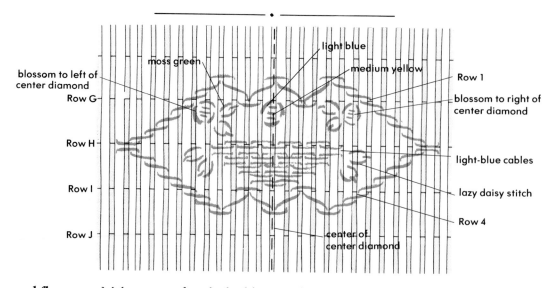

4. The vases and flowers. Make a **vase** of stacked cable stitches at the center of each diamond as follows. Using light-blue embroidery floss, start the stacked cables on the upper edge of Row H in the "valley" to the left of the fourth pleat left of the center of each diamond. Beginning with a down cable, work a row of 9 cables. Turn the work 180 degrees and work another row of 9 cables starting back to back with the first cable in the preceding row, as shown.

Repeat, turning the work at the beginning of each row, and starting back to back with the first cable in the pre-

ceding row, until the work tapers down to 3 cables, completing the vase.

The flowers. Work three large blossoms, following the instructions on page 189, in the space above each vase. Make the centers of medium yellow and surround them with light-blue cables. Work one or two lazy daisy leaves in moss green close to the blossoms or at random near the vase. Make an additional blossom with leaves to each side of the center diamond in the area under the vine.

Sewing the pillow sham

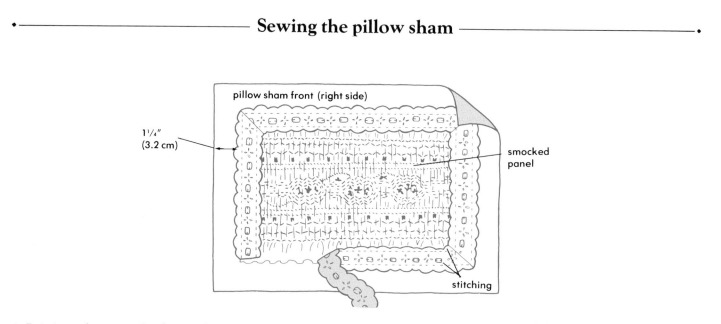

6. Joining the smocked panel to the pillow sham front. Before joining the smocked panel to the back of the pillow sham, remove the gathering threads from the smocking, pin the panel to an ironing board, and steam the smocked panel to a length of 10½″ (26.7 cm).

Center the smocked panel, wrong side down, on the right side of the pillow case front and baste it in place along the edges.

The beading. Thread the ribbon through the eyelet beading. Pin the beading over the raw edges of the smocked panel, mitering the corners and keeping the outside edge of the beading about 1¼″ (3.2 cm) from the edge of the front piece.

Stitch the beading in place about ½″ (13 mm) in from the outermost edge on each side, or wherever seems most suitable relative to the pattern of the beading.

7. Assembling the back. Finish one long edge of each back piece with a narrow topstitched hem. With right sides up, pin the upper section over the lower section, overlapping the hemmed edges by 1″ (2.5 cm). Baste the pieces together across the ends of the overlapping edges.

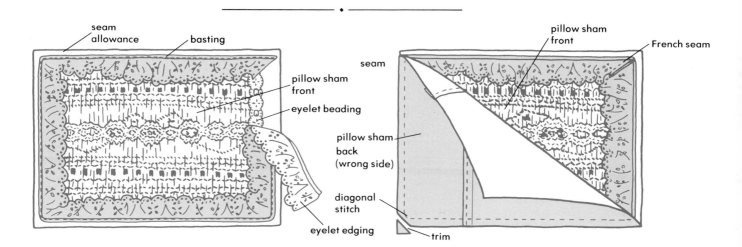

8. Finishing the pillow sham. With right sides together and the finished edge of the eyelet facing the center of the pillow, baste the eyelet to the edges of the pillow front ⁵⁄₈″ (16 mm) from the edge. Join the ends of the eyelet neatly with a French seam.

Pin, then stitch the front and back, right sides together, ⁵⁄₈″ (16 mm) from the edge, making two diagonal stitches at each corner. Clip off the seam allowances at each corner, and turn the sham right side out. Slip the pillow into the case through the back opening.

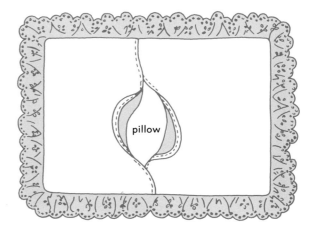

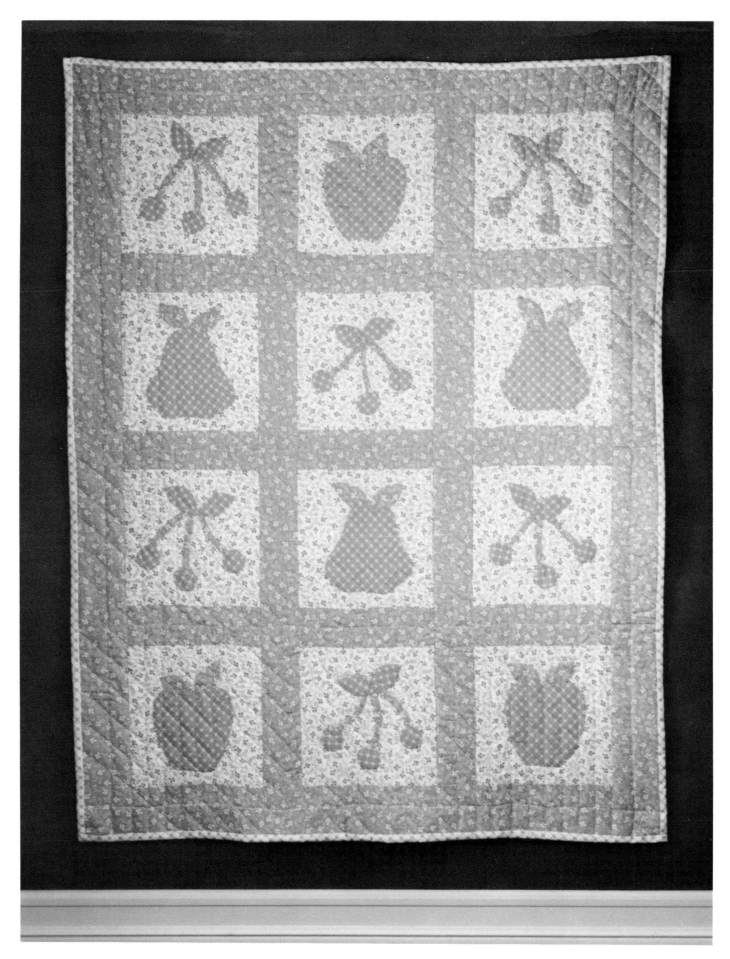

Appliquéd Crib Quilt

Here's the perfect quilt for a new baby and for a new quilter. Its small size—about 43″ × 55″ (109 × 140 cm), which fits a standard crib—makes it easy to handle. And the design calls into play several techniques associated with quilt-making: appliqué, piecing, and both hand and machine quilting. The best fabric choice is a lightweight, firmly woven cotton or cotton blend in soft pastels or bright crayon colors.

Materials

To make this quilt, you will need 45″-wide (114-cm) fabrics in four coordinating prints or solid colors:

Color A, for square blocks: 1 yard (.95 m)

Color B, for borders and joining strips: 1⅝ yards (1.5 m)

Color C, for appliqués: ¾ yard (.7 m)

Color D, for backing: 1⅝ yards (1.5 m)

Sewing thread to match all fabrics

4 spools of quilting thread to match color A

1 package crib-size batting

Tracing paper

Carbon paper

Lightweight cardboard

Quilting foot for sewing machine

Cutting the fabric

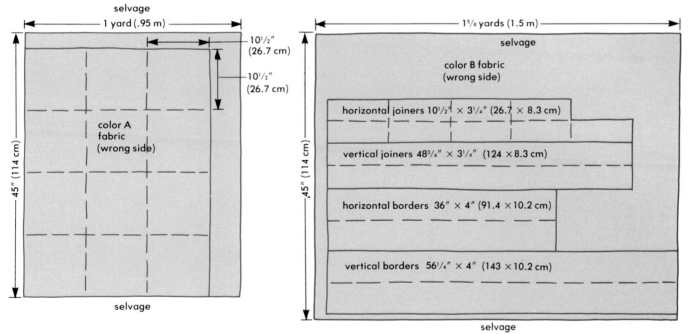

selvage

1 yard (.95 m)

10½″ (26.7 cm)

10½″ (26.7 cm)

color A fabric (wrong side)

45″ (114 cm)

selvage

1⅝ yards (1.5 m)

selvage

color B fabric (wrong side)

horizontal joiners 10½″ × 3¼″ (26.7 × 8.3 cm)

vertical joiners 48¾″ × 3¼″ (124 × 8.3 cm)

horizontal borders 36″ × 4″ (91.4 × 10.2 cm)

vertical borders 56¼″ × 4″ (143 × 10.2 cm)

45″ (114 cm)

selvage

1. Cutting the blocks and borders. All the pieces, except for those to be appliquéd, are straight strips or squares, which can be shaped more accurately and quickly by tearing the fabric than by cutting it. Most closely woven cottons will tear cleanly; if you are in doubt about the fabric you have, test a small piece first. Start each tear with a snip into the selvage or crosswise edge, then pull the fabric apart in the direction of the cut.

The blocks. For the color A blocks, first tear four equal 10½″-wide (26.7-cm) lengthwise strips, then tear the strips crosswise at 10½″ (26.7-cm) intervals to form squares.

The border strips. Tear the border strips of color B along the lengthwise grain of the fabric as follows: two 56¼″ × 4″ (143 × 10.2-cm) strips to border the long sides of the quilt; two 36″ × 4″ (91.4 × 10.2-cm) strips to border the short sides of the quilt; two 48¾″ × 3¼″ (124 × 8.3-cm) strips to join the blocks lengthwise; and nine 10½″ × 3¼″ (26.7 × 8.3-cm) strips to join the blocks horizontally.

After you've torn the pieces, press each one to correct any distortion caused by the tearing.

Note: If you're timid about tearing the fabric, or your fabric doesn't tear well, use a yardstick or a T-square and pencil to measure and mark the pieces on the wrong side of the fabric, and then cut them.

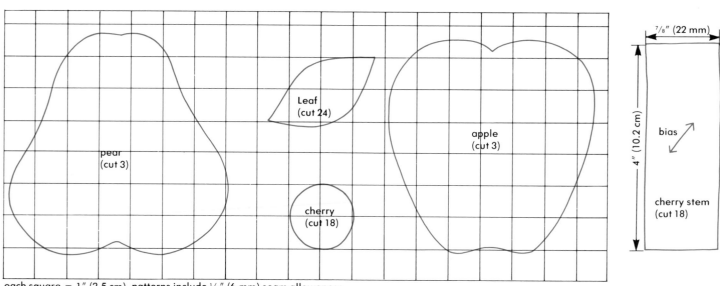

each square = 1″ (2.5 cm) patterns include ¼″ (6-mm) seam allowances

2. Cutting the appliqué pieces. Enlarge the pattern for the cherry, leaf, pear, and apple motifs to the scale indicated, following the directions on page 175. Trace the designs, then, using carbon paper and a sharp pencil, transfer each to lightweight cardboard and cut it out to make a template.

Fold fabric C, keeping the wrong side out, into three layers. Place the template on the top layer and trace around

it, then pin the layers together, and cut them out at the same time. Cut eighteen cherries, three pears, three apples, and twelve leaves from color C fabric (to go with the cherries). Cut twelve leaves from color B fabric.

For the cherry stems, cut several ⅞″-wide (22-mm) bias strips from color B equaling at least 2 yards (1.9 m) in length altogether. Do not cut color D yet.

Assembling the quilt

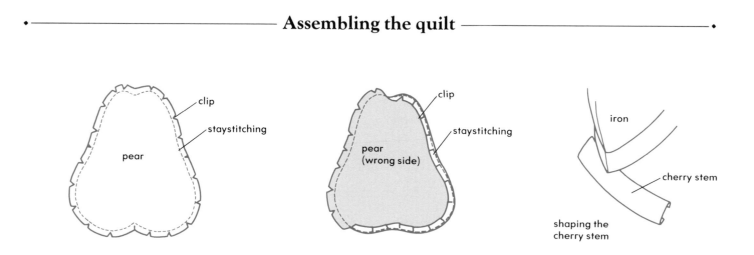

3. Appliquéing the blocks. First staystitch around each appliqué shape, except for the stems, ¼″ (6 mm) from the edge, using twelve to fifteen stitches per inch (2.5 cm). If you prefer, you may do this by hand, using a fine running stitch. Notch the edge of the fabric at the curves, then, with your fingers, press the edges under along the stitching line, rolling the stitching to the underside as you sew the appliqué in place.

The stems. To prepare the stems, press the long edges of the bias strips under ¼″ (6 mm). Cut the strips into 4″ (10.2-cm) lengths, and shape each piece into a gentle curve with a steam iron.

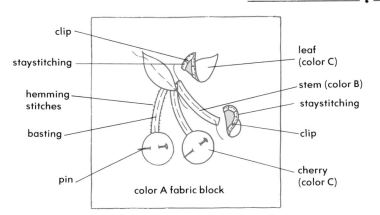

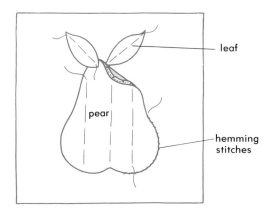

Stitching the appliqué. To attach the cherries, arrange three cherries, three stems, and two leaves on a color A square, as shown, hiding the stem ends under the cherries and leaves. When you are satisfied with the arrangement, pin the pieces in place, then baste them down the center. Using matching thread, hem the appliqués in place around the edges. Make six cherry blocks.

The pear blocks: Arrange one pear and two leaves on a square, lapping the top of the pear over one leaf and tucking it under the other. Pin, baste, and sew the piece in place as for the cherries. Make three pear blocks.

The apple blocks: Make three apple blocks in exactly the same fashion as the pear blocks.

4. Joining the blocks and strips. On a large table or on the floor, lay out the appliquéd blocks and the joining strips as shown, alternating motifs (omit the borders for now). With right sides together and stitching ¼" (6-mm) seams, join the first vertical row of four blocks and three short joining strips. Press the seam allowances open. Join the remaining two rows of blocks and strips in the same way.

Now seam the vertical joining strips to the long edges of the block-and-strip rows, as shown, being careful to match all intersections. Press the seam allowances open.

Joining the border. Seam the short border strips to the top and bottom edges of the large pieced rectangle; press the seam allowances open. Seam the long border strips to the side edges in the same way. The quilt top is now complete.

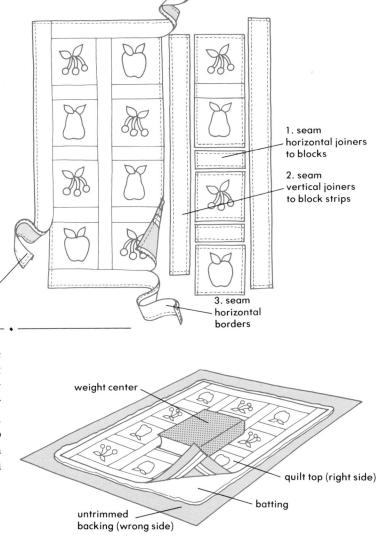

5. Assembling the quilt layers. Work on a large table or on the floor; the quilt must lie flat. Place the uncut backing fabric wrong side up on your work surface. Center the batting over the backing, smoothing it out. Now center the quilt top right side up over the batting. Place a large, heavy book or other weight at the center of the quilt top to keep the layers from shifting. Smooth the three layers from the center out to the edges, pinning them together as you work. Remove the weight.

49

6. Basting the layers together. To hold the layers together for quilting, baste them together, *starting at the center and working out to the edges* for each line of stitching. It is absolutely vital to do this; otherwise, you will get lumps, bumps, and wrinkles in your work. Making fairly small stitches (or one long and two short, as shown), baste the quilt as follows, *always starting at the center:*

1. across the center, horizontally, bisecting the middle row of joining strips;

2. down the center, vertically, bisecting the middle row of blocks;

3. diagonally, to each corner;

4. horizontally, through the remaining joining strips;

5. vertically, through the remaining joining strips;

6. around the border, about 1/2″ (13 mm) in from the edges. Remove all the pins.

Trim the batting even with the quilt top. Leave the backing untrimmed at this point.

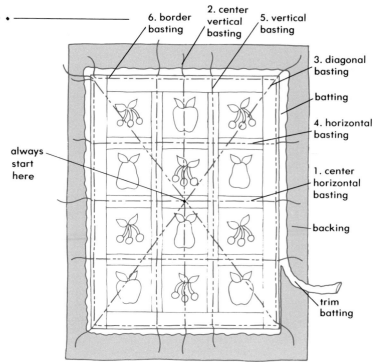

7. The hand quilting. Using a single strand of quilting thread, sew a row of running stitches 1/8″ (3 mm) outside all the edges of the appliqué pieces. This is known as outline quilting. First knot the end of the thread, bring the needle up from the backing side, and give the thread a tug to bury the knot in the batting. Then make small stitches—about 1/8″ (3 mm) long and 1/8″ (3 mm) apart—working with an up-and-down motion through all three layers. To end off the thread, make a knot and bury it in the batting as you did to start.

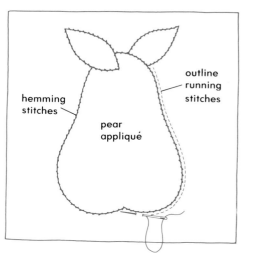

8. The machine quilting. Thread your machine and bobbin with quilting thread, and put on a quilting foot to help keep the stitching straight and evenly spaced. Before you start to work on the actual quilt, test-quilt a sample to determine the settings that work best on your machine and fabrics. Using scraps of fabric and batting, baste a three-layer test sample together. Loosen the top tension and the pressure and set the stitch length to eight to ten per inch (2.5 cm). Adjust these settings until your test sample is satisfactory.

If necessary, set up an extra table or chair near your machine to help support the weight of the quilt. Whenever possible, quilt from the center out to the edges, just as you

did when basting. Roll up the extra fabric to the right of your machine, as shown. The machine quilting is done in two parts: vertical and diagonal.

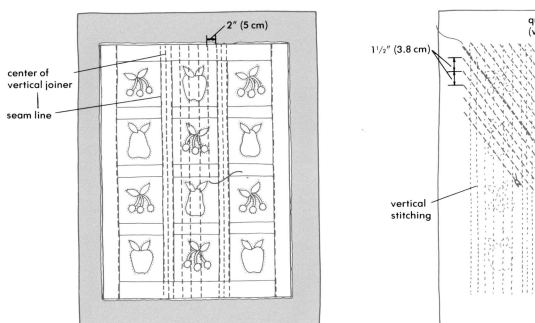

center of
vertical joiner

seam line

2″ (5 cm)

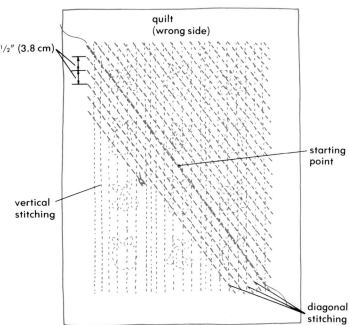

quilt
(wrong side)

1½″ (3.8 cm)

starting
point

vertical
stitching

diagonal
stitching

Vertical quilting. Working on the right, or top, side of the quilt, stitch in the following order, always starting at the center:

1. lengthwise, on the seam lines joining the vertical strips to the blocks;

2. lengthwise, bisecting the vertical strips;

3. lengthwise, in four rows spaced 2″ (5 cm) apart, through each row of blocks.

The diagonal quilting. Working on the wrong, or backing, side of the quilt and using either of the diagonal basting lines as a guide, start at the center and stitch out to one corner, keeping the diagonal 1½″ (3.8 cm) from the guideline of stitches. Finish that diagonal to the opposite corner. Stitch additional diagonals parallel to the first two across the entire quilt at 1½″ (3.8-cm) intervals. Do not stitch diagonals in any other direction.

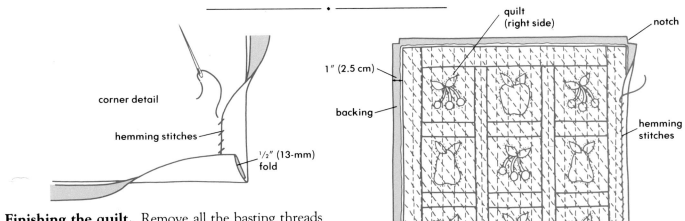

corner detail

hemming stitches

½″ (13-mm)
fold

quilt
(right side)

notch

1″ (2.5 cm)

backing

hemming
stitches

½″ (13-mm)
binding

½″ (13-mm) fold

9. Finishing the quilt. Remove all the basting threads and cut off any thread ends. Press the corners and edges of the quilt to straighten them, if necessary. Trim the backing so it is 1″ (2.5 cm) larger all around than the top and batting. Notch out all four corners of the backing almost to the corner of the quilt, as shown.

Fold the edges of the backing to the right side of the quilt. Turn the raw edges under ½″ (13 mm) to form a ½″-wide (13-mm) binding, and pin the binding edges in place. Hem or slipstitch the binding in place.

51

Bunting

There's no denying that one of life's great joys is a good snooze. The baby in the picture would surely agree. And, if it could wake up and talk, it would probably acknowledge that a bunting is an ideal sleeping environment—soft, warm, and cozy. Actually, a bunting, with its attached hood and mittens, is just a scaled-down, modified version of a sleeping bag. Traditionally, buntings are made from blanket or quilted fabric, to provide warmth without great weight. Since it may be hard to locate blanket fabric by the yard, your best bet is to buy a twin-bed-size blanket and cut out the bunting pieces from it. A blanket this size will allow you to make a matching carriage blanket (page 36) as well. Choose wool or a synthetic fabric; the latter is relatively inexpensive and is machine-washable, too.

Materials

1 twin-bed blanket, or 1½ yards (1.4 m) blanket fabric

¼ yard (.25 m) lining fabric

1 yard (.95 m) of 1″-wide (2.5-cm) Velcro fastener

1 yard (.95 m) of ½″-wide (13-mm) double-faced satin ribbon

A package of 2″-wide (5-cm) blanket binding

Embroidery floss: 1 skein each pink, green, and white

A commercial bunting pattern. All pattern companies offer buntings, usually as part of a layette. If there's a choice of sizes, buy the six-month rather than the newborn size, which is quickly outgrown. Try to find a style with an attached hood and mittens and a raglan sleeve.

Cutting the fabric

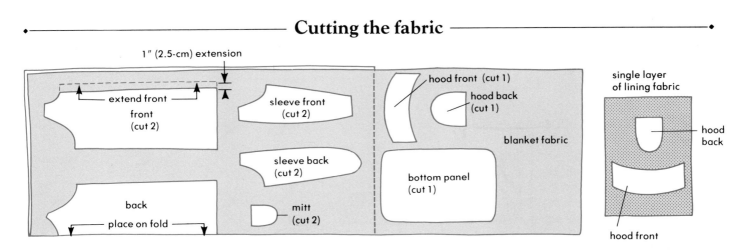

1. Adjusting the pattern. If the bunting pattern calls for a zipper down the center front, you will need to extend the front edges of the pattern to form an overlap for the closure. To do this, add 1″ (2.5 cm), or half the finished (folded) width of the blanket binding, to the center front edge of the pattern piece, as shown.

2. Cutting the fabric. If you are using a new blanket for the fabric, cut off the binding, then fold the blanket in half lengthwise. Lay out any pattern pieces that must be cut double or on the fold, pin them to the blanket, and cut them out. Open the remaining blanket fabric, and lay out and cut the rest of the pieces. The leftover blanket fabric can be used to make the eyelet-bound blanket on page 36, if desired.

Cut out the hood lining following the directions on the pattern.

Assembling the bunting

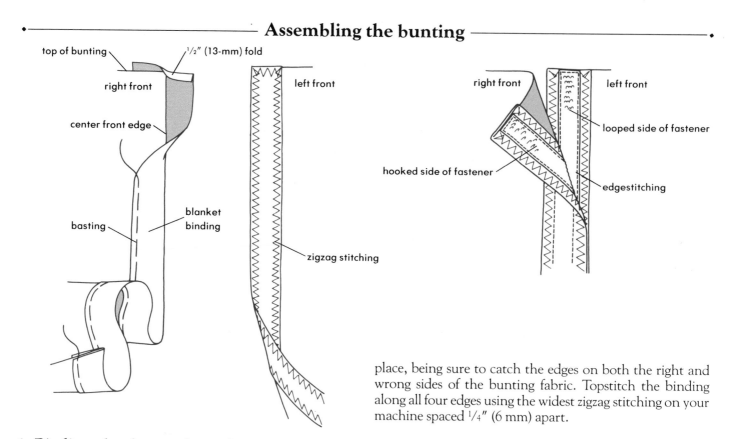

top of bunting

right front

center front edge

basting

blanket binding

½" (13-mm) fold

left front

zigzag stitching

right front

left front

looped side of fastener

hooked side of fastener

edgestitching

1. Binding the front edges. Cut two lengths of binding, each ½" (13 mm) longer than the center front edge of the bunting. With the extra length at the top, slip a strip of binding over the center front edge of each front piece to enclose it. Then fold the end of each strip of binding down over the raw edge of the blanket fabric, tucking it under the binding that runs down the front edge. Baste the binding in place, being sure to catch the edges on both the right and wrong sides of the bunting fabric. Topstitch the binding along all four edges using the widest zigzag stitching on your machine spaced ¼" (6 mm) apart.

2. Attaching the fastener. Cut the Velcro fastener the same length as the center front edges of the bunting. Center and pin the loop half of the fastener over the binding on top of the left front. Pin the hook half of the fastener to the wrong side of the right front, centering it between the rows of decorative stitching. Edgestitch both fastener halves in place around all four sides.

3. The shoulder and upper sleeve seams. Using the flat-felled method, stitch the raglan seams. Starting at the neck edge, stitch the upper arm seams as far as the elbows, using a regular plain seam; the rest of these seams will be stitched later. (*Note:* If your bunting has set-in rather than raglan sleeves, stitch flat-felled shoulder seams.) For either style, do not stitch the side seams or finish the sleeve seams yet.

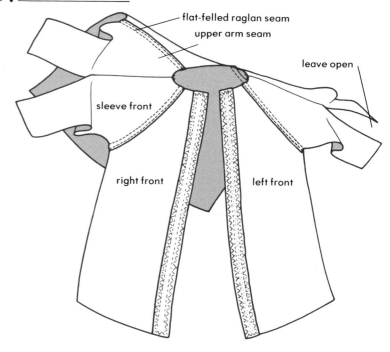

flat-felled raglan seam

upper arm seam

leave open

sleeve front

right front

left front

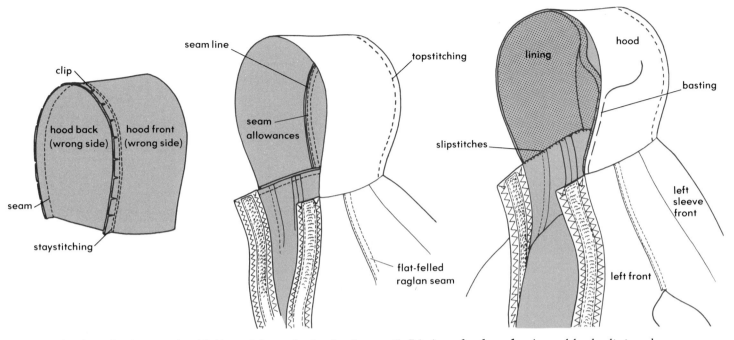

4. The hood. Staystitch ¼″ (6 mm) from the back edge of the hood front piece and clip the edge at intervals almost to the stitching. With right sides together, pin this edge to the curved edge of the hood back. Stitch the edges together. Press the seam allowances toward the front, then topstitch through them ¼″ (6 mm) from the seam line to simulate a flat-felled seam.

With right sides together and matching the center backs, pin the neck edge of the hood to the bunting neck edge; stitch. Press the seam allowances up toward the hood.

5. Lining the hood. Assemble the lining the same way as the hood, omitting the topstitching. Press the seam allowances under around the front and neck edges.

Matching front edges and seams, insert the lining wrong side out into the hood; pin, then baste the lining to the bunting along the front edge. Pin the pressed edge of the lining over the hood/bunting neck seam and slipstitch the lining in place.

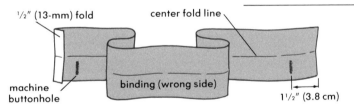

6. Binding the hood. Cut a strip of binding 1″ (2.5 cm) longer than the front edge measurement of the hood. Unfold the binding. Placed 1½″ (3.8 cm) in from each end and centered between the fold line and one edge, make a ½″-long (13-mm) machine buttonhole parallel to the binding ends. Then press both ends of the binding under ½″ (13 mm).

With the buttonholes on the outside, slip the binding over the front edge of the hood; then baste and sew it in place with zigzag stitching as on center front edges of the bunting. Slipstitch the binding ends in place.

The casing. To create a casing, make two rows of topstitching ¾″ (19 mm) apart along the center of the binding. Attach a safety pin to the end of the ribbon and draw it through the casing.

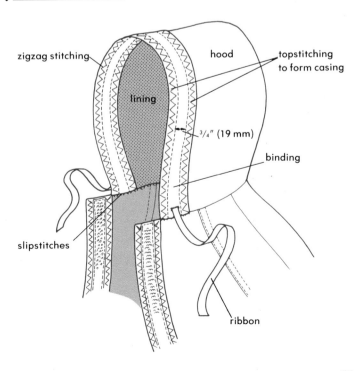

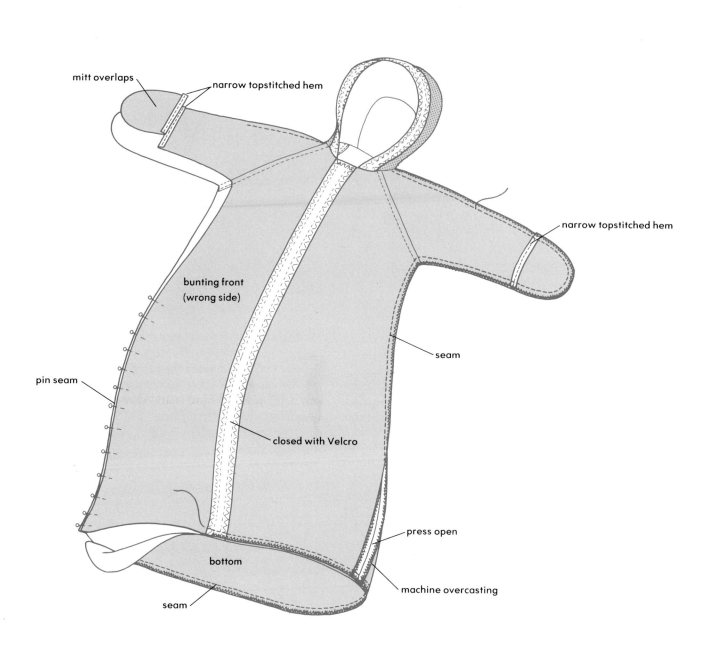

mitt overlaps

narrow topstitched hem

narrow topstitched hem

bunting front
(wrong side)

seam

pin seam

closed with Velcro

press open

bottom

machine overcasting

seam

7. Finishing the bunting. Finish the top edge of the mitt pieces and the lower edges of the sleeves with narrow topstitched hems. Lap and pin the mitts to the sleeves as your pattern directs.

The side and sleeve seams. With right sides together and beginning at the elbow, pin the upper arm, mitt, sleeve underarm, and side edges together; stitch. Press the side seams open. Finish the edges with machine overcasting.

The bottom piece. Lap and press the center front edges closed. Then pin and stitch the bottom piece to the lower edge of the bunting as your pattern directs. Finish the seam edges with machine overcasting. Open the center front to turn the bunting right side out.

The embroidery

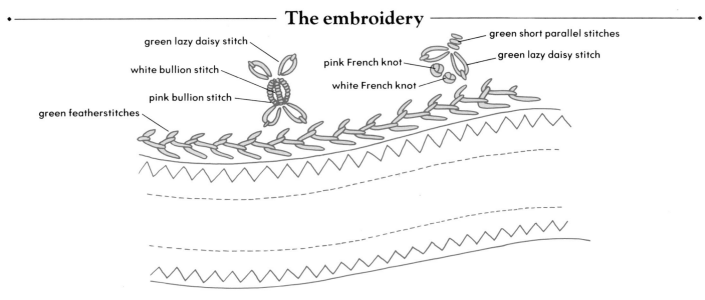

The featherstitched borders. Using two strands of embroidery floss, work the embroidery design as follows. Sew a line of green featherstitches along the inner edge of the ribbon binding on both sides of the front and around the front of the hood.

The flowers on the hood. Make a flower at the top center front of the hood next to the featherstitching, as shown. Make the blossom with an 1/8″-long (3-mm) white bullion stitch at the center, surrounded by two slightly longer pink bullion stitches. Then sew two lazy daisy leaves at each end of the blossom.

Sew two bunches of flowers on each side of the center flower at 2 1/2″ (6.4-cm) intervals. Make each bunch of flowers with one white and one pink French knot stitched side by side, and flanked by two lazy daisy stitches. Then sew a 1/2″-long (13-mm) stem below the flowers with short parallel stitches of green floss.

The flowers on the bunting front. Make one large blossom 1″ (2.5 cm) from the ribbon at the corner of the neck on the left front side of the bunting. First make a pink French knot, then make two blossoms of bullion stitches next to it and 1/4″ (6 mm) apart, exactly like the blossom at the center of the hood. Last, sew three green lazy daisy stitches, one on each side of the blossoms, as shown.

Sew a small bunch of flowers (like the ones on the hood) 1/2″ (13 mm) to the right and slightly below the larger flower.

Sew a small blossom consisting of one white French knot and one green lazy daisy stitch 1/4″ (6 mm) below and between the large flower and bunch of flowers, as illustrated.

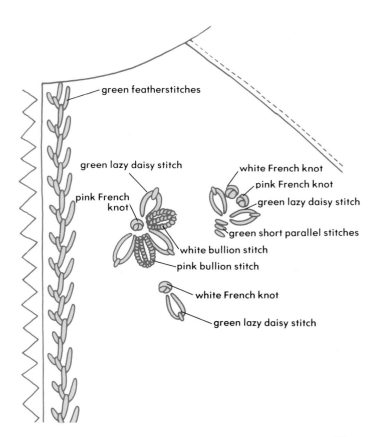

Smocked Pincushion

When pins were a rarity, before the turn of the century, one of the most treasured gifts a baby could receive was a pincushion, complete with pins. One example, from 1779, is decorated with pins cleverly arranged to spell out the year, a design of hearts, and the greeting: "Welcome, little stranger." This smocked pincushion is an easy sewing and smocking project that can easily be done in a day. It is stuffed with batting, sawdust, and sand, the latter of which adds a pleasant weight at the same time it conveniently helps to keep pins sharp. This project makes a lovely modern welcome for today's "little strangers."

Materials

An 8″ × 12″ (20.3 × 30.5-cm) piece of medium-weight closely woven white fabric, such as chino, sateen, or twill (to hold the filling)

White sewing thread

Polyester stuffing or scraps of quilt batting

1 cup clean sand

1 cup sawdust, available from local builders or lumberyards

¼ yard (.25 m) white broadcloth

A 5″ × 6¼″ (12.7 × 15.9-cm) scrap of velvet or corduroy

1¼ yards (1.2 m) of ¾″-wide (19-mm) lace trim

6-strand embroidery floss: one skein each of light blue, pale green, green, and yellow

1 yard (.95 m) of ⅛″-wide (3-mm) double-faced satin ribbon

The cushion

1. Assembling the inner cushion cover. Cut two 5″ × 6¼″ (12.7 × 15.9-cm) rectangles of the closely woven white fabric. Align the pieces, right sides together, and stitch them ⅝″ (16 mm) from the edges, turning each corner with two diagonal stitches and leaving a 2″ (5-cm) opening on one long side. (This way of turning the corners will make them look nearly square when turned.) Trim the corners outside the stitching, and turn the cushion right side out.

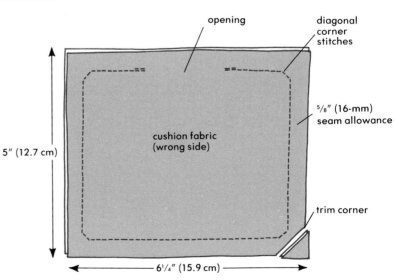

opening

diagonal corner stitches

⅝″ (16-mm) seam allowance

cushion fabric (wrong side)

5″ (12.7 cm)

trim corner

6¼″ (15.9 cm)

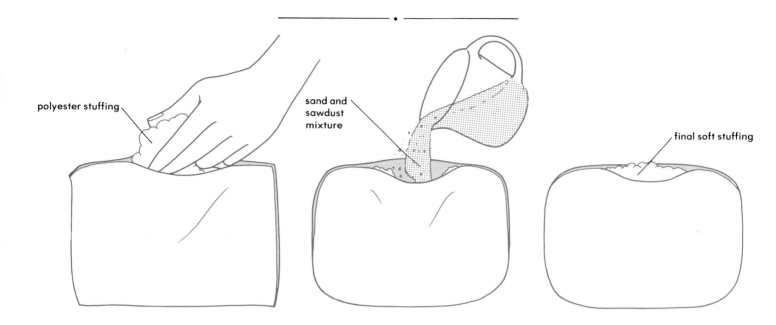

polyester stuffing

sand and sawdust mixture

final soft stuffing

2. Stuffing the cushion. Work the polyester batting or fiber stuffing into the corners and along the seams on the inside of the cushion cover. Mix the sawdust and sand, and pour it into the cover. When the cushion is pleasingly plump, place a piece of batting or a wad of stuffing on top of the mixture, along the opening. Turn under the seam allowances along the opening and slipstitch the edges together.

The smocked cushion cover

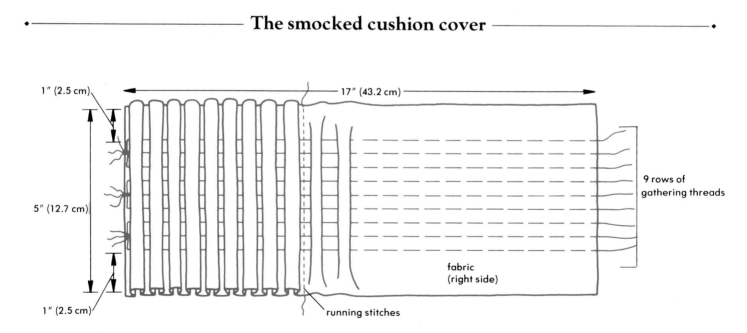

1" (2.5 cm)

17" (43.2 cm)

5" (12.7 cm)

1" (2.5 cm)

9 rows of gathering threads

fabric (right side)

running stitches

1. Preparing the smocked panel. Cut a rectangle of white broadcloth that measures 17" × 5" (43.2 × 12.7 cm). Transfer or make nine rows of gathering dots across the entire length of the fabric, leaving a 1" (2.5-cm) margin above and below the rows. The seven inner rows are for the smocking pattern, and the auxiliary rows above and below the smocking help to stabilize the pleats. Stitch and gather the fabric, beginning and ending at the very edge. (You will smock right over the seam line into the seam allowances.) Pull up the fabric along the gathering threads to a width of 6" (15.2 cm), and knot the threads. Sew a row of running stitches, using colored thread, down the center of the pleats.

The smocking and embroidery

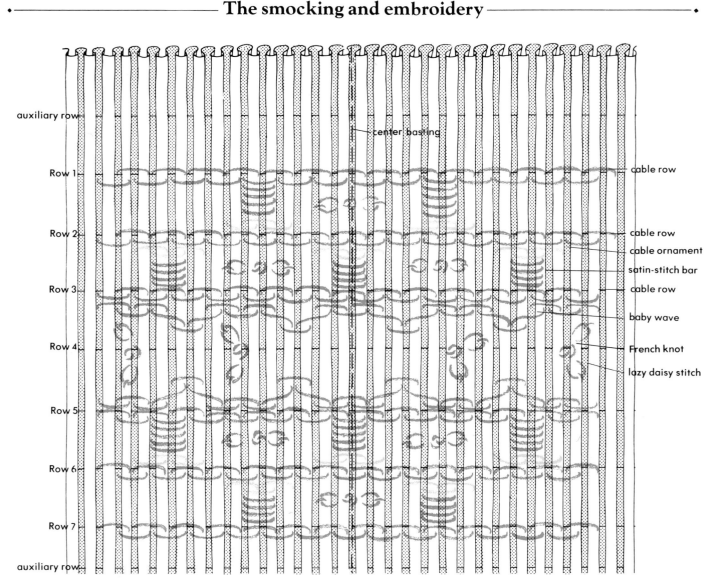

auxiliary row

center basting

Row 1 — cable row

Row 2 — cable row
— cable ornament
— satin-stitch bar
Row 3 — cable row
— baby wave

Row 4 — French knot
— lazy daisy stitch

Row 5

Row 6

Row 7

auxiliary row

2. The smocking. Skip the auxiliary row of gathering stitches at the top, and begin the first row of **smocking** (Row 1) along the second gathering row. Work Rows 1 through 7 with three or four strands of light-blue embroidery floss as follows:

Rows 1 and 7: Work cable stitches across both rows in light blue.

Rows 2 and 6: Using light-blue embroidery floss, work cable stitches across both rows and then make cable ornaments above and below each entire row, following the diagram and skipping two cables between each ornament.

Rows 3 and 5: Using light-blue embroidery floss, work cable stitches across both rows. Then work a row of baby waves separated by single cable stitches just below Row 3 and above Row 5.

3. The embroidery. Sew the embroidery using three or four strands of embroidery floss.

The bars. Using pale-green embroidery floss, make a bar of vertical satin stitches over the top of two pleats, placing them 5 cable spaces to the right and 5 cable spaces to the left of the center line. Work the satin stitches side by side between Rows 1 and 2 and between Rows 6 and 7. Work 3 bars between Rows 2 and 3 and between Rows 5 and 6, starting with a bar in the center and one on either side, about 9 cables away.

The blossoms and leaves. Stitch four yellow blossoms made of one or two yellow French knots and two or three bright-green 3/16″-long (5-mm) lazy daisy leaves across the center of Row 4, spacing them between every other baby wave and cable pattern. Then work blossoms with single French knot centers and one or two leaves in the spaces between the satin-stitch bars or at random on the smocked pincushion top.

The finishing touches

1. Steaming the smocking. Remove the gathering threads from the smocking, and steam the smocking to fit the rectangle of velvet or corduroy.

2. The lace trim. Baste the lace trim, right side up, to the right side of the smocked top ⅝″ (16 mm) from the edges, mitering the corners. Stitch both edges of the lace to the panel.

With right sides together and the scalloped side of the lace turned in, baste a second strip of lace along the outer seam line of the first strip, making a tuck in each corner so the lace can be folded out from the edge of the cushion when the top and bottom of the cover are assembled.

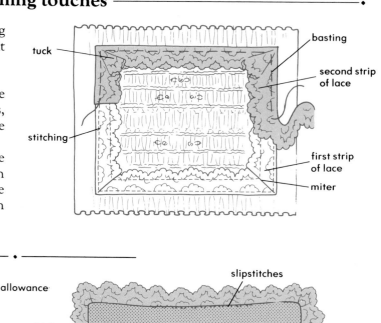

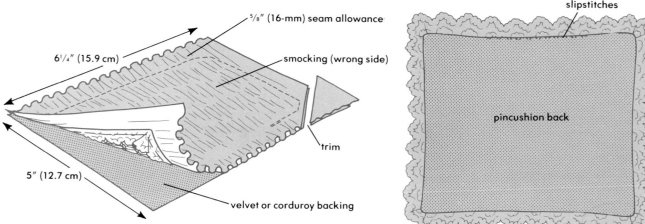

3. Joining the front and back. With right sides together, align the edges of the smocked top and the velvet or corduroy bottom and stitch them together, leaving ⅝″ (16-mm) seam allowances and a large enough opening in the long side to insert the inner cushion. Stitch the corners with two diagonal stitches as you did the inner cushion. Trim the seam allowances at the corners and turn the cushion cover right side out.

Tuck the inner cushion into the cover. Turn under the seam allowances along the opening and slipstitch the edges together.

4. The ribbon trim. Beginning and ending at the center of one long edge, stitch a band of ribbon, by hand, around the pincushion between the rows of lace, overlapping the end slightly before cutting it.

The bow. Tie a 2″-long (5-cm) bow in the remaining ribbon and trim the ends diagonally. Stitch the bow over the ends of the ribbon on the cushion.

Following the instructions on page 189, work a large blossom over the knot of the bow using yellow floss for the center and bright-green stitches around it.

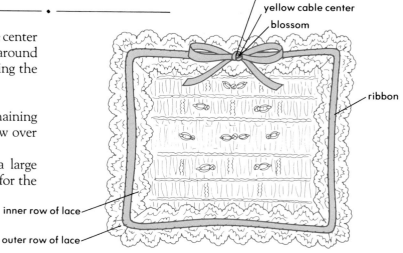

Teddy Bear

Teddy Bear

Around the turn of the century, a cartoon appeared showing that intrepid hunter, President Theodore Roosevelt, sparing the life of a bear cub. Ever since then, stuffed toy bears have been known as *teddy bears*. But stuffed animals had been the special friends of children for many generations before that time. Even today, when funny frogs and big birds on TV seem as real as people to a small child, a wonderfully furry teddy bear that willingly cuddles up to comfort a child through the night is still as welcome a gift as parents or relatives can give.

Materials

½ yard (.5 m) of 54"-wide (137-cm) medium brown fake fur (medium or short pile) fabric

Brown heavy-duty sewing thread

Polyester fiber for stuffing

2 brown and black ⅝"-diameter (16-mm) safety eyes

2 yards (1.9 m) thin black yarn

1 yard (.95 m) of 1"-wide (2.5-cm) red ribbon

Cutting the fabric

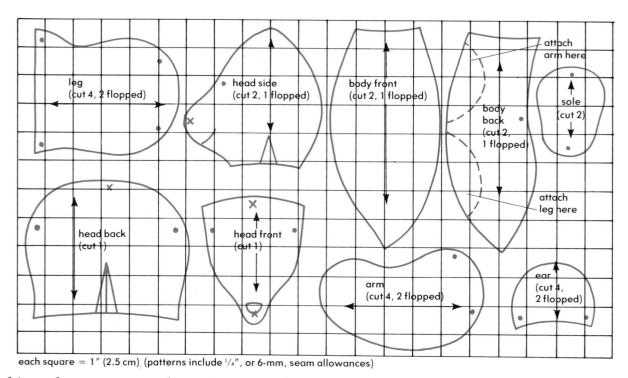

each square = 1" (2.5 cm) (patterns include ¼", or 6-mm, seam allowances)

1. Making the pattern and cutting out the fabric. Enlarge the pattern pieces to the scale indicated and cut them out following the instructions on page 175. Pin the pattern pieces to the wrong side of the fabric, so the arrows are aligned on the lengthwise grain and the nap is running down from the top of each pattern piece. Cut out and transfer the markings for the following: 1 head back, 1 head front, 1 head side, 1 body front, 1 body back, 2 arms, 2 legs, 2 soles, and 2 ears. Turn the following pattern pieces over sideways so they face in the opposite direction and cut them out, transferring any pattern markings: 1 head side, 1 body front, 1 body back, 2 arms, 2 legs, and 2 ears.

Assembling the bear

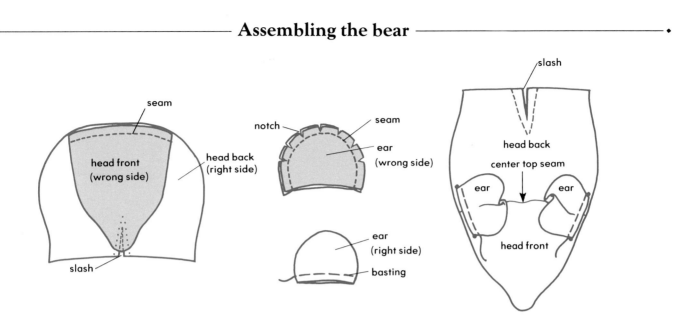

1. The head. Staystitch along the outside lines of the dart on the head back; then slash along the center line of the dart, stopping ¼″ (6 mm) short of the point.

Pin the head front to the head back, matching the center markings, and stitch them together.

The ears. To make each ear, align a pair of ear pieces right sides together, and pin. Stitch the pieces together leaving the slightly curved lower edge open. Notch the seam allowances, and turn each ear right side out. Baste the lower edges together along the seam line.

Baste one ear to each side of the head, right sides together, matching the dots and keeping the raw edges parallel.

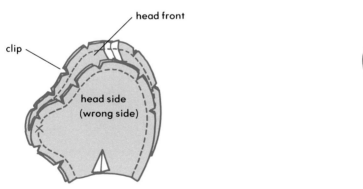

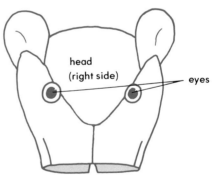

The head sides. Stitch the dart on each head side section, slash along the fold of the dart, and then press it open. With the right sides together, align the edges of one head side with the head back and front, matching the X at the nose, the dots, and the back neck edge, and stitch them together. Attach the second head side in the same manner. Clip the seam allowances along the inner curves and turn the head right side out.

The eyes. Attach the eyes by pushing the shank end of each one through the fabric ¾″ (19 mm) from the end of the nose and just below the seam line so the top of the eye touches the seam line. Attach the safety clasp on the underside of the head.

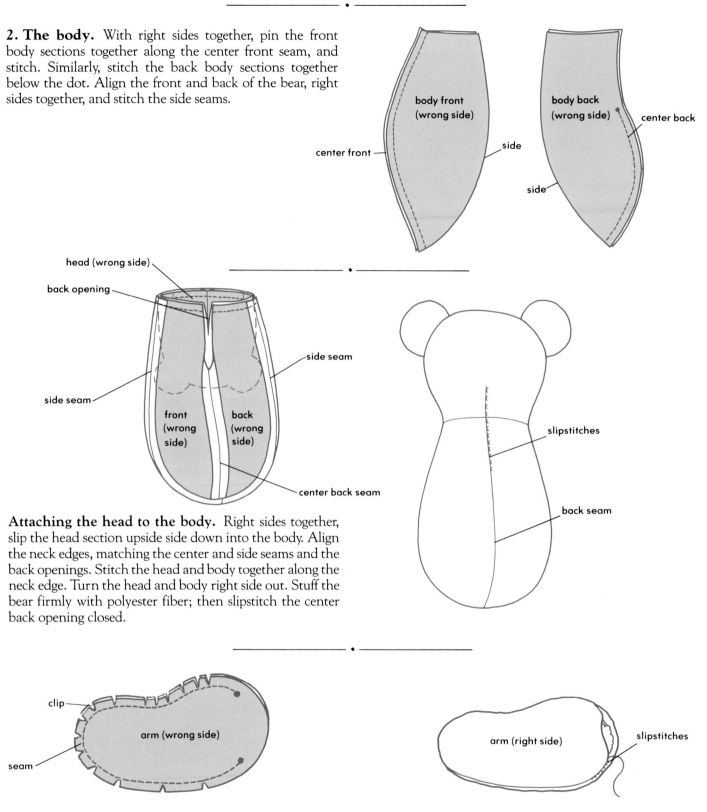

2. The body. With right sides together, pin the front body sections together along the center front seam, and stitch. Similarly, stitch the back body sections together below the dot. Align the front and back of the bear, right sides together, and stitch the side seams.

Attaching the head to the body. Right sides together, slip the head section upside side down into the body. Align the neck edges, matching the center and side seams and the back openings. Stitch the head and body together along the neck edge. Turn the head and body right side out. Stuff the bear firmly with polyester fiber; then slipstitch the center back opening closed.

3. The arms and legs. Align two **arm** sections, right sides together, pin, and join them, leaving an opening between the dots. Clip the seam allowances along the inner curves and turn the arm right side out. In a similar fashion, join the other arm sections.

Stuff the arms firmly with polyester fiber, but leave the end with the opening rather flat. Turn under ¼" (6 mm) of fabric around the opening, then slipstitch the opening closed.

The legs. Align two leg sections, right sides together, pin, and join them, leaving an opening between the dots at each end. Pin the sole to the straight edge of the leg, matching the dots. Clip the seam allowance on the leg edge if necessary to make it fit the curve of the sole. Stitch the sole and leg together. Clip the seam allowances along the inner curve of the leg, and turn the leg right side out. Stuff the leg firmly, but leave the curved end rather flat. Turn ¹/₄″ (6 mm) of fabric under along the opening, then slipstitch the opening closed. Repeat for the other leg.

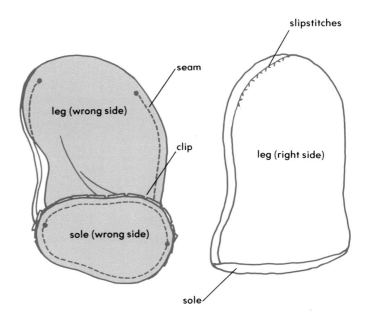

seam

slipstitches

leg (wrong side)

clip

leg (right side)

sole (wrong side)

sole

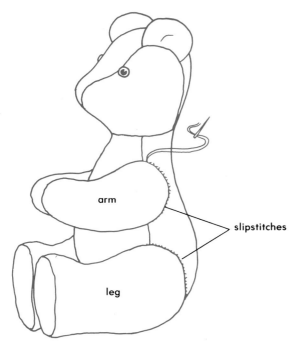

arm

slipstitches

leg

Attaching the arms and legs. Position the arms and legs along the sides and back of the body as indicated in the illustration. Using a needle with doubled thread, slipstitch the tops of the legs and arms securely to the body.

4. The finishing touches. Using a large needle and black yarn, embroider the **nose** with sixteen to eighteen ⁷/₁₆″- to ⁵/₈″-long (11- to 16-mm) satin stitches sewed in the shape of an upside down pyramid that is ¹/₂″ (13 mm) wide at the top.

The mouth. For the mouth, make three 1¹/₈″-long (2.9-cm) straight stitches ³/₈″ (9.5 mm) below the bottom of the nose. Using black yarn, tack the center of the mouth in place at the center front seam line, making the stitch about ¹/₄″ (6 mm) below the ends of the mouth to pull it into a smile.

The bow. Tie a ribbon around the bear's neck into a pretty bow and neatly clip the ends of the ribbon.

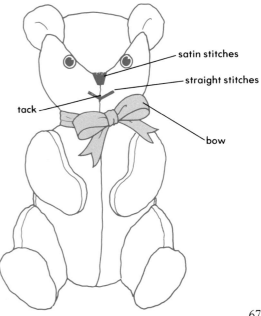

satin stitches

straight stitches

tack

bow

Christening Classics

n the Western world, long clothes have traditionally been worn by the socially prominent, by the clergy, and certainly by most women on important occasions such as weddings. The more exalted the personage, the longer the clothes: witness the sumptuous trains of royalty that trail for yards. This distinction has extended to little children, too, even to babes in arms. At his christening in 1491, the future Henry VIII wore robes that measured three ells in length, something over eleven feet! Several attendants were required just to bear the royal baby's train to the font.

In those days the christening robe was actually a mantle, open down the front, since the child was bound hand and foot in his swaddling clothes and wrapped in numerous other garments. Swaddling clothes disappeared, mercifully, during the eighteenth century, but the tradition of elaborate robes for the christening of royal babies, aristocratic babies, and anyone else who could afford it remained firmly entrenched. Although christening mantles and dresses grew shorter over the centuries, a very elaborate dress for the christening service still distinguished any baby of consequence. And today, many mothers who value fine handiwork follow this centuries-old tradition, making beautifully crafted garments for their own children.

White has been the preferred color for christening robes for 200 years, and the robes have invariably been ornamented with fine white embroidery. Panels of raised satin stitches, called Ayrshire work, on the bodice and down the front of the skirt to the hem, were widely prized in England during the nineteenth century. While most garments became less elaborate as the Victorian Age drew to a close, embroidery, fancy tucks, and yards of lace remained part of the requisite style for christening clothes.

The robes in museums and private collections from former times exhibit exceptionally delicate and precise handiwork rarely seen today. Some French convents used to specialize in making christening dresses; with painstaking care, the nuns created elaborately worked dresses, sewing every stitch by hand. The christening dress described in this chapter uses a center panel design that was created long ago in such a convent. Fortunately, machine techniques now closely imitate beautiful handwork in a fraction of the time it used to take; thus, even the busiest seamstress can find time to create this heirloom.

Cornelius Vanderbilt, Jr. poses calmly for his christening portrait, taken in 1898. His mother, Mrs. Cornelius Vanderbilt III, has dressed him in the long clothes traditional for christenings, some four feet of embroidered and lace-trimmed white satin.

Christening Dress and Slip

Every stitch was sewn by hand in this lovely heirloom christening gown worn by three generations of Priscilla Alden's descendants.

Special Materials and Techniques

Choosing the right materials

The fabrics. Very fine 100% cotton fabrics have a soft, lustrous quality that makes them ideal for baby wear. Batiste is the best fabric choice because it is soft, sheer, and dainty. Cotton lawn is somewhat crisper and heavier. Avoid using a fabric with a high percentage of synthetic fibers; they can cause sewing problems such as puckering. Such fabrics may also be treated with resins, which yellow permanently with age.

Cotton batiste imported from Switzerland is the best quality and, of course, the most expensive. If imported fabric is out of the question because of price or availability, try to find a domestic batiste of very good quality. They are readily available for about one-half to one-third the cost per yard of the imported fabric.

Choose a fabric with fine, closely woven threads. The more threads per inch, the better the fabric. Look for threads that cross each other at right angles.

Since lightweight cottons are sheer, buy enough fabric to make a matching slip (see page 80). Most slips are very simple in style and have only a ruffle or flounce at the bottom to give body to the dress. Such long slips were formerly called "gertrudes."

The trims. Trims of 100% cotton have the softness and delicacy so desirable for trimming baby's clothing. Many cotton trims are imported, and their prices reflect this fact. If you have trouble finding cotton trims in your locality, consult the mail-order sources in the Appendix. They are worth the expense if your budget permits. Most of the laces and eyelets sold in stores today have a percentage of synthetic fibers, and they are available at reasonable prices in a variety of patterns and styles. If you choose a synthetic trim, be sure it has a soft hand and a delicate look.

Lace and embroidery trims.
Lace insertion is lace with straight edges on both sides. It is sewed between two panels or sections of fabric, lace, or beading.

Beading is lace insertion with holes in it through which ribbon can be woven.

Edgings have one decorative edge and one plain edge that is often unfinished and must be trimmed before sewing. Edgings can be made of embroidered tape, eyelet, embroidered net, or lace, and they come in many widths. Some edgings are gathered into a binding. These are usually too bulky to use with delicate fabrics.

Ribbon. Double-faced satin ribbon has the same satin weave on both sides. It is softer and more lustrous than single-faced ribbon, and does not show a wrong side when tied in a bow, making it the obvious choice for trimming a fine garment.

Thread and needles. For this project, two-ply cotton thread known variously as lingerie thread or hand-sewing thread, is worth searching out. It blends into the lace and helps make machine techniques resemble painstaking handwork. One large spool is usually enough, so in this case price should not be a deterrent. Availability, however, might be a problem. Again, see the mail-order sources in the Appendix, or find a notions shop with a large selection of threads and brave down any incredulous stares.

For work on fine cotton and lace, use a very fine sewing-machine needle—size 9 or 11 (American), or 70 or 80 (European). For hand sewing, use a sharp, slender needle of short to medium length.

Fine sewing techniques

The look of fine hand sewing can be duplicated a number of ways by machine. Even the thread you use can make a difference when sewing a fine fabric, such as batiste or lawn. Thread your machine and wind the bobbin with two-ply lingerie thread. To gather such fine fabrics, loosen the upper thread tension of the machine, and set it at 14 to 16 stitches to the inch (2.5 cm). This technique results in tiny, elegant pleats when the bobbin thread is pulled.

Other sewing skills needed for the christening dress involve the stitching of lace. Whether you are joining lace to lace or lace to fabric, the machine-whipped finish shown here is both easy and fool proof.

Machine whipping a tiny hem. Cleanly trim the raw edge of the fabric. Stitch along the edge of the fabric so that the left side of the zigzag stitching goes through the fabric and the right side goes completely over the raw edge. To prevent stretching along curved, bias, or diagonal edges, first staystitch, using 16 to 18 stitches per inch (2.5 cm) and stitching 1/4″ (6 mm) away from the raw edge of the

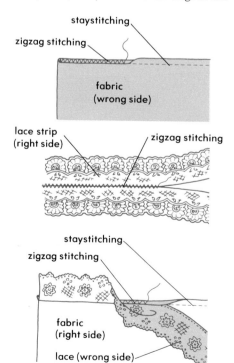

fabric. Then trim the fabric to within 1/16″ (1.5 mm) of the stitching and machine whip a tiny hem along the edge, catching the stitching and the edge of the fabric.

Joining strips of lace. Position two lace strips next to each other, right sides up, with the edges touching. Feed the strips through the machine so that the left side of the zigzag stitching sews through the left strip and the right side of the zigzag stitching sews through the right strip. The joining will be nearly invisible.

Whipping lace and fabric together. First staystitch 1/8″ (3mm) from the fabric edge. Then place the lace edging over the fabric, right sides together and aligning the raw edges, and pin. Set the machine for a medium-width zigzag stitch at about 20 stitches to the inch (2.5 cm). Arrange the fabric so that one side of the stitching falls just over the raw edges of the lace and the staystitching on the fabric. Stitch the lace to the fabric. Then fold the lace back over the stitches and press.

Christening Dress

Making a christening dress is an ambitious project, but it can be a richly satisfying experience that results in a future heirloom. Choose your fabrics and trimmings carefully. Practice each sewing technique on scraps until you have mastered it, and allow plenty of time to complete the project. Keep the dress carefully folded and wrapped in tissue, out of the way of any household activity between work sessions. Be sure to wash your hands and dust your sewing area each time you resume work. Refer to the "Dressmaking Skills" section for any unfamiliar sewing techniques.

Materials

8 yards (7.3 m) of ¼"-wide (6-mm) double-faced satin ribbon

12½" (32 cm) of ⅛"-wide (3-mm) elastic

White two-ply lingerie thread

White sewing thread

Four ¼"-diameter (6-mm) pearl sew-through buttons

White cotton batiste or lawn: 3 yards (2.7 m) of 42"- to 48"-wide (106- to 121-cm)

8 yards (7.3 m) of ⅝"-wide (16-mm) lace insertion

4 yards (3.7 m) of ⅝"-wide (16-mm) lace beading

7 yards (6.4 m) of 3"-wide (7.6-cm) cotton eyelet edging

Cutting the fabric

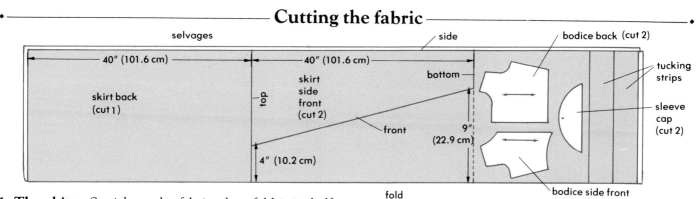

1. The skirt. Straighten the fabric, then fold it in half lengthwise, right sides together. For the skirt front and back, cut two pieces the full width of the fabric and 40" (102 cm) long—36" (91.4 cm) for the length of the skirt, plus 4" (10.2 cm) for tucks.

With the fabric still folded, measure 4" (10.2 cm) from the fold along one end of one of the pieces of fabric and mark it with a small, light pencil dot. This will be the inside edge of the top of the skirt side front. Measure and mark a point 9" (23 cm) from the fold on the bottom of the front piece. Connect the dots with a straight line. The sections along the selvages will be the skirt side front pieces. Cut the fabric through both layers along the line to form space for the lace panel that will be inserted down the front of the dress.

2. The bodice. Enlarge the bodice side front, bodice back, sleeve cap, and sleeve edge patterns, and cut the first three out of the remaining fabric, following the instructions on page 175. Put the sleeve edge pattern aside for later use.

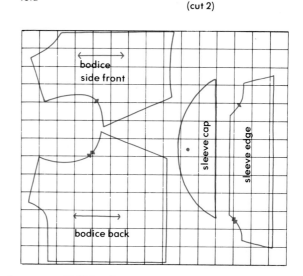

each square = 1" (2.5 cm)

patterns include ⅝" (16-mm) seam allowances, except where otherwise indicated

73

Assembling the bodice

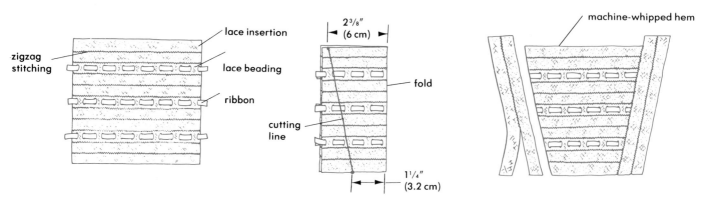

1. The lace bodice panel. Cut eight 5″ (12.7-cm) lengths of lace insertion and three 5″ (12.7-cm) lengths of lace beading. Join the strips by using the machine whipping technique illustrated earlier and alternating two strips of lace insertion with one strip of beading until all of the strips are joined. When all the strips are joined, the center panel should match the length of the bodice side front. If necessary, add extra strips, alternating them in the same manner.

Shaping the panel. Thread the double-faced white satin ribbon through all the strips of beading. Fold the lace panel in half perpendicular to the strips of lace. Place a pin 2³/₈″ (6 cm) from the fold on the top edge of the lace panel. Then place another pin 1¹/₄″ (3.2 cm) from the fold on the lower edge of the panel. Connect the two points with a straight line, then cut along the line through both layers of fabric. Staystitch along both cut edges just inside the raw edges. Cut four more strips of insertion lace about ¹/₂″ (13 mm) longer than the sides of the bodice panel. Join the strips lengthwise in pairs, and then join one pair of strips to each side of the panel, aligning the bottom edges.

2. The bodice front. Cut two strips of eyelet edging the length of the bodice from shoulder to waistline. Trim the unfinished edge of the eyelet so that each strip is 2″ (5 cm) wide.

With wrong sides together, align one diagonal side edge of the center panel with the diagonal edge of the corresponding bodice side front.

With right sides together, align the cut edge of one eyelet strip along the side of the center insert panel that is already aligned with the side front piece. Make sure that the lower edges are even and that the finished edge of the eyelet faces in. Pin through all three layers. Stitch ¹/₄″ (6 mm) from the edge, and trim the seam allowances to a scant ¹/₈″ (3 mm). Fold the fabric bodice and the eyelet away from the center panel, and press. Topstitch along the seamed edge of the eyelet edging through the bodice, enclosing the seam allowances. By hand, stitch a vertical tuck in the eyelet at the lower edge of the bodice to make the edging 1″ (2.5 cm) wide.

Trim away the extra lace and eyelet at the neckline in a gradual curve that conforms to the shape of the bodice.

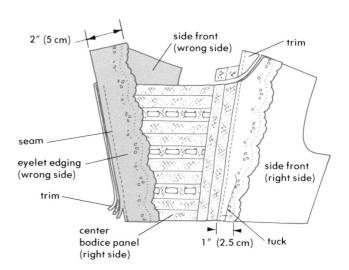

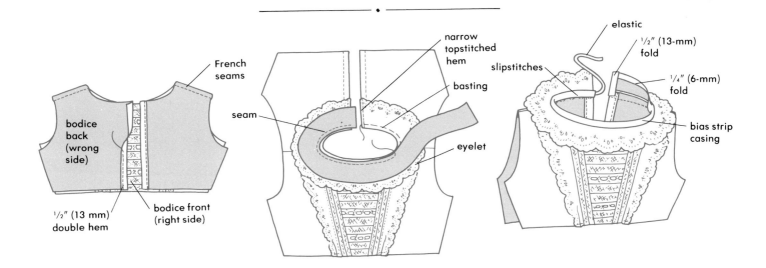

3. Joining the bodice and finishing the neck.

To **join** the bodice pieces, first turn under and stitch a 1/2" (13-mm) double hem along the center edges of the bodice backs. Join the backs to the front at the shoulders with tiny French seams.

The neck. For the neck ruffle, cut a strip of eyelet edging the length of the neck edge plus a little extra for a narrow hem at each end. Trim away the unfinished edge so the eyelet is 2 1/2" (6.4 cm) wide. Roll and stitch the ends of the eyelet. With right sides up, pin the eyelet to the neck edge and baste 1/4" (6 mm) from the edge.

From the white fabric, cut a 1 1/4"-wide (3.2-cm) bias strip that is 1" (2.5 cm) longer than the neck edge. With right sides together and edges matching, pin the bias strip to the neck edge, so that 1/2" (13 mm) of the strip extends beyond each center back edge. Stitch through all layers 1/4" (6 mm) from the edges. Fold the bias strip over the seam allowances to encase them, turning the long raw edge under 1/4" (6 mm) and turning the ends under, even with the neck edge. Slipstitch the casing to the inside of the neck along the seam line.

Take the 12 1/2" (32-cm) length of 1/8"-wide (3-mm) elastic and, using a small safety pin at the end as a guide, run it through the casing. Tack the elastic in place at each end of the casing with a few hand stitches. Slipstitch the ends of the casing closed.

4. The sleeves and buttonholes.

Using the pattern pieces as a guide, cut two **sleeve** edges from the eyelet edging, placing the lower (longest, straight) edge of the pattern along the finished decorative edge of the eyelet.

With right sides together, join an eyelet sleeve edge to each sleeve cap with a tiny French seam. Sew a row of fine gathering stitches—14 to 16 stitches per inch (2.5 cm), with the upper tension of the machine loosened—on the curved edge of each sleeve cap, just inside the seam line. With right sides together, pin a sleeve to each armhole, pulling the bottom (bobbin) gathering threads to fit the sleeves to the armhole. Adjust the fullness, and pin about every 1/2" (13 mm). Stitch along the seam line. Make another row of stitching through the seam allowances 1/8" (3 mm) from the seam line and trim the seam allowances close to the stitching.

Using a French seam, stitch the side and sleeve seams.

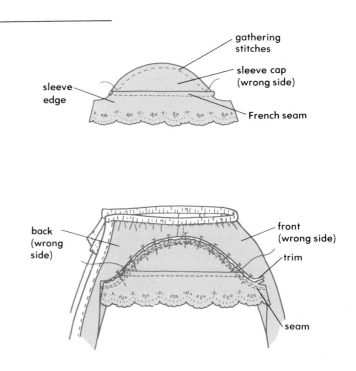

The buttonholes. Make three ¹/₂″-long (13-mm) buttonholes on the right bodice back and one buttonhole on the left bodice back. Sew the first buttonhole on the right back side 1¹/₄″ (3.2 cm) below the neck edge in the middle of the hem along the edge. Space the other two buttonholes the same distance apart below the first one. Stitch the buttonhole on the left bodice back ³/₄″ (19 mm) above the bottom edge and just to the left of the center back hem.

Make a thread loop buttonhole at the edge of the neck opening on the right bodice back. Sew a ¹/₄″-diameter (6-mm) button on the opposite neck edge.

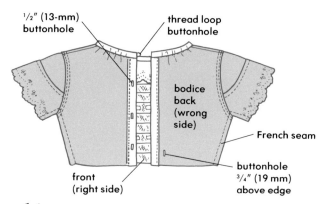

Assembling the skirt

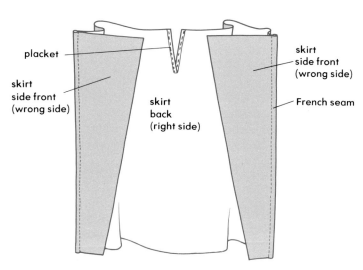

1. The side seams, placket, and hem. **Seam** the skirt pieces by stitching the skirt back to the side fronts along the side edges with tiny French seams. Press the seam allowances toward the back.

The placket. Make a 3″-long (7.6-cm) placket at the center back of the skirt, following the directions on page

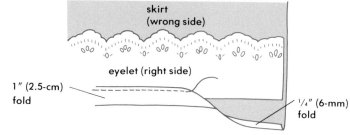

178. To maintain the delicate proportions of the dress, cut a 1¹/₈″-wide (2.9-cm) placket strip.

The hem and hem tuck. Turn under and press a ¹/₄″ (6-mm) fold along the lower edge of the skirt. Then turn under and press an additional 1″ (2.5 cm) of fabric. Cut a length of eyelet edging to fit the lower edge of the skirt. Trim the unfinished edge of the eyelet to make it 3″ (7.6 cm) wide. With wrong sides together, tuck ¹/₄″ (6 mm) of the unfinished edge of the eyelet under the top edge of the hem. Pin, then baste along the top edge of the hem. Then stitch through all layers from the inside of the skirt. Press the eyelet down away from the skirt so that it shows below the hem, and press the resulting tuck down.

3. The tucks. To stitch the tucks, loosen the upper tension of your machine slightly and adjust the stitch length to eight stitches per inch (2.5 cm).

Tucks tend to pucker, especially on sheer fabrics. To minimize this problem, be sure to use a fine needle for stitching the christening dress. As you stitch, hold the fabric taut, with your left hand behind the needle and your right hand in front, pulling it through the machine gently. If the fabric puckers, place a strip of tissue paper between the feed dog and the fabric and stitch through it. Tear away the paper after stitching.

After determining where the fold of your first tuck will be and folding and pinning the fabric down to that point on the right side, measure at intervals along the entire length of

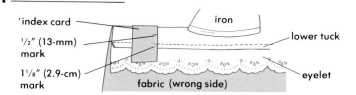

the tuck to make sure it is even. Press, and stitch the desired distance from the fold. Be sure to stitch from the side that will be seen so you can control the finished look.

Press each tuck three times; first, along the fold before you stitch it; second, from the wrong side after stitching; and third, from the right side with the fabric flat, to press the tuck into position.

While you are still at the ironing board, measure the distance to the next fold and press it in place.

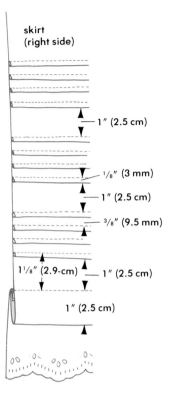

skirt
(right side)

1″ (2.5 cm)

1/8″ (3 mm)

1″ (2.5 cm)

3/8″ (9.5 mm)

1 1/8″ (2.9-cm) 1″ (2.5 cm)

1″ (2.5 cm)

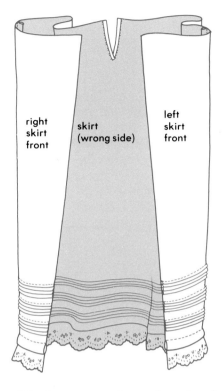

right skirt front

skirt (wrong side)

left skirt front

The skirt tucks. Decorate the bottom of the skirt with three groups of four 1/8-wide (3-mm) tucks, spacing each group so the fold of the first tuck is 1″ (2.5 cm) above the stitching of the last tuck. To start a group of tucks, measure 1 1/8″ (2.9 cm) from the stitching of the last tuck to the fold line of the first tuck in the group. An index card marked for

the length will facilitate measuring and spacing the tucks, as shown at the bottom of the opposite page.

To make each tuck within a group, measure 1/2″ (13 mm) from the stitching line of the last tuck to the fold of the next in a similar fashion. The resulting stitching lines in each group will be 3/8″ (9.5 mm) apart.

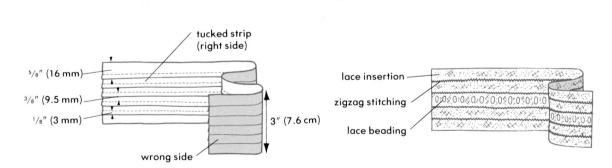

tucked strip (right side)

5/8″ (16 mm)

3/8″ (9.5 mm)

1/8″ (3 mm)

wrong side

3″ (7.6 cm)

lace insertion

zigzag stitching

lace beading

4. The center front skirt panel. To make the **tucked sections,** cut two 4 1/4″-wide (10.8-cm) strips of the white dress fabric equal to the entire width of the fabric; cut along a pulled thread to keep the grain of the fabric straight. Then cut the long strips into shorter single strips of each of the following lengths: 12″, 14″, 16″, 18″, and 20″ (30.5, 35.6, 40.6, 45.7, and 50.8 cm).

The tucks. Beginning with a fold parallel to and 5/8″ (16 mm) from one long edge, make five 1/8″-deep (3-mm) tucks

on each strip, spacing the stitching between them 3/8″ (9.5 mm) apart. The finished width of the tucked strip should be 3″ (7.6 cm).

The lace sections. Cut four strips of lace insertion and one strip of beading to each of the following lengths: 12″, 14″, 16″, and 18″ (30.5, 35.6, 40.6, and 45.7 cm). Aligning the five strips of similar length, stitch two lengths of lace insertion to each side of the beading strips, as described earlier.

lace panel
(wrong side)

zigzag
stitching

tucked strip
(right side)

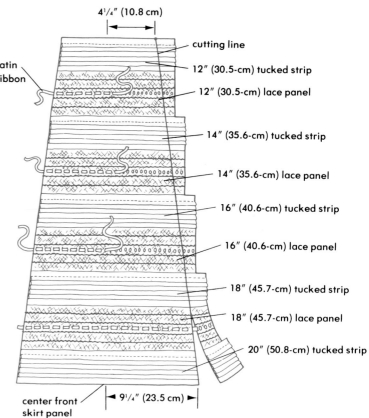

satin
ribbon

4¹/₄" (10.8 cm)

cutting line

12" (30.5-cm) tucked strip

12" (30.5-cm) lace panel

14" (35.6-cm) tucked strip

14" (35.6-cm) lace panel

16" (40.6-cm) tucked strip

16" (40.6-cm) lace panel

18" (45.7-cm) tucked strip

18" (45.7-cm) lace panel

20" (50.8-cm) tucked strip

center front
skirt panel

9¹/₄" (23.5 cm)

Joining the tucked and lace sections. Align the 12"-long (30.5-cm) tucked strip and the 12"-long (30.5-cm) lace panel, right sides together, and join them using the machine-whipped seam technique described earlier.

In the same fashion, join the other strips of similar length. Matching the center of each piece vertically, working from the shortest (14", 35.6 cm) to the longest (20", 50.8 cm), and alternating tucked and lace sections, in that order, machine whip the sections, right sides together, along the edges.

Shaping the center panel. To shape the center panel, mark a point 4¹/₄" (10.8 cm) to each side of the center along the top edge of the 12" (30.5-cm) tucked strip. Mark a point 9¹/₄" (23.5 cm) to each side of the center along the lower edge of the 20" (50.8-cm) tucked strip. Connect the marks on each side with a straight line and cut along the lines.

Thread satin ribbon through the lace beading strips, leaving ¹/₂" (13 mm) extending beyond the edge at each end.

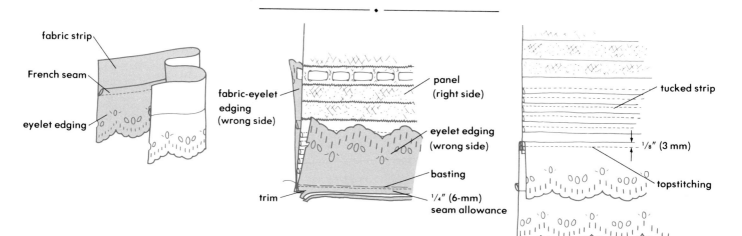

fabric strip

French seam

eyelet edging

fabric-eyelet
edging
(wrong side)

panel
(right side)

eyelet edging
(wrong side)

basing

¹/₄" (6-mm)
seam allowance

trim

tucked strip

¹/₈" (3 mm)

topstitching

5. The eyelet edging. Cut a 2" × 20" (5 × 50.8-cm) strip of dress fabric and a 20" (50.8-cm) length of eyelet. Stitch them together with a French seam. With wrong sides together, pin, then baste the fabric-eyelet strip to the bottom of the center panel, leaving a ¹/₄" (6-mm) seam allowance. When the edging is folded down, the center panel should be the same length as the skirt side fronts. Adjust the width of the fabric strip along the bottom, if necessary.

Cut an 18¹/₂" (47-cm) length of eyelet. With right sides together, align the unfinished edge of the eyelet with the lower edge of the center panel. Fold back the fabric-eyelet

strip, and then baste them together, leaving a ¹/₄" (6-mm) seam allowance.

Stitch the seam, joining both edgings to the center panel. Trim the seam allowances to a scant ¹/₈" (3 mm). Press both edgings down over the seam allowance, and topstitch ¹/₈" (3 mm) below the seam.

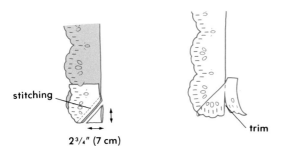

stitching

2³/₄" (7 cm)

trim

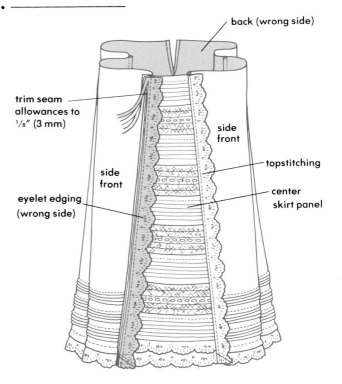

back (wrong side)

trim seam
allowances to
¹/₈" (3 mm)

side
front

topstitching

center
skirt panel

side
front

eyelet edging
(wrong side)

6. Attaching the center front panel. Cut two strips of eyelet edging the length of the diagonal edge of the center panel plus 4″ (10.2 cm). Trim the unfinished edge of the eyelet to make the eyelet 3″ (7.6 cm) wide. Turn the strips so the finished edge of one faces left and the other faces right.

Mitering the bottom of the eyelet. Fold up 3¹/₂″ to 4″ (9 to 10.2 cm) at the lower edge of each eyelet strip, wrong sides together, so the patterned edges of the eyelet match, and pin. Starting on the unfinished edge, measure and mark a point 2³/₄″ (7 cm) from the lower corner along the fold. Make a mark the same distance from the corner along the unfinished edge. Using a pencil, lightly draw a line between the points. Cut along that line. Finish the edges with a French seam. Fold down and press the mitered end of the eyelet, and trim the excess fabric that extends beyond the long unfinished edge of the eyelet.

With wrong sides together, align the diagonal edges of the center panel and the side front sections. With right sides together and lower edges even, align the mitered edging and

the center panel. Pin through all three layers. Stitch ¹/₄″ (6 mm) from the edge. Trim the seam allowances to a scant ¹/₈″ (3 mm). Fold the side front and the edging away from the center skirt, and press. Topstitch along the seamed edge of the eyelet edging through the side front, enclosing the seam allowances.

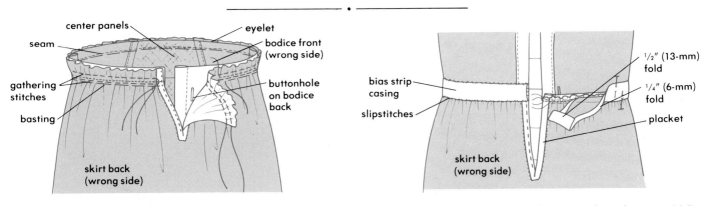

center panels

seam

eyelet

bodice front
(wrong side)

buttonhole
on bodice
back

gathering
stitches

basting

skirt back
(wrong side)

bias strip
casing

slipstitches

skirt back
(wrong side)

¹/₂″ (13-mm)
fold

¹/₄″ (6-mm)
fold

placket

7. Gathering the skirt. Using ordinary white sewing thread and starting and ending at the center back placket, sew one row of fine gathering stitches just inside the ⁵/₈″ (16 mm) seam line at the top edge of the skirt and another row ³/₈″ (9.5 mm) from the edge.

Joining the skirt and bodice. With right sides together, pin the skirt to the bodice, aligning the center back edges, the side seams, the eyelet, the side front seams, and the center front. Pull up the bobbin threads to gather the skirt until it fits the bodice, distributing the fullness evenly. Baste,

then seam the skirt and bodice together, leaving ⁵/₈″ (16-mm) seam allowances. Press the seam allowances toward the bodice, and then trim them to ¹/₄″ (6 mm).

The bias casing. Cut a 1″-wide (2.5-cm) bias strip from the white dress fabric to fit the waistline of the dress, plus 1″ (2.5 cm). Turn under ¹/₄″ (6 mm) on each long edge and ¹/₂″ (13 mm) on each end of the strip. Pin the lower edge of the casing along the waist seam line and the top edge to the bodice. Slipstitch the casing in place.

8. The finishing touches. Thread 3 yards (2.7 m) of ¼″ (6-mm) ribbon through the casing, bringing it out through the buttonhole on the left side. Sew four buttons in position on the left back. When the dress is on the baby, draw up the ribbon in the casing to fit the baby's waist and tie a bow at the center back.

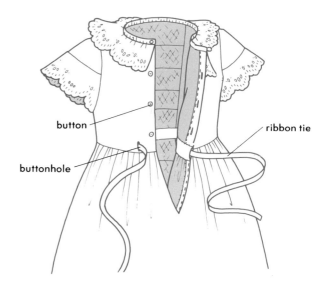

button

ribbon tie

buttonhole

Christening Slip

The christening slip is designed with a narrow bodice to minimize bulk around the baby's waist and with a ruffled four-gore skirt to support the skirt of the christening dress shown on page 70 .

Materials

2½ yards (2.4 m) of 42″- to 48″-wide (107-to 122 cm) batiste

3 yards (2.9 m) of ¾″-wide (19-mm) lace edging

Four ¼″-diameter (6-mm) mother-of-pearl buttons

Cutting the fabric

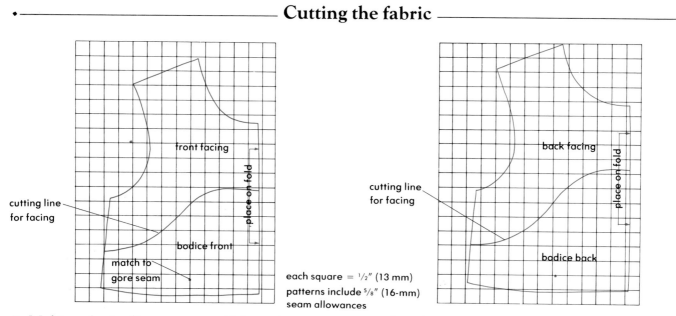

front facing

place on fold

cutting line
for facing

bodice front

match to
gore seam

back facing

place on fold

cutting line
for facing

bodice back

each square = ½″ (13 mm)
patterns include ⅝″ (16-mm)
seam allowances

1. Making the bodice patterns. Enlarge the patterns for the bodice and its facings according to the scale indicated, and cut them out following the instructions on page 175. Transfer pattern markings to the patterns.

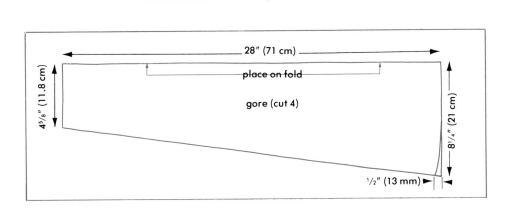

2. Making the gore pattern. The skirt is cut in four identically shaped gores tapered to reduce bulk at the waist and give fullness at the hem.

To make the gore pattern, draw a straight 28″-long (71-cm) line on a long piece of paper, and mark it for placement along the fold of the fabric.

Make a 4⅝″-long (11.8-cm) line at one end of and at right angles to the first line. Make a similar 8¼″-long (21-cm) line at the other end of the first line.

Connect the ends of both lines with a diagonal line. Mark a point on the diagonal line ½″ (13 mm) from the wider end. Connect the ½″ (13-mm) mark and the end of the 28″-long (71-cm) line with a curved line to shape the bottom of the gore.

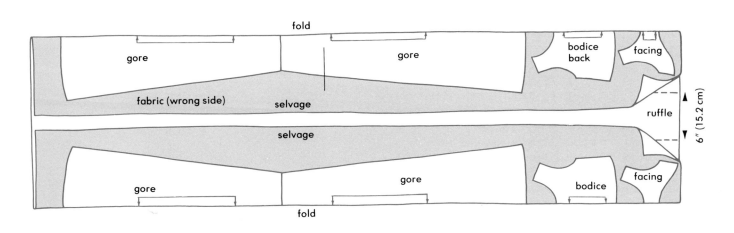

3. Cutting the fabric. Fold both sides of the fabric lengthwise to the center, wrong side out. Cut four gores, one front and one back facing piece and one front and one back bodice piece with the center edge of each pattern piece placed along the folds of the fabric.

Cut a 6″-wide (15.2-cm) strip of fabric equal to the entire length of the fabric for the ruffle.

Assembling the slip

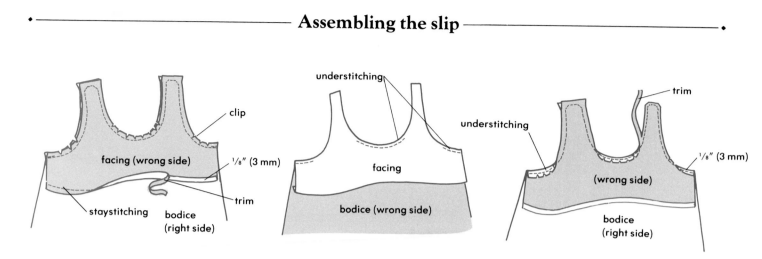

1. Facing the bodice. Staystitch the facings ⁵⁄₈″ (16 mm) from the bottom edge, and press the edge under along the stitching line. Trim the fabric to ¹⁄₈″ (3 mm) outside the line of staystitching.

Join a facing piece to each bodice section, right sides together, along the outer edges, making a diagonal stitch or two at both corners of each shoulder strap, as shown. Clip the curved edges. Turn the front and back sections of the bodice right side out, and press. Understitch the facing about 2″ (5 cm) along the center front and center back of the bodice and along the bottom edge of the armhole on each side.

Turn the bodice pieces wrong side out again, and trim the seam allowances to a scant ¹⁄₈″ (3 mm) outside the entire seam line. Also trim the corners of the shoulder straps. Turn the bodice right side out.

2. Finishing the bodice. Join the side seams of the bodice and facings with French seams; slipstitch the bottom edge of the facings to the bodice.

Make two buttonhole loops at the end of each back shoulder strap. Stitch a button in each corresponding position about ³⁄₈″ (9.5 mm) from the end of each front shoulder strap so the back will overlap the front when buttoned.

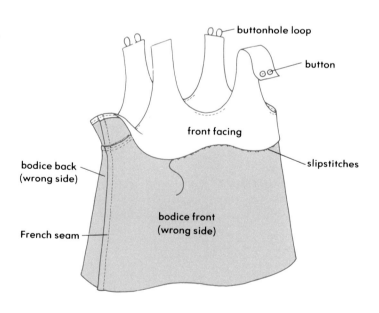

3. The skirt. Join the long edges of the gores of the skirt with French seams, leaving one seam open. Stitch two rows of gathering stitches around the top of the skirt at the waist, one ¼″ (6 mm) from the edge, the second ¼″ (6 mm) from the first row of stitching.

The ruffle. Stitch two rows of gathering stitches across the top of the ruffle, one ¼″ (6 mm) from the edge and the other ¼″ (6 mm) below the first.

Make a machine-whipped hem along the bottom edge of the ruffle, as follows. Place the lace edging along the bottom of the ruffle with the raw edges aligned and right sides together, and join them with very closely spaced overcast or zigzag stitches that run off the edge of the fabric. Then fold down the lace and press it. (If you don't have a machine that does overcast or zigzag stitching, make a narrow topstitched hem along the bottom of the ruffle. Then stitch the lace edging, wrong side down over the right side of the ruffle, along the hem edge.)

Attaching the ruffle. Join the skirt and ruffle with a French seam.

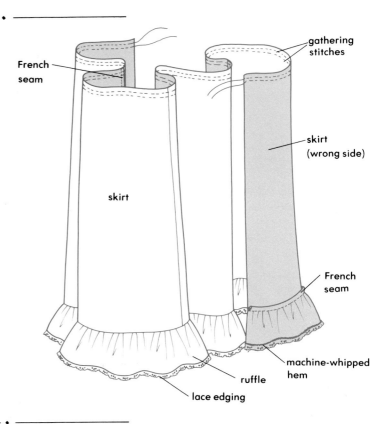

4. Finishing the slip. Gather the top of the skirt evenly along the threads to fit the bodice. Turn the skirt right side out; turn the bodice wrong side out and slip it inside the skirt so that the wrong sides are together and the seams of two of the gores match the pattern markings on the bodice. Sew the bodice to the skirt with a French seam.

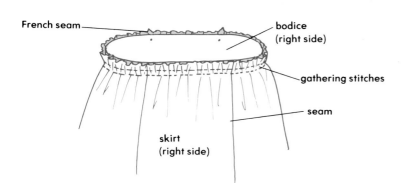

Smocking Favorites

The ancient art of smocking, undoubtedly the oldest decorative construction technique represented in this book, retains all its vitality today as a hand-crafted adornment for children's clothes. What we now call a smock was, in Anglo-Saxon times, a sort of shift or chemise, worn by women as an undergarment beneath a woolen dress. It became the fashion to decorate the upper part of the undergarment with fine stitching, and to cut the neck of the overdress lower to display this handiwork.

By the thirteenth century in England, the smock had become a peasant worker's garment, elaborately embroidered around the collar and yoke and even down the sides and at the wrists. This fine stitching, which we know as smocking, served then as now to gather the loose-fitting fabric together in flexible pleats at those crucial points where a fabric is pulled most. It also added welcome warmth around the shoulders during the chilly seasons of the year.

Over the centuries a tradition arose of employing certain stitches to signify the wearer's trade. A farmer's smock, for example, might be worked around the collar and yoke with cart wheels and ears of corn, while a woodsman's garment might be trimmed with trees and branches. A woman might even add her own personal touches to a smock, such as lover's knots and hearts, affectionately applied to a husband's or son's garment.

Today, of course, such durable symbolism has disappeared; about the only people who still wear pleated work garments are choir boys and bishops. But the art of fine smocking is far from dead. During the nineteenth century it became a popular technique for sewing children's garments, and so it remains today. For not only is smocking a wonderfully attractive and varied decoration, and thus a source of pride for the seamstress, but the flexibility afforded by the pleats is especially accommodating to growing shoulders and expanding tummies.

The projects that follow—an infant's nightgown of smocked Viyella, and a toddler's smocked cotton dress in two variations—demonstrate that smocking is not only a challenging art, but also becomes addictive to anyone fond of fine needlework.

The thoughtful child watching her young friend weave a circlet of summer flowers wears a smocked dress, that perennial child's garment combining free-flowing practicality and attractive handworked decoration. Jessie Willcox Smith, the foremost illustrator of children in her time, painted this charming childhood idyll for the cover of Harper's Bazaar *in 1910.*

Smocked Nightie

This nightgown is actually a daygown for a small baby. The basic silhouette is somewhat reminiscent of the dress worn by Sweet Pea in *Popeye*, but this version is much more elegant. It is made from Viyella, a wonderfully soft wool and cotton blend that is machine washable and lasts for years. The gown's extra length allows freedom of movement, while the drawstring at the bottom keeps the baby snug. When the drawstring is open, the gown flows in a traditional manner so that the baby looks special in Daddy's or Granny's arms. See the "Dressmaking Skills" section for any unfamiliar techniques, such as those involving smocking.

Materials

2 yards (1.9 m) of 44″-wide (112-cm) Viyella or other soft fabric

2 skeins of six-strand embroidery floss: one white and one in desired color

3 size 4/0 silver snaps

A ¼″-diameter (6-mm) mother-of-pearl shank button

1½ yards (1.4 m) of ⅜″-wide (9.5-mm) double-faced white satin ribbon

½ yard (.5 m) of ¼″-wide (6-mm) white lace edging

Making the pattern and cutting the fabric

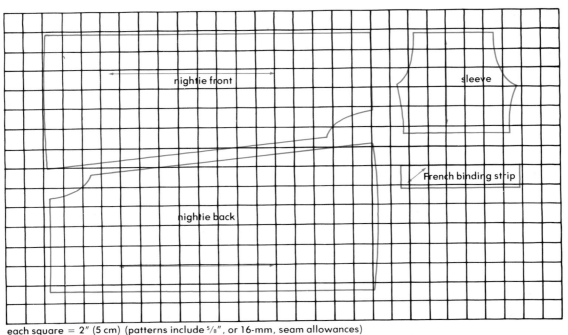

each square = 2″ (5 cm) (patterns include ⅝″, or 16-mm, seam allowances)

1. Making the pattern. Enlarge the nightgown pattern according to the scale indicated and cut it out, following the instructions on page 175.

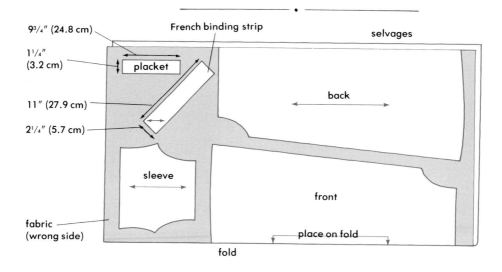

2. Cutting the fabric.

Fold the fabric in half lengthwise, right sides together, aligning the selvages. Lay the center front along the fold of the fabric.

Place the pattern for the back parallel to the front, and follow the diagram to cut out the remaining pieces. In ad-

dition, cut a 1¼″ × 9¾″ (3.2 × 24.8-cm) strip of fabric for the placket at the back opening and a 2¼″ × 11″ (5.7 × 27.9-cm) bias strip for the French binding around the neckline.

Assembling the nightie

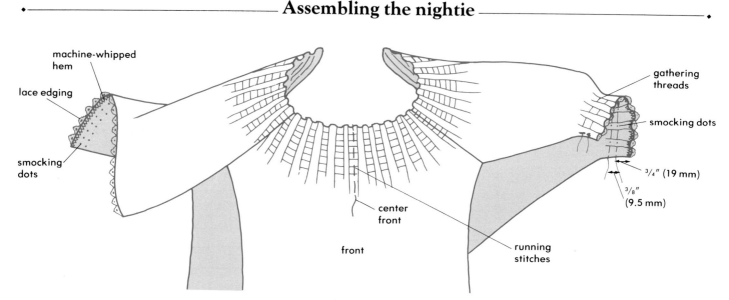

1. Preparing the fabric for smocking.

First, prepare the **sleeves.** Mark two rows of smocking dots along the bottom edge of each sleeve, placing the first row approximately ¾″ (19 mm) from the edge and the second row ⅜″ (9.5 mm) above the first.

The lace trim. Using the machine-whipping technique, stitch a row of lace trim just along the inside edge of each sleeve bottom.

Joining the front, back, and sleeves. Align the neck and shoulder edges of the sleeves with the corresponding edges of the front and back pieces, wrong sides together, and join them with French seams. By hand or with a pleating

machine, make seven rows of gathering stitches around the neck edge. If using hot-iron transfer dots, follow the instructions for marking curved areas for smocking in the "Dressmaking Skills" section. Place the first row approximately ¼″ (6 mm) from the raw edge. The first row is an auxiliary row and will fall just inside the seam line to help keep the smocked pleats from twisting. Pull the gathering threads to form even pleats in the fabric so that the first row of gathering measures 12½″ (31.8 cm) around the neck edge, and the bottom row of smocking measures 23″ (58.5 cm). Knot the threads. Pull the gathering threads in the sleeves until the sleeve measures 2″ (5 cm) across. Count the pleats across the front and mark the "valley" between the two centermost pleats with a row of basting stitches.

The smocking

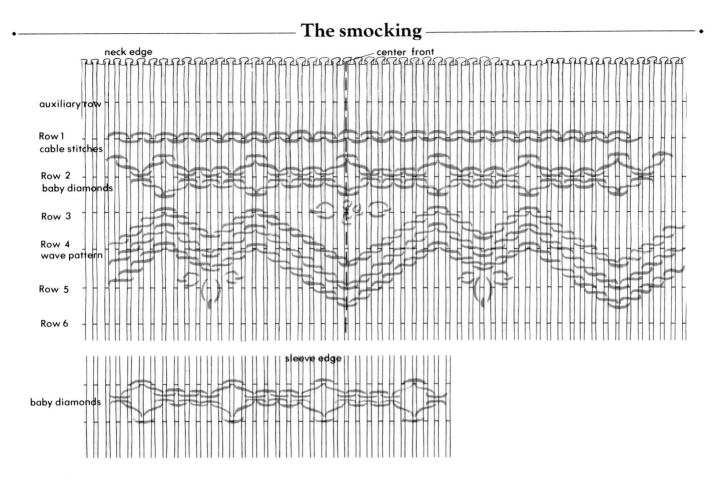

1. Smocking the neck edge. Work the smocking design around the neck of the nightie as follows:

Row 1: Work cable stitches across the entire row, starting and ending at the back opening.

Row 2: Starting at the center front, midway between Rows 1 and 2, sew an up cable over the basting stitches. Wave down to Row 2 and stitch 5 cables. Wave up midway to Row 1. Continue this pattern of baby waves and cables to the back of the nightie.

Starting at the center front again and turning the work 180 degrees, make a baby wave *up to Row 2*, and continue the baby wave and cable pattern around the other side of the nightie.

Starting at the right back edge of the nightie, work the same baby wave and cable pattern around the entire nightie, copying the row above exactly in the type of stitch used, but stitching in the opposite direction, up or down, to form baby diamonds, as shown.

Rows 3 to 6: Begin the wave pattern at the center front midway between Rows 4 and 5 with a down cable. Wave up with 7 small waves to just below Row 3, and make an up cable. Wave down 3, make a down cable, wave up 3, and make an up cable. Wave down 7 steps and repeat the pattern all the way around to the back of the nightie. Note that the upper turning cables should fall in line with the bottom points of the baby diamonds above.

Finish the first row of the wave pattern by rotating the work 180 degrees, and starting at the center front. Sew a seven-step wave *down* to Row 3, then make the three-step waves. Continue the pattern to the back of the nightie.

Start the second and third rows of the wave pattern at the back of the nightie, 1/2" (13 mm) apart, with whatever stitch the previous row ended on, and follow the pattern around the entire garment.

The flowers. Work three lazy daisy stitches below each small wave along the front of the nightie, as shown, making the center one 3/8" (9.5 mm) long, and the two at the sides 1/4" (6 mm) long. Then, in the center of the space above the large waves at the front of the nightie, work a cluster of one white and three French knots of the desired color flanked by two white lazy daisy stitches.

Remove the gathering stitches across the front, except for those along the auxiliary row and Row 1, and steam the completed smocking.

Smocking the sleeve edge. Starting with a down cable midway between the two rows of gathering stitches, work a row of up baby waves linked by 5 cables across the sleeve edge. Then start with an up cable back to back with the first down cable made in the previous row, and work a second row of down baby waves and cables to form baby diamonds, as shown. Begin and end both rows 1/2" (13 mm) from each end.

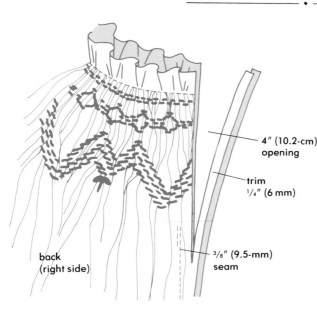

4" (10.2-cm) opening

trim ¼" (6 mm)

back (right side)

⅜" (9.5-mm) seam

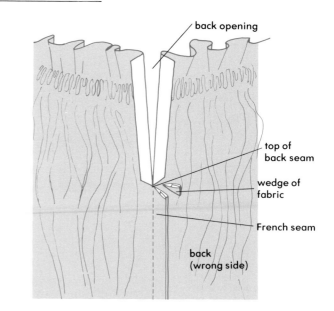

back opening

top of back seam

wedge of fabric

French seam

back (wrong side)

3. Seaming the back. Align the back edges, wrong sides together, and stitch the center back seam ⅜" (9.5 mm) from the edges, leaving a 4"-long (10.2-cm) opening at the top. Staystitch ⅜" (9.5 mm) from each edge of the opening above the seam to hold the smocking in place. Trim ¼"

(6 mm) from the seam allowances, and then encase them in a French seam, leaving the placket section open. Clip a small wedge from the seam allowance so the point of the wedge points to the top of the stitching line.

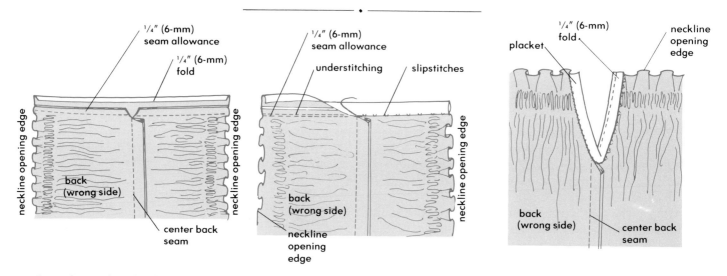

¼" (6-mm) seam allowance

¼" (6-mm) fold

neckline opening edge

back (wrong side)

center back seam

¼" (6-mm) seam allowance

understitching

slipstitches

neckline opening edge

back (wrong side)

neckline opening edge

¼" (6-mm) fold

neckline opening edge

placket

neckline opening edge

back (wrong side)

center back seam

4. Attaching the placket. Press under ¼" (6 mm) along one long edge of the placket strip. Spread out the back opening of the nightgown, and pin the long raw edge of the placket strip to the opening edge, right sides together and ends flush.

With the garment facing up, stitch the placket to the back opening along the seam line; do not stitch over the center back seam allowance. Leaving the needle in the fabric, lift the presser foot of the machine, pivot the work, and set the presser foot down again. Sew down the other side of the placket.

Finishing the placket. Turn the placket strip away from the nightgown and understitch the seam line on the right side along its entire length, catching the seam allowances below. Fold the placket strip over to the wrong side of the nightie, encasing the seam allowances, so the folded edge of the strip meets the placket seam line, and slipstitch it in place.

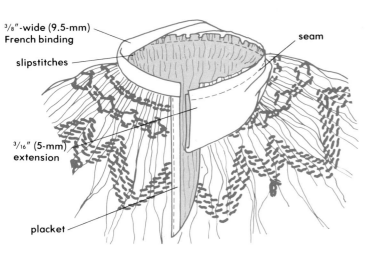

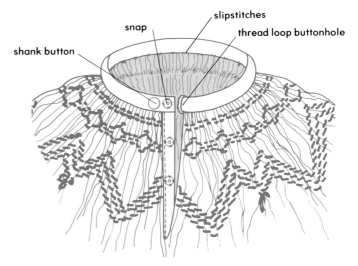

5. Finishing the neckline. Attach the 2¼″-wide (5.7-cm) strip of **French binding** around the neckline (see page 178), making the finished width ⅜″ (9.5 mm) and leaving a ³⁄₁₆″-long (5-mm) extension beyond the edge on the right back. Tuck in and slipstitch the ends at the center back so they are completely smooth.

The fastening. Sew three pairs of snaps along the placket, one at the top and the other two equally spaced below the first.

Make a thread loop buttonhole at the very end of the binding on the right side of the placket edge. Sew the shank button in place on the left side to the left of the snap.

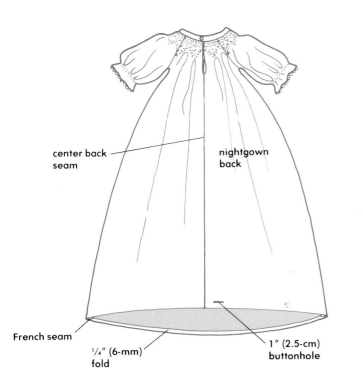

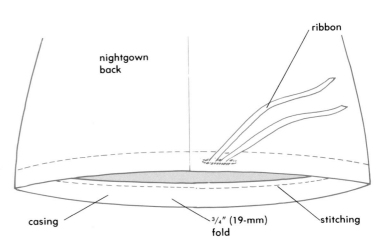

6. Completing the nightie. Sew up each side and underarm seam in one continuous French seam.

The casing hem. To make a casing at the bottom of the nightgown, make a 1″-long (2.5-cm) horizontal buttonhole that is 1½″ (3.8 cm) above the bottom raw edge and just to the right of the center back seam. Press under ¼″ (6 mm) of fabric along the bottom, then press under another ¾″ (19 mm); stitch the fold in place to form a casing. Thread the satin ribbon through the casing and tie the ends into a small bow at the buttonhole opening. Trim the ends of the ribbon diagonally.

Bishop Dress

The art of smocking, or decoratively securing pleats to control a large piece of fabric, was all the rage in Europe during the fifteenth century. Today the technique is most often seen on dainty dresses for little girls. The dresses can be made in almost any fabric and can have either short or long sleeves. The short-sleeved style shown here is made in two variations: Version I is done in a traditional calico and has a collar; Version II is made of dotted swiss and has a bound neckline and fagoting on the sleeves. The smocking pattern is also different for each dress, but the pattern is essentially the same as the one used for the smocked nightie.

The bishop dress got its name because it resembles a vestment, or ceremonial garment, worn by an Anglican bishop. Every mail-order source has some version of it, and one of the major pattern companies has already issued one. Although there may be some minor style variations among patterns, there is little that can go wrong with a dress as simple as this. With its deep hem, raglan sleeves, and absence of waistline definition, the dress can be used for a good two years or more.

Refer to the "Dressmaking Skills" section for further instructions on smocking and smocking stitches, and for help with unfamiliar techniques.

Materials

A commercial pattern for a bishop dress

1½ yards (1.4 m) of 44"-wide (112-cm) sprigged calico, for Version I, or dotted swiss, for Version II

¼ yard (.25 m) contrasting white fabric, for the collar of Version I and the fagoted trim of Version II

¼ yard (.25 m) lightweight iron-on interfacing, for the calico dress only

2 skeins 6-strand embroidery floss in desired color for the calico dress, or 1 skein each of light and dark floss in the desired hue and 1 skein of bright green for the dotted swiss

3 small snaps

A ³/₁₆"-diameter (5-mm) mother-of-pearl shank button

Note: The amounts of materials are based on a size 2 dress.

Adjusting the pattern and cutting the fabric

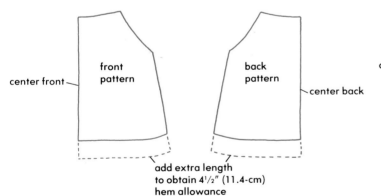

add extra length
to obtain 4½" (11.4-cm)
hem allowance

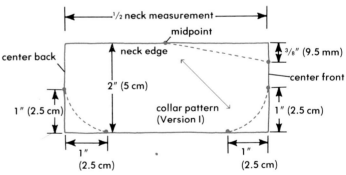

1. Adjusting the pattern. If necessary, extend the length of the dress pattern so that there is a 4½" (11.4-cm) hem allowance at the bottom.

Version I: Making a collar pattern. If there is no collar pattern, draw a rectangle using half of the finished dress neck measurement as the rectangle's length and 2" (5 cm) as its width. (If your pattern does not give a finished neck measurement, simply make the rectangle 12", or 30.5 cm, long for a size 2 dress. For each larger or smaller dress size, add or subtract ¼", or 6 mm, respectively.)

Make a dot midway along one long edge of the rectangle to divide it in half. This will be the neck edge. On the right-hand side of the rectangle, measure down ³/₈" (9.5 mm) from the neck edge, and mark the point with a dot. Mark this side the center front and the opposite side the center back. Connect these two dots as shown.

Mark off 1" (2.5 cm) from either side of each lower corner, then connect each pair of dots to round off the lower corners. Add a seam allowance (the same as on the dress) all around, and cut out the pattern.

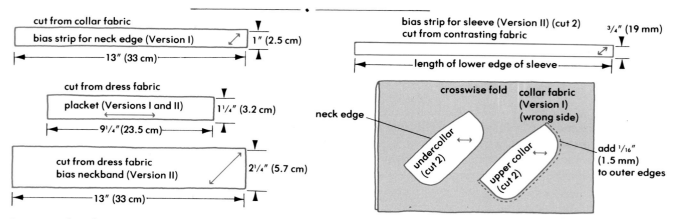

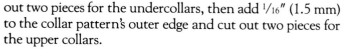

2. Cutting out the dress.

Cut out the dress pieces following the cutting layout from your pattern. From the dress fabric, cut a straight 1¼" × 9¼" (3.2 × 23.5-cm) strip for the placket.

Version I. From the collar fabric, cut a 1" × 13" (2.5 × 33-cm) bias strip. Fold the fabric crosswise, and place the collar pattern on it so the neck edge is on the true bias. Cut out two pieces for the undercollars, then add ¹⁄₁₆" (1.5 mm) to the collar pattern's outer edge and cut out two pieces for the upper collars.

Version II. From the dress fabric, cut a 2¼" × 13" (5.7 × 33-cm) bias strip for the neckband. From the white trim fabric, cut two ¾"-wide (19-mm) bias strips long enough to fit along the lower edge of each sleeve.

Assembling the dress

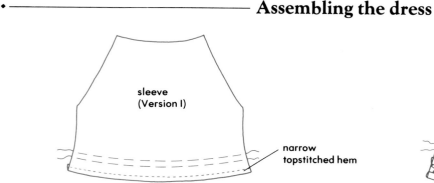

1. Preparing the sleeves for smocking.

Make a narrow topstitched hem along the lower edge of each sleeve. Mark two rows of smocking dots along the lower sleeve edge, placing the first row ¾" (19 mm) from the edge and the second row ⅜" (9.5 mm) above the first. Pregather the smocking dots.

Version II. Using the white bias strips and the dark-blue floss, follow the directions for fagoting given on page 122 for the smocked dress to finish the lower edges of the sleeves.

2. Preparing the neckline for smocking.

Following the pattern seam allowances, join the sleeves to the back and front pieces of the dress with French seams.

The placket. If your pattern has a center back seam, leave it open and follow the placket instructions given for the smocked nightie (page 90). If not, mark a 4"-long (10.2-cm) placket line along the center back. Machine-staystitch ¼" (6 mm) away from the top of the marked line, tapering to a V at the bottom point, then up to a point ¼" (6 mm) from the opposite side of the line. Slash between the stitching lines to the point of the V, being careful not to cut into the staystitching.

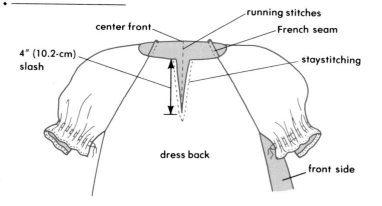

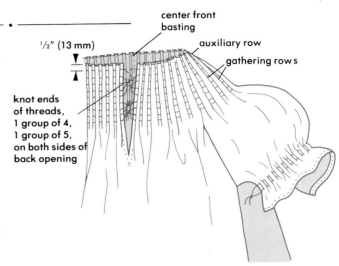

Pleating the fabric. By hand or with a pleating machine, make nine rows of gathering stitches along the neck edge. If you are working by hand, use hot-iron transfer dots, and follow the technique for slashing the dot pattern given in the "Dressmaking Skills" section and marking to within ¹/₂″ (13 mm) of the center back. Place the initial or auxiliary row of dots approximately ¹/₂″ (13 mm) from the raw edge of the fabric. Space the other rows about ³/₈″ (9.5 mm) apart. When completed, the auxiliary row will fall just inside the seam line to help keep the smocked pleats from twisting. Pregather the smocking dots along the neckline edge. Count the number of pleats across the front of the dress and mark the "valley" between the two center pleats with a row of basting stitches.

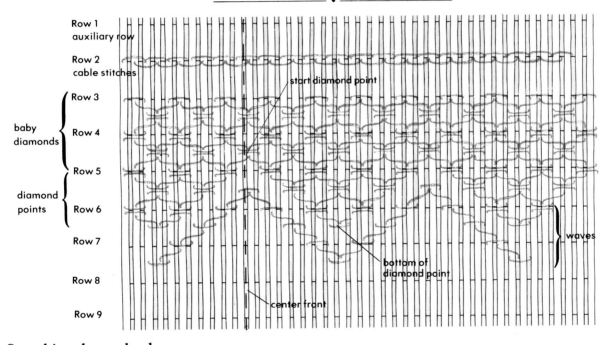

3. Smocking the neck edge.

Version I

Row 2: Start the design on Row 2. Work cable stitches across the entire row, beginning and ending at the center back.

Rows 3 to 5: Starting midway between Rows 3 and 4, make four rows of baby waves around the entire dress, resulting in three complete rows of baby diamonds.

Rows 5 to 6¹/₂: The diamond points. To form diamond points that fall symmetrically across the front of the dress, stitch an up cable back to back with the first down cable that forms the bottom point of a diamond to the right of the center front on Row 5. Wave down to midway between Rows 5 and 6 and stitch 3 complete baby waves, touching the bottom points of four diamonds on Row 5. Turn the work and stitch 2 complete baby waves to Row 6. Turn the work and stitch a complete baby wave to complete the di-

amond point. Fasten off the thread and work another diamond point for each subsequent group of four baby diamonds, around to the back of the dress.

To complete the pattern, turn the work 180 degrees and return to the center front. Start with an up cable back to back with the first up cable that forms the top of a diamond on Row 5, and complete diamond points around the other side of the dress, reversing the direction of the stitches so both sides of the dress match.

The waves: Outline the diamond points as follows, making an up cable at the top of each diamond and a down cable at the lowest point. Descend down the left side of each diamond point with down waves, and ascend up the right side of each diamond with up waves. Keep a half step below the previous row and make sure to align the stitches with the row above. Remove all the gathering threads, except the auxiliary row along the neck edge.

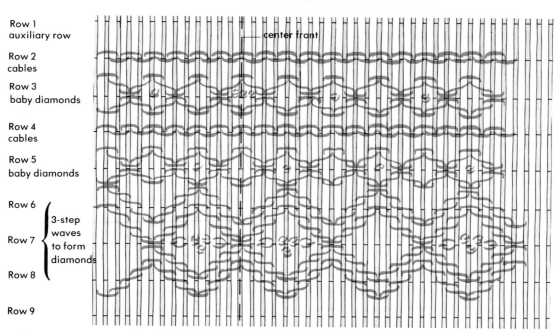

Row 1
auxiliary row

Row 2
cables

Row 3
baby diamonds

Row 4
cables

Row 5
baby diamonds

Row 6

Row 7 } 3-step waves to form diamonds

Row 8

Row 9

Version II

Following the chart, work the design in the lighter hue.

Rows 2 and 4: Stitch cables across each row.

Rows 3 and 5: To center the design, work a row of baby diamonds across each row. Start at the center front of the dress with an up cable over the center basting, midway between Rows 2 and 3. Then make baby waves down to Row 3 and back all the way around one side of the neck to the back. Turn the work 180 degrees and start at the center to finish the row of baby waves. Once the design is centered, the remaining rows of baby waves on Rows 3 and 5 can be stitched to form baby diamonds, starting and ending at the center back. Simply align the stitches from row to row.

Row 6: Starting half a space below Row 6 at the center front, make a down cable in line with the bottoms of the baby diamonds above. Wave up 3 steps, and stitch an up cable back to back with the bottom of the first baby diamond to the right of the center front. Wave down 3 and make a down cable in line with the bottom of the next diamond. Repeat this wave pattern around the dress, keeping the cables aligned with the bottoms of the di-

amonds to form hearts. Rotate the work and start at center front to finish the row.

Row 7: Work a similar row of waves ¹⁄₂″ (13 mm) below the first, starting and ending at the center back.

Row 8: Work a row of large diamonds by making another row of three-step waves, in the opposite direction of the first two rows, making sure to keep the cables aligned. Start and end at the center back.

Row 9: Work a similar row of waves ¹⁄₂″ (13 mm) below the first.

The embroidery: Using the darker hue and bright-green embroidery floss, work flowers with French knot centers and lazy daisy leaves as explained in "Dressmaking Skills." Place a flower in the center of each large diamond at either side of the center front. Then skip a diamond on each side and add a flower to the adjacent diamond, as shown.

Work a flower in the baby diamond at the center of the top row, then stitch French knot blossoms in alternating diamonds along that row. Work a row of French knots in alternating baby diamonds along Row 5, as shown.

Remove all the gathering threads except the auxiliary row.

4. Smocking the sleeve edges.

Rows 1 and 2: Work cable stitches just above Row 1 and below Row 2. Then work a row of baby diamonds between the cable rows. Steam-block the completed smocking.

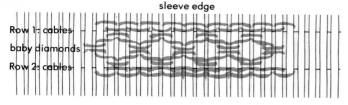

sleeve edge

Row 1: cables

baby diamonds

Row 2: cables

Version II. Add a French knot flower (above) to the center of every other diamond, as for the neckline smocking.

5. Finishing the placket. Following the instructions in the "Dressmaking Skills" section, apply the placket strip to the back opening. If the dress already has a back opening, finish it according to the pattern instructions.

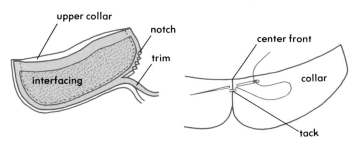

6. Making the collar (Version I). Cut out two under-collar pieces from the iron-on interfacing, and trim away the seam allowances around the interfacing pieces. Center a piece of interfacing on the wrong side of each undercollar piece and fuse them together.

With right sides together, pin the upper collar to the undercollar along the outer edges, and stitch. Trim the seam allowances, notch the curves, and turn the collar right side out. Press the outer edges, being careful not to stretch the neck edges. At this point, the collar will not lie flat, as the upper collar is slightly larger than the undercollar; this is as it should be so that the upper collar can roll smoothly over

the undercollar once it is sewed to the dress. With right sides facing up, tack the two collar sections together, using a few hand stitches at the center front.

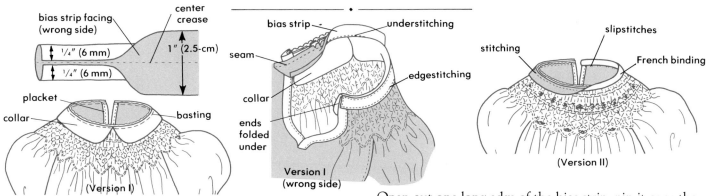

7. Finishing the neckline.

Version I. Prepare the 1″ × 13″ (2.5 × 33-cm) bias strip by pressing it in half lengthwise. Open out the strip, then fold each long edge to the inside to meet the center crease line; press along both folded edges. Now shape the strip by pressing it into a curve to match the neck edge.

Position the collar along the neck of the dress so that the center of the collar is exactly over the center front line of the dress and each collar section lies evenly on each side. Pin, then baste the collar to the dress, placing the basting stitches between the first two gathering rows of the smocked neckline.

Open out one long edge of the bias strip; pin it over the collar right sides together so that the crease along the edge is directly over the collar basting. Stitch the strip in place along the crease line. Grade the seam allowances, then clip them at the curves. Extend the bias strip and the seam allowances away from the dress and understitch them together.

Turn the bias strip to the inside of the dress, turning under the seam allowances at the ends of the strip. Edge-stitch the lower edge of the strip in place.

Version II. Using the 2¼″-wide (5.7-cm) bias strip cut earlier, finish the neckline with French binding.

Finishing the dress

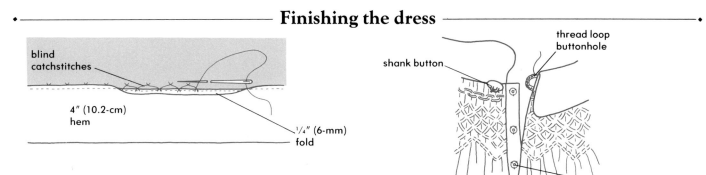

1. The side seams. Sew each side and underarm seam of the dress in one continuous French seam.

2. The hem. Turn under ¼″ (6 mm) along the bottom edge of the dress, and edgestitch. Turn up a 4″ (10.2-cm) hem and blind-catchstitch it to the dress.

3. The fastenings. Sew the snaps along the placket opening. Make a thread loop buttonhole at the right-hand edge of the neckline overlap, then sew the shank button in place on the other side, opposite the loop.

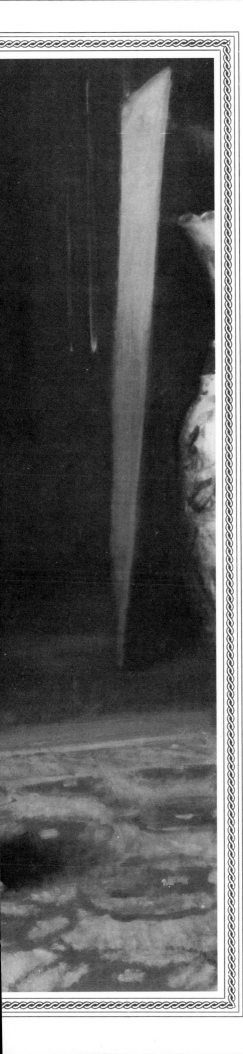

Pinafores

ittle girls have been wearing pinafores for more than a hundred years. The graceful style is practical as well as pretty, and its popularity has not diminished over the years, nor is it likely to in the near future.

In the nineteenth century, most dresses for little girls were made with no-nonsense serges and twills meant to take the wear and tear inflicted by active young bodies and to last long enough to be passed on to younger sisters. They were also meant to keep those bodies warm in houses heated only by fireplaces. In those days, it was far more difficult to keep clothes clean than it is now, so dresses were usually made in dark colors that minimized soil and, incidentally, reflected the more limited color palette of the period.

Hence, the invention of the pinafore. Pinafore fabric was washable, light in weight, relatively inexpensive and easy to replace, and—almost always—white. In fact, the origin of the word and the garment comes from the early custom of pinning an apron on the front (afore) of a dress to prevent soil. As to color, the freshness of white, its compatibility with every color, and the becoming way it highlights a child's face make it the choice for most pinafores even today. Then, too, a white pinafore immediately dresses up the simplest of frocks, especially if accented with a ruffle, some eyelet or lace, a bow or two, or even a few embroidered flowers.

Best of all, a pinafore can be easily and quickly made in a number of traditional styles, as seen in the projects that follow. Its silhouette can be crisp and tailored as in the lace-trimmed piqué "bubble" pinafore on page 110, or it may be soft and ruffled like that most famous of all pinafores worn by the storybook figure of Alice in *Through the Looking-Glass* (page 104). Whatever its style, the "pinney" is sure to enhance the figure of any little girl at the same time it protects her best dress.

The effectiveness of the pinafore is dramatically captured by John Singer Sargent in this arresting portrait of Edward Boit's daughters, painted in 1882 (at left). The one element in the painting that unifies the four sisters is the pinafore worn by each, a factor that also suggests the enormous popularity of the garment.

Shoulder-Tie Pinafore

This pinafore can be adapted nicely to long dresses, and when made up in different fabrics with matching bloomers, it can serve as a sundress. The measurements need not be compulsively accurate; there is a good deal of leeway with the tied straps. Both the front and back sections of the pin- afore are the same, which simplifies the project tremendously. In fact, the pinafore can be made, from start to finish, in only a few hours. Unfamiliar stitches and techniques are explained in the "Dressmaking Skills" section of this book.

Materials

A length of 44"-wide (112-cm) white cotton or cotton-blend broadcloth equal to twice the desired finished length of the pinafore (see Step 1 under "Measuring and cutting") plus 1/2 yard (.5 m)

White sewing thread

Embroidery floss: a few strands each of pink, blue and green

1/2 yard (.5 m) of 1"-wide (2.5-cm) elastic

Measuring and cutting
---

1. Taking accurate measurements. Measure the child while she is wearing the dress that will be worn under the pinafore. To figure the width of the pinafore fabric, measure across the chest from armhole to armhole, and triple the measurement. For the finished length of the pinafore, measure from 1" (2.5 cm) below the collarbone to 1 1/2" (3.8 cm) or 2" (5 cm) above the hem of the dress, and add 7" (17.8 cm) to that measurement.

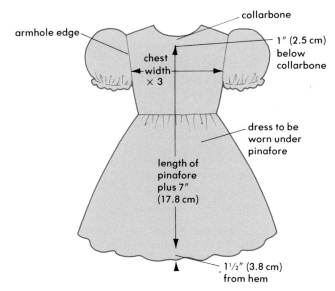

2. Marking and cutting the fabric. Cut the selvages from the fabric edges, then fold the fabric in half crosswise. Following the diagram, cut two rectangles whose sides equal the width and length of the pinafore (as just measured), aligning the length with the grain of the fabric. Cut four 3″ × 23″ (7.6 × 58.4-cm) ties, also along the grain of the fabric.

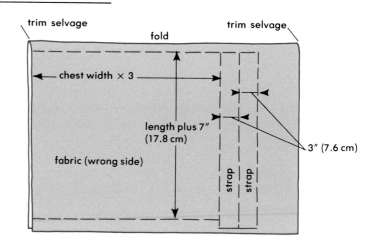

Assembling the pinafore

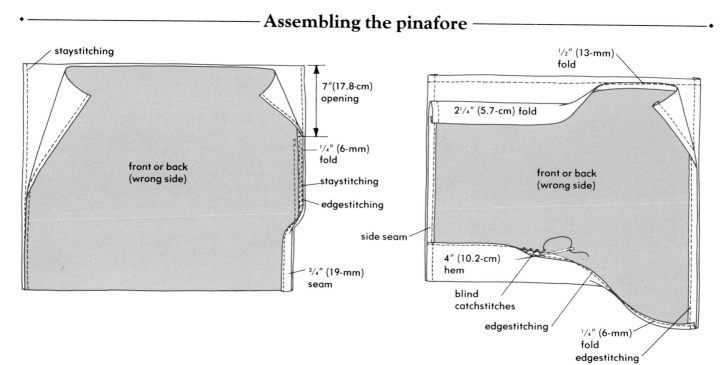

1. Joining the front and back. Staystitch ¹⁄₄″ (6 mm) in from the side edges of each front and back rectangle. Turn under a narrow hem just inside each line of staystitching, and edgestitch it in place. (The side seams are open at the top and the seam allowances become self-facings for the armholes.) Align the edges of the rectangles right sides together, and stitch the sides, leaving ³⁄₄″ (19-mm) seam allowances and a 7″-long (17.8-cm) opening at the top for each armhole and casing. Press the seam allowances open along the entire length of each seam.

2. The casing and hem. To prepare the casing for the elastic, staystitch ¹⁄₂″ (13 mm) down from the top edges of the front and back sections. Press the raw edges under just inside the staystitching, using the staystitching as a guide. Fold the edges down again 2¹⁄₄″ (5.7 cm), and press.

The hem. Fold under the bottom edge of the pinafore ¹⁄₄″ (6 mm), and edgestitch. Turn the hem up 4″ (10.2 cm), and secure it with blind catchstitches.

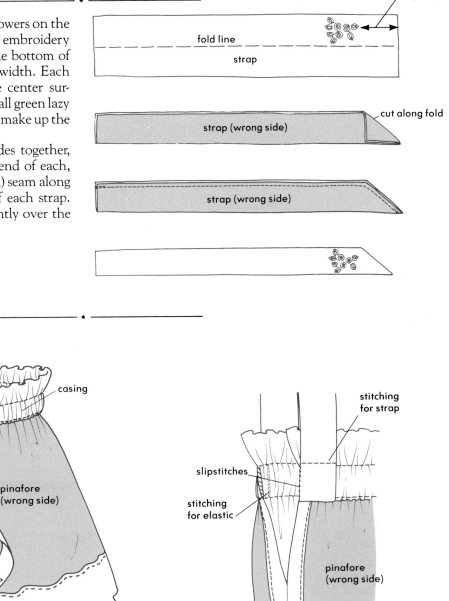

3. The straps. Embroider a circlet of three flowers on the right side of each strap, using three strands of embroidery floss and placing the design 2″ (5 cm) from the bottom of the strap and centering it on one half of the width. Each flower consists of a blue French knot at the center surrounded by three pink outline stitches. Two small green lazy daisy stitches, approximately ³/₁₆″ (5-mm) long, make up the leaves.

Fold the straps in half lengthwise, right sides together, and pin. Fold up a corner diagonally at one end of each, then cut along the fold line. Stitch a ¹/₄″ (6-mm) seam along the open side and across the diagonal end of each strap. Turn the straps right side out and press; go lightly over the embroidery work to avoid flattening it.

4. Finishing the pinafore. Attach a strap at each armhole edge by inserting and pinning the cut end under the folded edge of casing so that the strap and armhole edges are aligned and the embroidered side of the strap is facing the wrong side of the pinafore. Stitch across the front and back sections and across the ends of the straps as close to the folded edge as possible.

Sew another row of stitching 1¹/₈″ (2.9 cm) above the first row to form the casing for the elastic.

The elastic. Cut two pieces of 1″-wide (2.5-cm) elastic equal to the front chest measurement, minus 1″ (2.5 cm).

Attach a safety pin to each end of one length of the elastic. The second pin will prevent the end of the elastic from being pulled through the casing. Insert the length of elastic through the casing on one side of the pinafore. To secure the elastic, pin the ends just inside the edge of the casing, and stitch them in place ¹/₂″ (13 mm) from each edge of the casing. Fold up each strap and tack it in place with a row of running stitches above the top row of stitching for the casing. Then slipstitch the ends of the casing closed, together with the shoulder strap, to hide the elastic. Repeat for the other side of the pinafore.

Alice in Wonderland Style
Pinafore

No character in literature is more closely identified with a particular garment than Lewis Carroll's Alice in Wonderland in her white pinafore. This version is actually adapted from *Through the Looking-Glass*, which was first published in 1871. For that story, John Tenniel, the illustrator, added a ruffle to the bottom of Alice's pinafore, making it all the more fetching. Of course, he retained the familiar full skirt, wide shoulder straps, and large bow at the back.

Traditional tucking has been added at the bottom of the skirt, reminiscent of the tucked effect seen in Tenniel's illustrations of the dress Alice wore under her pinafore, and ruffled eyelet trimming is used on both the skirt and the shoulder straps.

Materials

A length of 44″-wide (112-cm) white organdy, batiste, or lawn equal to the length of the pinafore (see Step 1 under "Measuring and cutting")

2 yards (1.9 m) of 2½″-wide (6.4-cm) white eyelet trimming

2 yards (1.9 m) of 4″- to 5″-wide (10.2- to 12.7-cm) white eyelet trimming

A piece of lightweight interfacing equal in size to the waistband

Two ⅝″-diameter (16-mm) mother-of-pearl or white sew-through buttons

White sewing thread

Measuring and cutting

1. Taking accurate measurements. Tie a string around the child's waist, and clip off the ends. For the length of the shoulder strap, measure the distance from the string directly below one shoulder in the front, up and over the shoulder and crossed over in the back, to the string directly below the opposite shoulder. For the length of the skirt, measure down from the string to the desired level on the child's leg. To obtain an accurate dimension for the waist, first cut the string (do not untie it), then measure its length.

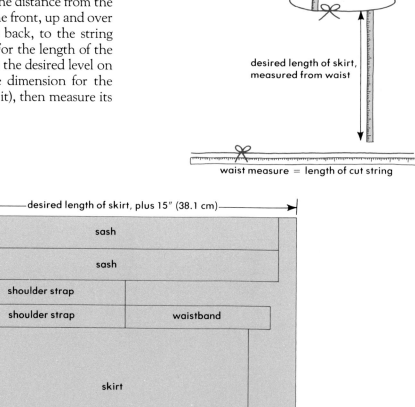

length of shoulder strap, measured from waist

measuring tape

string around waist

desired length of skirt, measured from waist

waist measure = length of cut string

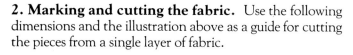

desired length of skirt, plus 15″ (38.1 cm)

selvage

sash

sash

shoulder strap

shoulder strap

waistband

44″ (112 cm)

skirt

selvage

fabric (wrong side)

2. Marking and cutting the fabric. Use the following dimensions and the illustration above as a guide for cutting the pieces from a single layer of fabric.

Shoulder strap: *width* = 3¾″ (9.5 cm); *length* = distance from front (below one shoulder), over the shoulder, to back (below the other shoulder), measured from the string around the waist, plus 2″ (5 cm).

Skirt: *width* = twice the waist measurement; *length* = distance from the string to the desired hem length, plus 6″ (15.2 cm).

Waistband: *width* = 3¾″ (9.5 cm); *length* = length of the string cut from around the waist, plus 2″ (5 cm).

Sash: *width* = 4½″ (11.4 cm); *length* = desired length of the skirt plus 12″ (30.5 cm).

Assembling the pinafore

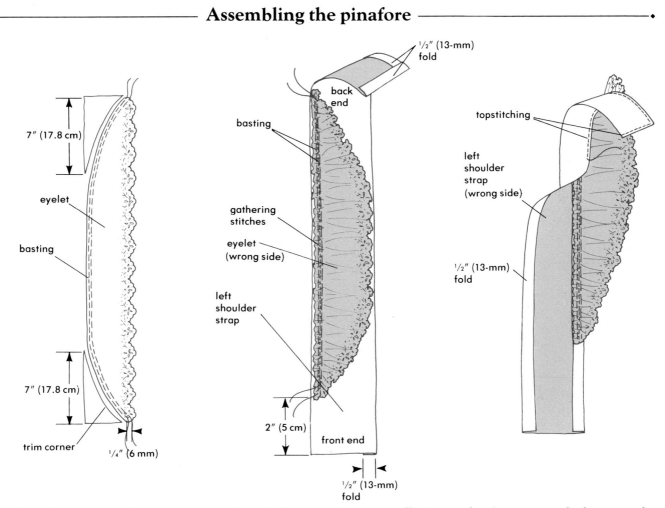

1. The shoulder straps. To prepare the eyelet trim for the shoulder straps, cut the 2¹/₂″-wide (6.4-cm) eyelet in two. Then measure and mark 7″ (17.8 cm) from each end of both eyelet strips on the unfinished edge. Starting at one end of each strip, ¹/₄″ (6 mm) above the finished edge, make a row of gathering stitches that curves gradually to within ¹/₄″ (6 mm) of the first 7″ (17.8-cm) mark; continue stitching ¹/₄″ (6 mm) inside the unfinished edge until you reach the second 7″ (17.8-cm) mark, and then curve the stitching line toward the finished edge, as you did at the opposite end. Make a second row of gathering stitches ¹/₄″ (6 mm) inside the first row. Trim the excess fabric at each end ¹/₄″ (6 mm) outside the outer stitching line.

Gathering and attaching the eyelet. Gather each eyelet strip evenly along the threads until it is 4″ (10.2 cm) shorter than the shoulder straps.

Center a ruffled strip of eyelet, wrong side down, on the right side of each shoulder strap, aligning the gathered edge on one long edge of the strap, and pin it in place. Stitch the eyelet to the shoulder straps between the two rows of gathering stitches. Press under ¹/₂″ (13 mm) of fabric along the free side of each shoulder strap.

Establishing the right and left straps. Lay the straps side by side, right side up, with the ruffled eyelet extending outward. Turn under the uppermost (back) end of each strap about ¹/₂″ (13 mm), and press.

Press each strap away from the ruffle, toward the seam allowance.

Turn the folded edge of each strap over the seam allowance, covering any stitches in the ruffle, align it with the seam between the ruffle and the shoulder strap on the opposite side of the fabric, and pin. Topstitch the back end and open side of the strap as close to the edge as possible.

2. The sash. Staystitch both long sides of each sash piece ⅛″ (3 mm) inside the edges. Turn a narrow, ⅛″ (3-mm) topstitched hem over the staystitching on one side of each sash piece.

Turn the sash pieces right side up, fold up one end of each piece diagonally to align it with the staystitched side, and pin. Starting at the pointed end of the sash pieces, stitch a ¼″ (6-mm) seam along the pinned edges. Trim the tip of each sash end, as shown, and turn the stitched end right side out. Turn and finish the other staystitched edge of each sash piece with a hem.

Sew two rows of gathering stitches across the unfinished end of each sash piece, gather the end along the thread to a width of 3¼″ (8.3 cm), knot the thread, and set the sash pieces aside.

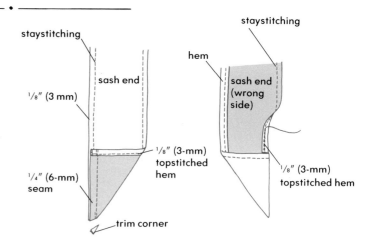

3. Gathering, hemming, and trimming the skirt. Sew two rows of gathering stitches along the top of the skirt, one ⅜″ (9.5 mm) below the edge, the other ¼″ (6 mm) below the first, stopping 1¼″ (3.2 cm) short of each end.

The hems. Turn under a ½″ (13-mm) double fold of fabric at each side of the skirt, edgestitch, and press.

Turn the bottom edge of the skirt under ½″ (13 mm), and press. Pin up a 2½″ (6.4-cm) hem along the bottom of the skirt, and edgestitch.

Attaching the eyelet. Measure a length of the wide eyelet equal to the width of the skirt, plus ½″ (13 mm). Staystitch the eyelet 3″ (7.6 cm) above the decorative edge, and trim it ⅛″ (3 mm) above the stitching. Turn and stitch a ⅛″ (3-mm) double hem at each end of the eyelet.

Baste the eyelet, right side up, to the right side of the skirt along the stitching for the skirt hem.

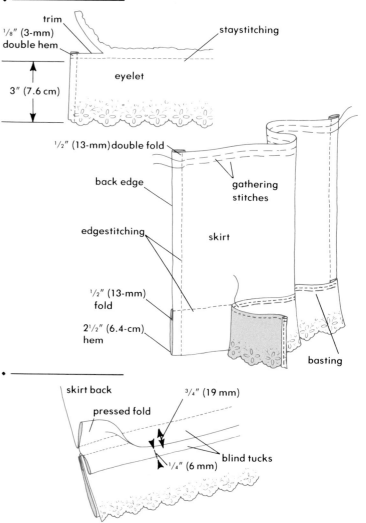

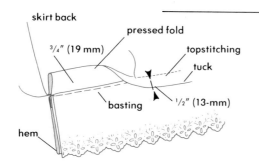

4. Tucking the skirt. Fold the skirt down ¾″ (19 mm) over the top of the eyelet, press the fold, and topstitch ½″ (13 mm) from the edge of the fold to form a tuck. Remove the basting from the eyelet.

Fold the skirt down to cover all but ¼″ (6 mm) of the first tuck. Press the fold, then stitch ¾″ (19 mm) above the edge of the fold.

Finishing the pinafore

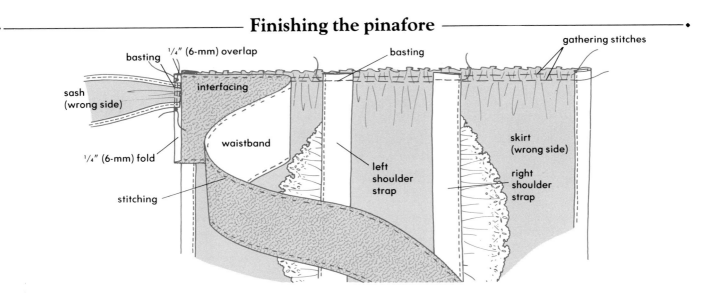

1. Attaching the waistband. First, cut a piece of lightweight **interfacing** identical to the size of the waistband, and stitch it around the edges or press it to the wrong side of the waistband fabric. (Any press-on interfacing should be tested first, as it may be too stiff; bias nonwoven interfacing is usually best.)

The waistband and shoulder straps. Gather the skirt evenly along the threads at the top until it is 1″ (2.6 cm) shorter than the waistband.

Pin the unfinished ends of the shoulder straps to the center front of the skirt (the opening is at the back), wrong sides together and about 3″ (7.6 cm) apart, with the edges aligned at the top and the eyelet facing out. Check the spacing for the straps by wrapping the skirt around the child, then sew the straps in place with basting stitches.

Center the waistband and pin it, right side down, along the wrong side of the top of the skirt, aligning the edges and covering the ends of the shoulder straps. The waistband should extend ½″ (13 mm) beyond each end of the skirt. Sew the waistband to the skirt between the rows of gathering stitches. Turn under and press a ¼″ (6 mm) fold at each end of the waistband.

The sashes. Baste a sash, wrong side up and across its gathered end, to each end of the waistband, close to the waist seam.

2. The finishing touches. Fold the **waistband** to the front of the skirt, covering the seam allowances and the gathering stitches, and pin it in place. Fold the shoulder straps up behind the waistband and pin them straight. Edgestitch around all four sides of the waistband.

The buttonholes. Make a ¾″-long (19-mm) buttonhole at the center about 1¼″ (3.2 cm) in from each end of the waistband. Try the pinafore on the child to correctly place the buttons on the shoulder straps. (By moving the buttons, the pinafore can be lengthened as the child grows.)

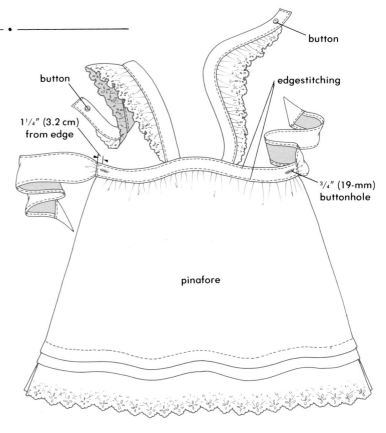

"Bubble" Pinafore

The bubble pinafore and its variations, reminiscent of Kate Greenaway's illustrations for Mother Goose and other stories, have been popular since the 1920s, when *McCall's* first published a pattern similar to the one illustrated here. This pinafore is usually worn by very young children, and it can double as a sundress when made with matching bloomers.

Piqué makes an ideal choice of fabric; it holds the crisp shape of the pinafore and can take the punishment a young child is likely to mete out. The major trimming is a pre-gathered lace edging attached to a strip of stiff netting that serves as a seam allowance. This type of lace is preferable to the bias-bound type, which can add too much bulk to a seam. Of course, you can always gather your own lace, but it is probably not worth the time since the pinafore itself is essentially a quick and easy afternoon's work. The trimming used around the handkerchief is a flat lace edging with no seam allowances. Some bubble pinafores have shoulder seams like this one, while others button over the shoulders; the bias facing technique shown will work just as well for either style. Unfamiliar sewing techniques can be found in the "Dressmaking Skills" section.

Materials

³/₄ yard (.70 m) of 44″-wide (112 cm) white cotton or cotton-blend piqué

A 3″ × 3″ (7.6 × 7.6-cm) square of fabric to match the dress worn with the pinafore or to match one of the colors in the dress

White sewing thread

5 yards (4.6 m) of ¹/₂″-wide (13-mm) white pregathered lace edging, attached to stiff netting

8 yards (7.3 m) white single-fold bias tape

A ¹/₂″-diameter (13-mm) sew-through mother-of-pearl button (optional)

¹/₂ yard (.5 m) ¹/₄″-wide (6-mm) flat lace edging

Note: The amounts of materials are based on a size 2 dress.

Cutting the fabric

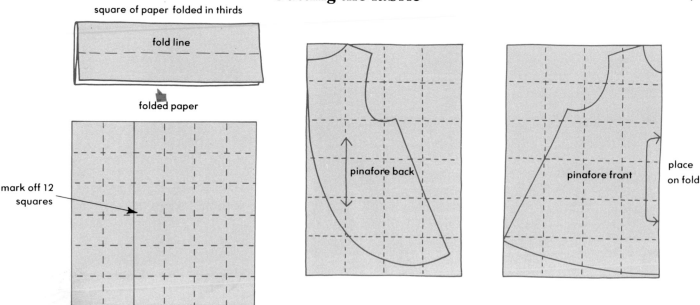

1. Making the pattern. Measure the child's back dress length and make a square of paper using that measurement for each side. Fold the square in thirds, one side over the other, like a letter. Now fold it in half in the same direction, to make six equal sections. Unfold the paper and repeat the same folding sequence in the opposite direction, making six

folded squares. Mark off two rows of the folded squares (12 altogether) along one side of the paper. Draw the pinafore front on the other side of the line, matching the illustration given here square for square. Fold another piece of paper and repeat for the back of the pinafore. The pattern includes ⁵/₈″ (16-mm) seam allowances.

2. Cutting the fabric. Fold the white piqué lengthwise, wrong side out, and pin the pattern pieces to it with the center front on the fold and the arrows aligned with the lengthwise grain of the fabric. Cut one front piece, two back pieces, one 3″-square (7.6-cm) pocket, and, if they are to be used, two 1³/₄″ × 26″ (4.4 × 66-cm) ties. If you are also making the dress to be worn under the pinafore, cut a 3″ × 3″ (7.6 × 7.6-cm) square from extra dress fabric to make the handkerchief; if you do not have matching fabric, use a solid color that picks up one of the minor colors in the dress.

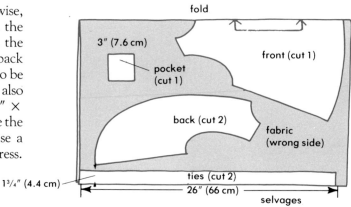

Assembling the pinafore

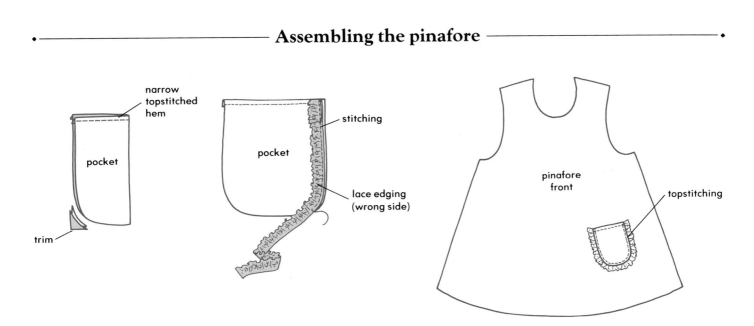

1. The pocket. Make a narrow topstitched hem along the upper edge of the pocket piece, then fold it in half vertically and trim both bottom corners together to round them off equally. Pin a length of lace edging around the unfinished edge of the pocket, right sides together, aligning the raw edges, and fold back the end of the lace at each top corner of the pocket. Stitch the lace in place $1/4''$ (6 mm) from the pocket edge. Notch the seam allowances at the curves, then turn them under, and press. Pin the pocket $2^1/2''$ (6.4 cm) to one side of the center front and about $2^3/4''$ (7 cm) from the bottom edge. Topstitch the pocket in place as close as possible to the folded edge.

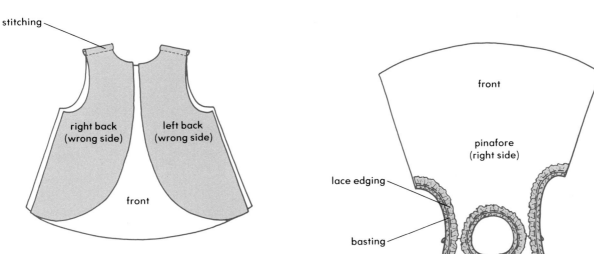

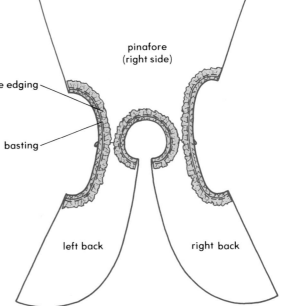

2. Attaching the lace edging. Align the front and back pieces of the pinafore, right sides together, along the shoulder edges, and join them with narrow French seams. (Do not stitch the side seams.)

Pin the lace edging along the pinafore neckline and armhole, right sides together. Baste the lace in place $1/2''$ (13 mm) in from its inner edge.

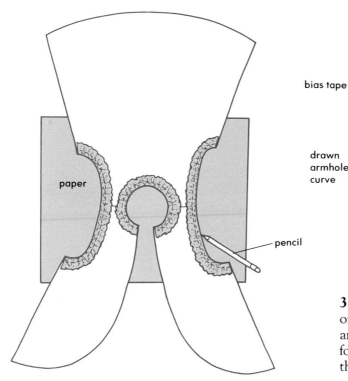

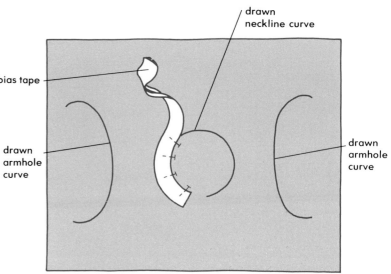

3. Preparing the bias binding. Lay the pinafore out flat on a piece of stiff paper, and draw an outline of the neckline and armhole curves on the paper. Pin the bias tape along the folded edge to the drawn curves, and steam-press the tape so that it conforms to the neck and armhole curves.

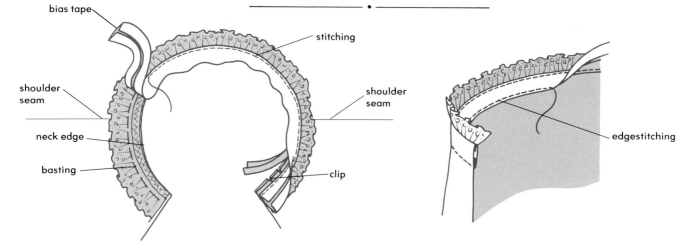

4. Attaching the bias binding. Pin the inside edge of the bias tape right side up so that it just covers the basting stitches in the lace. Then stitch as close as possible to the folded edge of the tape. Trim the seam allowance of the pinafore to ¼″ (6 mm), and clip it along the curves. Turn the bias tape over the trimmed seam allowances to the wrong side of the pinafore, and edgestitch it in place along the remaining folded edge. To prevent puckers from forming between the two rows of stitching on the front and back of the pinafore, do not pull the fabric taut when sewing the bias tape in place. Press the binding without flattening the lace.

5. The ties. Fold each tie in half lengthwise, right sides together, and pin. Fold a corner at one end of each tie diagonally, then cut along the fold line. Stitch a ¼″ (6-mm) seam along the open side and the diagonal end of each tie. Turn each tie right side out, and press it flat.

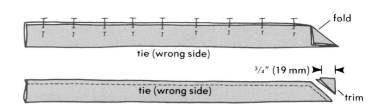

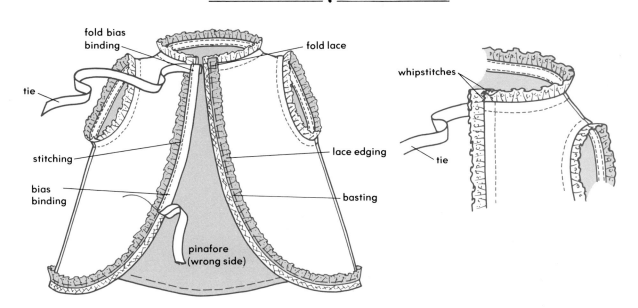

6. Finishing the pinafore. Join the back pieces of the pinafore to the front at each side with narrow French seams.

The lace edging. Pin lace edging from one top back neck edge, down the back, around the bottom, and up to the other neck edge of the pinafore in the same manner as for the neckline and armhole, so the ends extend $1/2''$ (13 mm) beyond the edge of the neckline. Fold back the ends of the lace even with the neckline, and baste the lace in place.

Attaching the ties. Position and baste a tie over the lace at the top of each back neck edge, aligning the raw edges of the ties with the raw edges of the center back opening.

Binding the outer edges. Pin and stitch the binding over the lace and ties as for the neckline and armhole edges, folding under $1/4''$ (6 mm) at each end to give it a smooth finish.

Whipstitch the ends of the lace together at the corner of the neckline. (If you wish to use a button instead of ties, sew a $1/2''$-diameter (13-mm) mother-of-pearl button at the neck edge of the left back opening and a $5/8''$ (16-mm) buttonhole on the right back neck edge.)

Making the hanky

1. The handkerchief. Sew the narrow lace edging to the edge of the handerchief fabric with a machine-whipped hem.

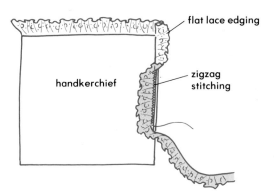

Yoke Variations

The ancient root of our word *yoke* has a curious history. In ancient Greece and Rome, *yoke* meant *joining*; later on, in Old German and Old English, it meant objects of joining that are not entirely forgotten even today: the heavy wooden beam joining a pair of oxen and the lighter beam on which the blushing milkmaid hangs her pails. On the other side of the world, the root has become *yoga*, which usually refers to a kind of spiritual joining.

In the world of sewing, the word *yoke* has taken on its own technical meaning: it refers to a fitted or shaped piece of a garment from which a looser piece hangs. A skirt, for example, may be constructed with a hip-yoke, a section that fits closely around the hips; the rest of the skirt, which may be gathered, pleated, or flared, falls from the yoke. On a dress, the yoke is the fitted section that rests across the shoulders and around the neck. In the typical yoked dress, the yoke serves to join the skirt and the sleeves. This construction will be discussed in the following chapter, which presents variations on the traditional yoke theme.

Four yoked garments are given here: a smocked dress, in which the yoke is joined to the smocked panels; a romper that has been adapted from the smocked dress; a long-sleeved corduroy dress with a plain yoke; and a gingham dress with an embroidered yoke. All of these garments are made along the same general lines, but each one is distinguished by at least one or two variations.

A yoked dress usually has two yokes, one across the front of the shoulders and one across the back. These two pieces may have the same depth or they may be different. A shallow yoke ends at about mid-armhole; that is, the seam that joins the yoke and the skirt falls within the curve of the armhole. On the other hand, a deep yoke ends below the armhole. Both types of yokes are used in these projects.

Many other variations on the yoke theme are possible. Yokes may be embellished with embroidery, appliqué, or other trimming, or they may be left completely unadorned. A yoke may be joined to any sort of collar or sleeves to complete the garment. But no matter what variations on the basic style are chosen, the yoked dress is ideal for a toddler because it's easy to fit and is also highly becoming to any member of the chubby-tummy set.

When Master Henry L. Wells had his portrait painted in 1845 by a now-unknown American artist, he was still young enough to be wearing dresses. His mother chose a gaily striped one with a shallow yoke joined to a tightly shirred bodice and a full skirt over his stiff pantalets.

Smocked Dress

White cotton broadcloth is a classic fabric choice for this dress because of its simplicity and elegance; besides, it makes a perfect background for the pastel smocking on the front

and sleeves and for the fagoting on the little round collar. Refer to the "Dressmaking Skills" section for any unfamiliar sewing techniques.

Materials

2 yards (1.9 m) of 45″-wide (114-cm) white cotton broadcloth

One package matching bias tape

Six-strand embroidery floss: 2 skeins each light pink and dark pink, and 1 each bright green and light blue

Three or four ³/₈″ (9.5-mm) buttons

Two size 4/0 snap fasteners

A commercial pattern with the following features: a shallow front yoke (one that ends at mid-armhole); a back with a similar yoke or a bodice that ends at the waist; short puffed sleeves; and a two-piece, round collar. It is not necessary for the pattern to come with a smocking design. (Note: Numerous yoke dress patterns specifically designed for smocking are sold by mail-order houses.)

A scrap of interfacing as large as the collar, optional.

Adjusting the pattern and cutting the fabric

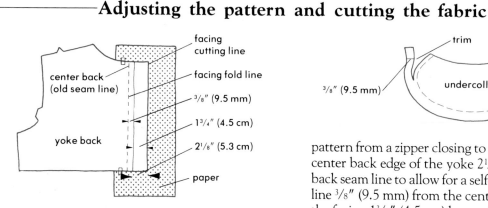

1. Pattern adjustments. Check the pattern to see what **type of closing** is called for. If there's a zipper, you may make the dress that way. However, the classic style has a button closing with a placket opening in the skirt. To change your

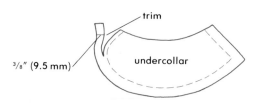

pattern from a zipper closing to a button closing, extend the center back edge of the yoke 2¹/₈″ (5.3 cm) from the center back seam line to allow for a self-facing. Mark the facing fold line ³/₈″ (9.5 mm) from the center back line, and the end of the facing 1³/₄″ (4.5 cm) beyond the facing fold line.

The collar. Trim away ³/₈″ (9.5 mm) from the outer edges of the collar to allow for the width of the fagoted trim; leave the neck edge as is. Use this pattern for the undercollar.

The skirt. If the front skirt of your yoke dress pattern does not have a smocking design, you must make sure that the skirt is large enough to pleat. The skirt must be at least three times wider than the yoke; it will be even prettier if it is four times wider. Increase the fullness accordingly by cutting the pattern down the middle from waist to hem, and taping an insert of paper at the center to give you the proper measurement. Repeat for the skirt back so the fullness will be balanced. (See the velvet dress instructions, page 142, for an illustration of this technique.)

The hem. Check the hem allowance, which will probably be 3″ (7.6 cm). When you cut out the skirt, plan on increasing the hem allowance to at least 4″ (10.2 cm) to allow for growth.

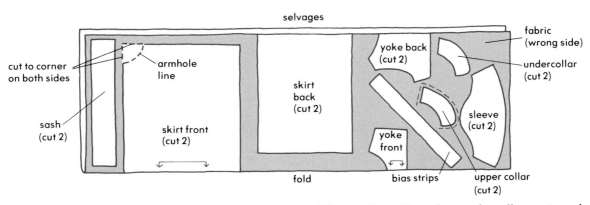

2. Cutting the fabric. If you are using a pattern specifically designed for smocking, follow the pattern directions to cut out the fabric. Otherwise, fold the fabric in half lengthwise, wrong side out, as shown, and lay out the pattern pieces, allowing enough room for the additional hem allowance on the skirt front and back. Don't cut out the armholes until after you've done the smocking. If your pattern doesn't have a special outer cutting line for the armhole corner, pin or chalk-mark lines extending the top and side edges of the skirt, as shown, to cut a full rectangle. Transfer any relevant pattern markings.

The collar. Cut the undercollar, using the adjusted pattern piece. Then cut the upper collar 1/16″ (1.5 mm) larger than the undercollar, along the outer edges only. Do not make any changes on the neck edges of the yoke or collar.

Bias strips. Measure the outer edge of the upper collar and add an inch (2.5 cm). Cut two 3/4″-wide (19-mm) bias strips equal to that length. Save the remnants of fabric to cut a strip for the placket later.

The smocking

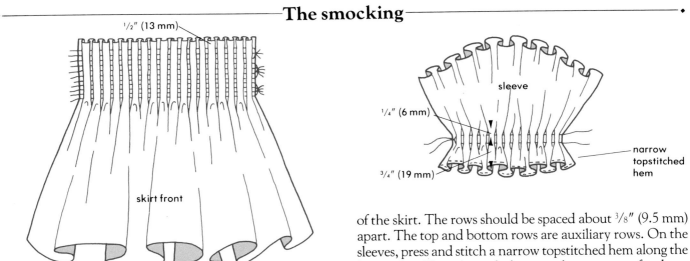

1. Preparing for smocking. By hand, using hot-iron transfer dots, or with a pleater, make eleven rows of gathering for smocking starting 1/2″ (13 mm) from the top edge of the skirt. The rows should be spaced about 3/8″ (9.5 mm) apart. The top and bottom rows are auxiliary rows. On the sleeves, press and stitch a narrow topstitched hem along the lower edge. Then, on each sleeve, make two rows of gathers, starting 3/4″ (19 mm) away from the hemmed edge.

Pull the top of the skirt and the sleeves along their respective gathering threads until they measure 1″ (2.5 cm) less than the required finished width, and knot the threads.

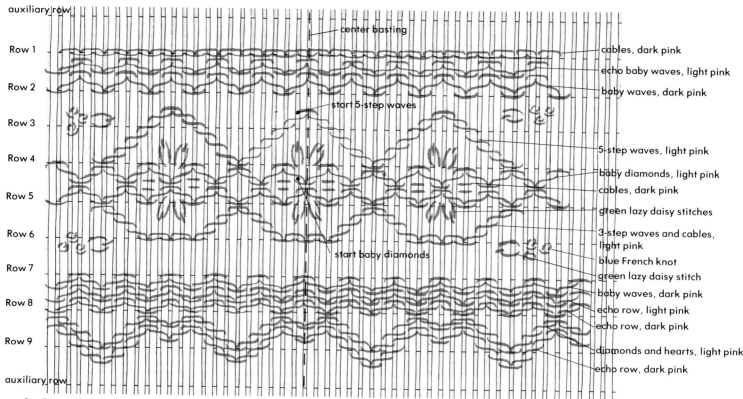

auxiliary row
Row 1
Row 2
Row 3
Row 4
Row 5
Row 6
Row 7
Row 8
Row 9
auxiliary row

center basting
start 5-step waves
start baby diamonds

cables, dark pink
echo baby waves, light pink
baby waves, dark pink
5-step waves, light pink
baby diamonds, light pink
cables, dark pink
green lazy daisy stitches
3-step waves and cables, light pink
blue French knot
green lazy daisy stitch
baby waves, dark pink
echo row, light pink
echo row, dark pink
diamonds and hearts, light pink
echo row, dark pink

2. Smocking the top of the skirt.

Row 1. Using four strands of dark-pink floss, cable-stitch across Row 1 to stabilize the pleats. Then, with sewing thread, baste along the "valley" between the two centermost pleats.

Rows 3, 4, and 5. Begin the larger design with light-pink floss. To center the design, stitch a down cable over the center basting midway between Rows 4 and 5. Then work a row of baby waves up to Row 4 and back all the way to the right edge of the skirt. Turn the work 180 degrees and start at the center again to finish the row of baby waves. Turn the work again, and, working from left to right, stitch another row of baby waves in the opposite direction and below the first row to form baby diamonds.

Five-step waves. Using light-pink floss, stitch an up cable over the center basting, midway between Rows 2 and 3. Then work a row of five-step waves down to Row 4 and back up to the starting level across the top of the baby diamonds, making sure that each lower cable is back to back with a cable at the top of a diamond, as shown. Complete the right half of the row. Then turn the work 180 degrees and work the left half of the row.

Row 2. Turn the work 180 degrees. Using dark-pink floss, work a row of baby waves from midway between Rows 1 and 2 down to Row 2 and back across the row, as shown, making sure that the tops of the baby waves are aligned with the tops of the large waves and the down cables are aligned with the up cables at the tops of the baby diamonds between Rows 4 and 5. Using light-pink floss, stitch an echo row of baby waves above the first, from midway between Rows 1 and 2 to the bottom of the cables in Row 1.

Rows 5 and 6. Between Rows 5 and 6, continuing to use light-pink floss, work three-step waves alternating with five cables making sure that the top of each wave is back-to-back with the bottom of every third baby diamond above, and the center cable in the group of cables is below the peak of the five-step wave above, as shown.

Rows 7 and 8. Using dark-pink floss, work a row of baby waves across Row 7 to one-third space below it and back. Work two echo rows of baby waves below the first, one-third space apart, making the center row light pink and the bottom row dark pink.

Rows 8 and 9. Using light-pink floss, complete a row of diamonds and hearts below the baby waves in Row 8. Make the diamonds coincide with the centers of the larger designs above, as shown.

Echo row. Work an echo row in dark pink one-quarter space below the diamonds and hearts, as shown.

Leaves, cables, and flowers. In the center of each large design, work two bright-green lazy daisy leaves between the baby diamonds, as shown. With dark pink, work two stacked cables at the center of each diamond that flanks the leaves. Make small flowers of two or three blue French knots and one or two green lazy daisy leaves around the second large diamond to each side of the center front, as shown.

Smocking the sleeves. Using dark-pink floss, stitch a row of cables across each row of gathering stitches. Remove the gathering threads.

Assembling the dress

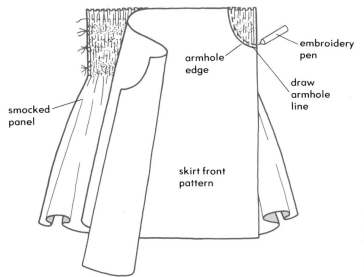

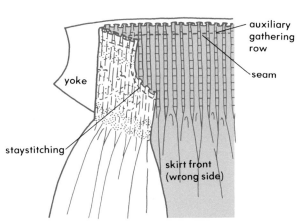

1. Joining the yoke and skirt fronts. Matching the top and side edges, place the skirt pattern (or armhole guide, if your pattern has one) over the smocked skirt. Using an embroidery marking pen with water-soluble ink,

mark the armhole cutting line and seam line. Remove the pattern.

Now staystitch the armhole curve just inside the seam line, then cut along the cutting line. Pull out all the gathering threads, except for the auxiliary row at the top. With right sides together, pin the top edge of the skirt to the lower edge of the yoke, aligning the armhole edges to make a continuous curve. Stitch the seam, finishing with a double-stitched finish. Steam-block the smocking and yoke seam.

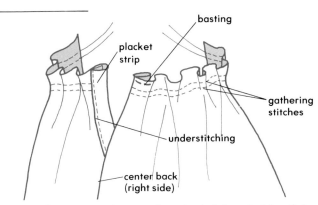

2. The skirt back and placket. On the skirt sections, make two rows of fine machine gathering stitches along the top edges. With wrong sides together, pin the center back edges and stitch from the lower edge up to the placket opening. Reinforce this point by backstitching, then finish with a French seam, and clip the seam allowance at the top of the seam almost to the stitching.

From the fabric remnants, cut a straight 1¼" (3.2-cm) strip the length of the entire placket opening. To attach the strip and finish the placket, follow the instructions given for the smocked nightie on page 90.

After the placket is hemmed to the inside of the skirt, turn the right-hand side to the inside of the skirt and baste

them together across the top. Let the left-hand side of the placket extend as an underlap.

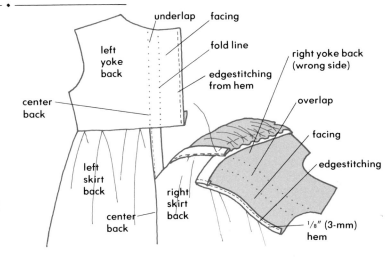

3. Joining the yoke and skirt backs. On the yoke back sections, press the raw edges of the facing under ⅛" (3 mm) and edgestitch along the fold. With right sides together, pin the left yoke to the left skirt back, matching side edges. At the opening edges, match the center back of the yoke to the placket seam, letting the facing extend as shown. Pull up the gathering threads until the skirt fits the yoke. Pin the right yoke to the right skirt back in the same way, matching the same points. Stitch the seams and finish as you did on the front. The lower edge of the yoke facings will be finished later.

Join the dress front and backs at the shoulders, finishing the seams as desired. Set the dress aside.

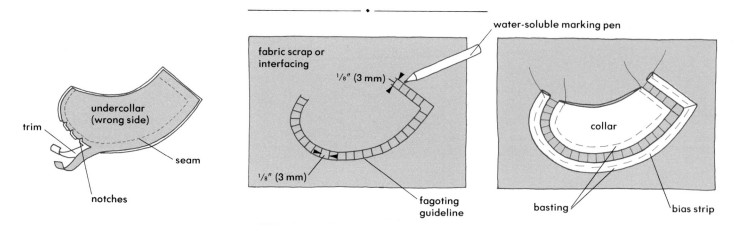

4. The collar. With right sides together, pin each upper collar to its corresponding undercollar, matching the outer edges, and easing in the extra fullness of the upper collar. Baste, and then stitch the seam. Grade and notch the seam allowances, and turn the collars right side out. Press, making sure the seam lies to the undercollar side around the entire outer edge.

Measure the finished outer edge of one of the collar sections, add 1″ (2.5 cm), and trim the bias strips to that length. With right sides together, fold each strip in half lengthwise and stitch the long open sides together ⅛″ (3 mm) from the raw edges. Turn the strips right side out.

Place one collar section right side up on a scrap of fabric or interfacing large enough to accommodate it; this will be the backing for the fagoting. Using an embroidery marking pen

with water-soluble ink, trace the outline of the collar on the backing. Remove the collar temporarily. Draw a curved line ⅛″ (3 mm) outside and parallel to the traced line. Then mark off the space between the lines with perpendicular lines ⅛″ (3 mm) apart; the resulting markings resemble a tiny railroad track. Position the collar section right side up on the backing again, along the inner line, and baste them together by hand.

Press a bias strip to conform to the outer curved line, with the seam edge of the strip along the line and the folded edge to the outside. If your collar has a corner, miter the bias strip to conform to the corner, slipstitching the miter in place before pressing the strip in place. Then baste the bias strip to the backing along the outer curved line, so the parallel markings are visible. Repeat for the other side of the collar.

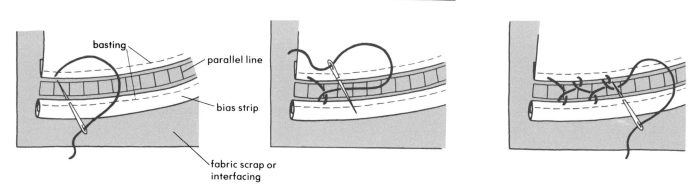

5. The fagoting. Fagoting is similar to smocking in that you work from left to right, one space at a time, but in fagoting the needle always points to the center. Thread an embroidery needle with three strands of dark-pink floss. Knot the end and hide it inside the collar seam. Bring the needle out at the first marking next to the collar.

Keeping the thread above the needle, insert the needle in the edge of the bias strip (not through the backing), one space to the right of where the needle emerged from the collar and with the needle pointing toward the collar. Pull the thread through. Now, with the thread below the needle, insert the needle in the collar, one space to the right

of the last stitch you took, and with the needle pointing toward the bias strip. Continue to alternate stitches from the bias strip to the collar, always moving one space to the right and keeping the needle pointing toward the center. Also, keep the thread above the needle when stitching through the bias strip, and below the needle when stitching through the collar. Be careful not to stitch through the interfacing. Finish with a fastening stitch in the collar. Remove the basting and lift the collar section from the scrap or interfacing. Work fagoting on the other collar section in the same way.

6. Attaching the collar. Place the collar sections side by side so the center front edges touch, and tack the edges together loosely at that spot. Then baste around the neck edges in one continuous step just inside the seam line.

Turn the center back facings to the right side along the fold lines and pin the upper edges along the neckline.

With right sides up, pin the collars to the neck edge of the dress, matching center fronts and backs. Baste, and remove the pins. Cut a piece of bias tape the length of the neck edge from center back to center back, less 1″ (2.5 cm). Then steam-press the tape so that one folded edge matches the curve of the neck edge.

Open out the fold of the tape that will be along the neck edge and, matching the fold line to the collar seam line and centering the tape, pin the tape to the collar. Stitch around

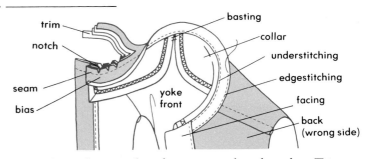

the neck on the seam line from one end to the other. Trim and notch the seam allowances; then understitch the bias tape to the seam allowances. Turn the ends of the tape to the inside. Pin the lower edge of the bias tape to the inside of the dress and edgestitch it in place. Turn the facings to the wrong side.

7. Finishing the dress. To attach the **sleeves,** make two rows of gathering stitches on the sleeve cap between the notches. With right sides together, pin the sleeve to the armhole edge, matching notches and symbols. Pull up the gathering threads until the sleeve fits the armhole, distributing the fullness evenly. Sew the sleeve to the armhole with a double-stitched seam.

The sash. Finish the side edges and free end of the sash as for the Alice in Wonderland style pinafore on page 108. Pin the raw ends of each sash to the bodice backs at the side edges, gathering or pleating them to fit; then baste the sashes in place.

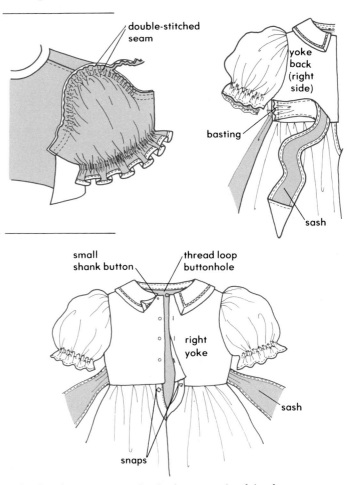

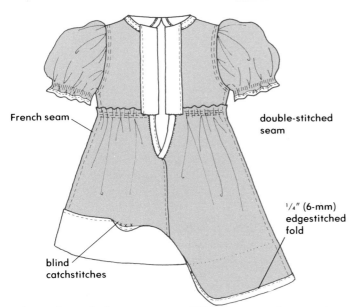

The side and sleeve seams. With wrong sides together, pin and baste the side and sleeve edges together. Then finish them with French seams.

The hem. Turn up the raw edge of the hem ¼″ (6 mm), and edgestitch along the fold; then turn up the hem and blind-catchstitch it in place.

The back opening. At the lower ends of the facings, turn the seam allowances under, and slipstitch the facing ends closed. Mark the right back for buttonholes, using your pattern as a guide, or the "Dressmaking Skills" section. If you like, make a thread loop buttonhole at the top of the right back. Make the buttonholes by hand or machine. Sew the buttons to the left back opposite the buttonholes. Sew a snap fastener at the top of the placket, placing the ball half on the inside of the right-hand placket and the socket half on the left-hand placket.

Smocked Romper

Here is the second variation on the yoke theme: a smocked romper for a little boy. It's so similar to the smocked dress that it can be made from the same pattern. All you need to do is convert the skirt pattern to snap-crotch pants, a fairly simple procedure explained below. Other modifications include a smocking design that features a pair of bunnies, a contrasting collar, and sleeves finished with French binding rather than smocking. Refer to the "Dressmaking Skills" section for unfamiliar sewing and smocking techniques.

Materials

1¾ yards (1.7 m) of 45″-wide (114-cm) light-gray cotton broadcloth

¼ yard (.25 m) white broadcloth

Six-strand embroidery floss: 2 skeins dark gray, 1 skein yellow, and small amount of white

One package light-gray bias tape

Three or four tiny pearl buttons

1 yard (.95) of ¼″-wide (6-mm) elastic

Two size 4/0 snap fasteners

Three medium-sized snap fasteners

Two small buttons, about ⅜″ (9.5 cm) in diameter, optional

A commercial pattern: Romper patterns are hard to find, except by mail, but any dress pattern with a mid-armhole yoke, a round collar, and puffed sleeves can be converted to rompers, using the directions that follow. If you made the smocked dress, you can use that pattern.

Adjusting the pattern and cutting the fabric

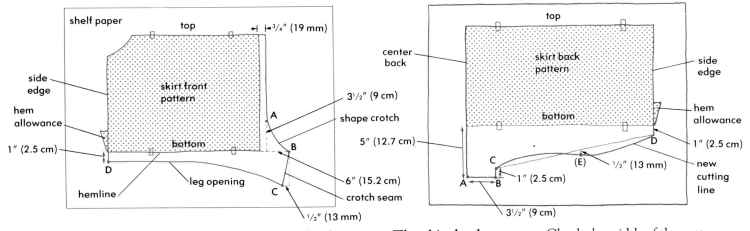

1. Adjusting the pattern. Before **adapting the skirt to a romper,** make sure that the skirt top is three or four times the desired finished width of the yoke. If it isn't, see the directions under the smocked yoke dress, page 119, for enlarging the pattern. Then fold and pin the hem allowance out of the way. Tape the pattern to a large sheet of paper, such as shelf paper. Draw a line ¾″ (19 mm) outside the center front line and parallel to it. Measure and mark point A on the line, 6″ (15.2 cm) up from the hemline. Extend the hemline 3½″ (9 cm) beyond the center front and mark the end point B. From point B, measure straight down 3½″ (9 cm). Then measure ½″ (13 mm) at a right angle to the left and mark it point C.

At the side edge, extend the cutting line down 1″ (2.5 cm) to mark point D. To shape the center front seam, connect points A and B with a curved line. To shape the crotch seam, connect points B and C with a straight line. To shape the leg opening, connect points D and C, forming a gentle curve as shown. Cut out the pattern along the new lines and the unchanged old ones.

The skirt back pattern. Check the width of the pattern as for the skirt front, and adjust it in the same manner, if necessary. Fold under the hem allowance and tape the pattern to paper as for the skirt front. Extend the center back cutting line down 5″ (12.7 cm) and mark the end point A. At a right angle to point A, draw a 3½″-long (9-cm) line, and mark the end point B. Directly up, at a right angle from point B, draw a 1″-long (2.5-cm) line, and mark the end point C. At the side edge, extend the cutting line down 1″ (2.5 cm), and mark the end point D. Lightly connect points C and D with a straight line and mark point E ½″ (13 mm) down from the midpoint of this line. Then connect points C and E with a curved line through point E, as shown. This is your new cutting line. Cut out the pattern.

The collar pattern. If you made the smocked dress, use the altered collar pattern for the romper. Otherwise, alter the pattern now, according to the directions for that dress, on page 118.

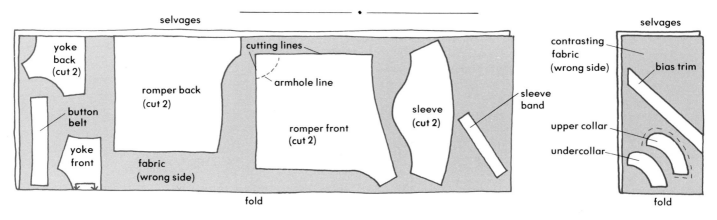

2. Cutting the fabric.

Fold the gray fabric in half lengthwise, wrong side out, and lay out all the pattern pieces except for the collar, as shown. Save the leftover fabric for cutting the button sash, sleeve bands, crotch facings, and placket strip later on. Cut the front and back skirt into rectangular pieces as for the smocked dress, page 119; the armholes are cut only after the smocking has been completed.

Fold the white fabric in half, wrong side out, along the lengthwise grain. Use the altered pattern to cut the undercollar sections. Cut two upper collar sections 1/16″ (1.5 mm) larger than the undercollar around the outer edges only. Do not change the neck edge. Save the rest of the white fabric for cutting bias strips later on.

The smocking

1. Preparing for smocking. With right sides together, pin and stitch the center front seam of the romper, finishing it as desired. By hand, using hot-iron transfer dots, or with a pleating machine, make ten rows of gathers for smocking across the top of the romper. Space the rows so that the top (auxiliary) row is outside the seam line and the next row is 1/8″ (3 mm) inside the seam line. The rows should be about 3/8″ (9.5 mm) apart.

Make three rows of gathering for smocking on each back half of the romper. Space the rows so the second row is 1/8″ (3 mm) inside the seam line.

Pull the gathering threads until the fabric is 1″ (2.5 cm) narrower than the desired finished width and knot the threads together in groups.

2. Smocking the front. Use four strands of dark-gray floss, except where otherwise noted.

Row 1. Work two rows of cables, back to back, along Row 1. Then, with regular thread, baste along the "valley" between the two centermost pleats closest to the center front seam.

Rows 2 and 3. Stitch an up cable across the center "valley" on Row 2. Wave down halfway to Row 3 and back. Continue working to the right, making baby waves to the end of the row. Finish the row by first turning the work 180 degrees. Then start at the center front and continue the pattern of baby waves. Turn the work again, and stitch a second row of baby waves below and back to back with the first row, working from the left side of the fabric to the right, forming baby diamonds.

Rows 6 and 7. Establish the bottom of the pattern by working another row of baby diamonds between Rows 6 and 7, keeping the stitches aligned with those in the diamonds above.

Windows: Mark the top and bottom points of the windows with a pin at the seventh diamond to the right and the seventh diamond to the left of the center. Place the pins between Rows 2 and 3 at the top and between Rows 6 and 7 at the bottom. Now work two more rows of baby waves, the first at the top of the window, from midway between Rows 3 and 4 up to Row 3 and back, the second at the bottom of the window, from midway between Rows 6 and 7 up to Row 6 and back, completing more baby diamonds. Carry the thread behind the space for diamonds 6 and 7 to form the top and bottom of the windows.

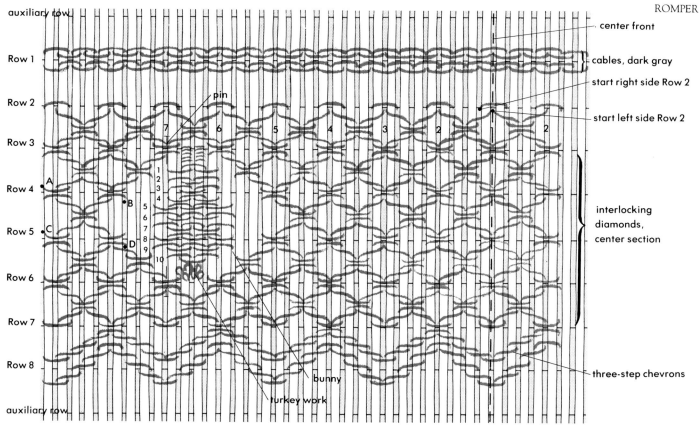

Labels in diagram: auxiliary row, Row 1, Row 2, Row 3, Row 4, Row 5, Row 6, Row 7, Row 8, auxiliary row, A, B, C, D, pin, bunny, turkey work, center front, cables, dark gray, start right side Row 2, start left side Row 2, interlocking diamonds, center section, three-step chevrons

ROMPER

To complete the windows, work three sections of the pattern separately with interlocking baby diamonds: the left side, center and right side.

The left side. Work the bottoms of the diamonds between Rows 3 and 4, starting at the left side (A). Turn the work 180 degrees, and bring the needle up at B. Complete another row of diamonds. Continue with two more rows of baby waves, turning the work at the end of each row and inserting the needle as indicated by letters C and D on the diagram. Work the center and right sections in corresponding fashion to complete the design, following the smocking diagram.

Rows 7 and 8. To complete the smocking design, work a row of gray three-step chevrons down from Row 7 to a quarter space above Row 8 and back. To center the chevrons, count the diamonds from the center to the left side of the fabric and make sure you begin stitching so the lowest cables will align with every other diamond, including the one at the center.

Echo row. Work an echo row of chevrons in yellow, half a space below the first row.

3. Smocking the back of the romper. Work four rows of double cables across the top of each back section as follows. Using dark-gray floss, work a row of cables just above Row 1, stopping or starting 1/4″ (6 mm) short of the center back seam line. Using yellow, work two more rows of cables below the first row. Using dark gray, stitch a row of cables just below Row 2.

Bunnies. Following the smocking diagram, work a yellow bunny with stacked cables in each window as explained below, and start each row as indicated by the dots on the diagram. It is not necessary to turn your work; simply carry the thread loosely on the wrong side of the fabric back to the left to begin each row. Work the rows in sequence; do not skip.

Row 1 (top of head): Starting below and to the left of the center of diamond 7, midway between rows 3 and 4, cable down, up, down.

Rows 2 and 3: Cable up, down, up.

Row 4: Cable down, up, down.

Rows 5 and 8: Cable down, up, down, up, down.

Rows 6, 7, and 9: Cable up, down, up, down, up.

Row 10: Cable up, down, up.

The ears. Work 5 up cables above the head over 1 pleat at each end of the topmost cable.

The tail. Make a turkey-work tail (see page 39), using white embroidery floss.

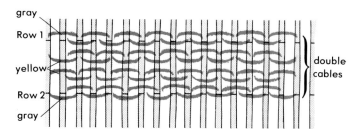

Diagram labels: gray, Row 1, yellow, Row 2, gray, double cables

127

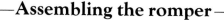

Assembling the romper

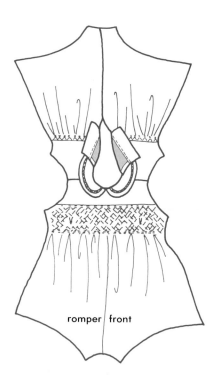

romper front

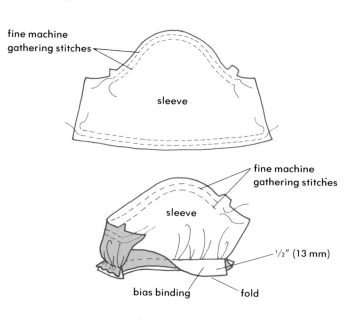

fine machine
gathering stitches

sleeve

fine machine
gathering stitches

sleeve

½" (13 mm)

bias binding   fold

1. Joining the major sections of the romper. The next steps are exactly the same as for the smocked dress, pages 121 to 123. Follow the directions given there for cutting the armholes, joining the yoke front to the romper front, making the placket, joining the yoke back to the romper back, joining the shoulders, and making and applying the collar. Use yellow floss for the fagoting on the collar.

2. The sleeves. Make two rows of fine machine gathering stitches on the sleeve cap between the notches and along the lower edge. Measure the child's upper arm at its fullest part. Cut two bias strips 1½" (3.8 cm) wide and 2" (5 cm) longer than the arm measurement. Gather the lower edge of the sleeves until they are the same length as the bias strips. Then, following the directions in the "Dressmaking Skills" section, finish the lower edges of the sleeves with French binding. Do not hem the binding until after the side and underarm seams have been stitched. The finished width of the binding should be ¼" (6 mm) wide. Sew the sleeves to the romper as for the smocked dress, page 123.

3. The belt and side seams. For a belt that buttons, measure the back of the romper from one side seam to the center and add 6" (15.2 cm). Cut two straight 3½"-wide (9-cm) strips the length of that measurement. For a tie belt, cut two 21"-long (53.3-cm) strips the same width.

For either belt, fold each strip in half lengthwise with right sides together. Stitch a ¼" (6-mm) seam along the long raw edges and along one end. Trim the corners, turn the strip right side out, and press. With right sides together, pin the raw ends of each strip to the side edges of the romper back, just below the armhole, and baste them in place.

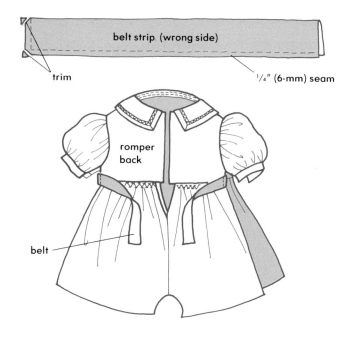

belt strip (wrong side)

trim

¼" (6-mm) seam

romper
back

belt

The side and sleeve seams. With the free ends of the sash tucked out of the way, and with wrong sides together, pin and baste the side and sleeve edges together. Then finish with French seams. Hem the sleeve binding to the inside, covering the seam allowances.

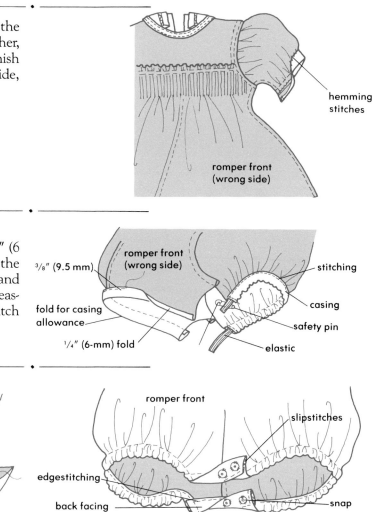

4. The leg casings. At each leg edge, press under ¼″ (6 mm), then ³⁄₈″ (9.5 mm). Edgestitch the inner fold to the romper to form a casing. Measure the child's upper leg and cut 2 pieces of elastic 1″ (2.5 cm) shorter than this measurement. Draw the elastic through the casings and stitch across the ends to secure them.

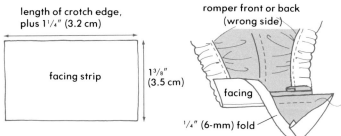

5. The crotch facings. Cut two straight strips 1³⁄₈″ (3.5 cm) wide and 1¼″ (3.2 cm) longer than the crotch edge of the front and back. Press under ¼″ (6 mm) along one long edge of each strip. With right sides together, and the ends extending evenly on both sides, pin the unpressed long edges of each strip to each one of the crotch edges and stitch a ⅝″ (16 mm) seam. Trim the seam allowances to ¼″ (6 mm). Turn in the raw ends of the facings and turn the facings to the wrong side of the rompers. Edgestitch the pressed edges in place. Turn the ends under, and slipstitch them closed. Sew the three snaps to the crotch facings, placing the ball half on the inside of the front and the socket half on the outside back.

6. Finishing the rompers. Finish the lower edge of the yoke facing, make buttonholes and sew on buttons and the size 4/0 snap fasteners to the placket as for the smocked yoke dress, page 123.

The belt. To complete the button belt, overlap the belt ends and sew a buttonhole in the right strap ½″ (13 mm) from the end. Pin the belt in place and determine the distance from the buttonhole to the center back. Mark and make a second buttonhole the same distance from the center at the opposite end of the belt piece. (Each side of the belt should extend about 3″ (7.6 cm) beyond the center.) Sew buttons onto the left belt strap corresponding to the buttonholes.

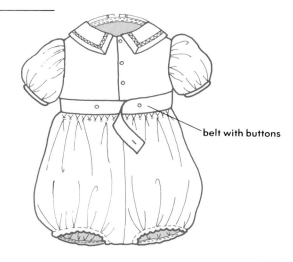

Lace-trimmed Corduroy Dress

Although it makes its initial appearance under the Alice in Wonderland style pinafore, the corduroy dress pictured here can be worn successfully all by itself. In this variation, the yoke dress has long sleeves gathered into cuffs, a stand-up band collar, and the crisp touch of lace at the neck and wrists.

Corduroy, like velvet, is a pile fabric. So, if you decide to make the dress from this fabric, be sure to read the section on working with velvet, page 140, since those hints apply to corduroy as well.

• ————— Materials ————— •

1³/₄ yards (1.17 m) of 45″-wide (114-cm) corduroy

One package matching 1″-wide (2.5-cm) bias tape

1 yard (.95 m) of ¹/₂″-wide (13-mm) flat lace trim

Two small snap fasteners

Four small pearl shank buttons

A commercial pattern: any pattern with a deep (below-the-armhole) yoke and a gathered skirt. A high round neck, with or without a collar, and long or short sleeves with gathered fullness at the shoulder are other pattern features to look for.

• ————— Adjusting the pattern and cutting the fabric ————— •

1. The skirt pattern. Lengthen the skirt pattern, if necessary, and make the hem allowance 4″ (10.2 cm) deep.

2. The yoke back. If you want to convert a zipper closing to a button-back closing, adjust the yoke back as for the smocked dress, on page 118.

3. The sleeves. If your dress has long sleeves, fine. If they're short and you want to make them long, proceed as follows. Tape the sleeve pattern to a long piece of shelf paper. Mark points A and B at the top of the underarm seam on the back and front sleeve edges, respectively. Then connect points A and B with a straight line. Measure the child's arm from shoulder to wrist and add 1″ (2.5 cm). Then draw a line this length, perpendicular to line AB, starting at C (the top of the sleeve cap). Mark D at the wrist end of the line. Draw a line through point D, parallel to and the same length as line AB. From each end of this line, measure 1¹/₂″ (3.8 cm) toward the center and mark these points E and F.

To draw the underarm edges, connect points A and E and points B and F with straight lines. To draw the wrist edge, connect points E and F with a line that curves ¹/₄″

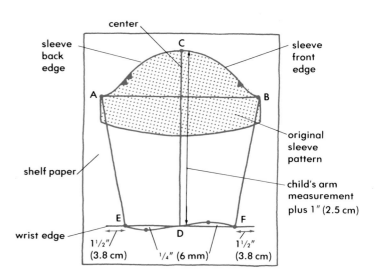

(6 mm) below the wristline, passes through point D, and then curves ¹/₄″ (6 mm) above the wristline before joining F, as shown. The new pattern includes ⁵/₈″ (16-mm) seam allowances.

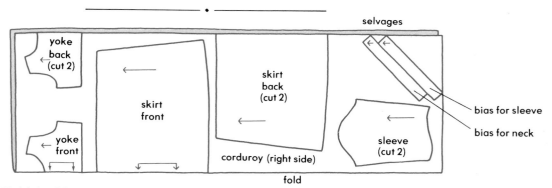

selvages

yoke
back
(cut 2)

skirt
front

skirt
back
(cut 2)

bias for sleeve

bias for neck

yoke
front

corduroy (right side)

sleeve
(cut 2)

fold

2. Cutting the fabric. Fold the fabric in half lengthwise, wrong sides together as for velvet, and lay out the pattern, omitting any collar pieces. Cut out the pieces and transfer any pattern markings as for velvet, page 140. Save the leftover fabric for cutting the placket strip and the neck and sleeve bias strips later on.

Assembling the dress

1. Joining the major sections of the dress. To join the **yoke front and skirt front,** make two rows of machine gathering stitches along the top of the skirt front. With right sides together, pin the skirt to the yoke, pulling up the gathers until the skirt fits the yoke. Stitch the seam and finish it as desired.

Joining the yoke back and skirt back. Gather and seam the skirt back, and finish the seam allowances as desired. Make the placket, as for the smocked nightie on page 90, finishing the seam as desired.

Sewing the shoulder seams and finishing the facing. Join the dress front to the back, right sides together, at the shoulders, and finish the seam allowances as desired. Finish the edges of the facings with a Hong Kong finish (page 140), and fold them under at the center back opening. Turn under the lower edges and sew them in place with hemming stitches.

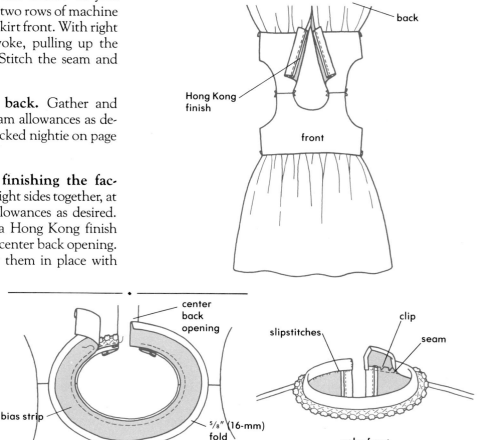

back

Hong Kong
finish

front

facing

back

lace trim

basting

center
back
opening

clip

slipstitches

seam

bias strip

⁵/₈″ (16-mm)
fold

yoke front

yoke front

2. Making and attaching the collar. First cut a piece of lace trim 1¹/₄″ (3.2 cm) longer than the measurement of the neck edge from fold line to fold line of the back facings. Cut a bias strip of corduroy the same length and 2¹/₂″ (5.7 cm) wide. With right sides up, pin the lace to the neck edge of the dress, with the inner edge just over the seam line. Turn the ends of the lace under ⁵/₈″ (16 mm) so they are even with the fold lines. Baste the lace in place.

The band collar. Press the bias strip in half lengthwise, wrong sides together, then press one long edge under ⁵/₈″ (16 mm). With right sides together and raw edges matching, pin the unpressed edge of the bias strip to the neck edge, so the ends extend equally on each side. Stitch, catching the inner edge of the lace. Clip, but do not trim, the seam allowances every ¹/₂″ (13 mm), and press them toward the bias strip. Fold the bias strip to the inside along the pressed center line, turning the ends in ⁵/₈″ (16 mm), and pin the folded edge over the seam line. Slipstitch the folded edge in place, then slipstitch the ends closed.

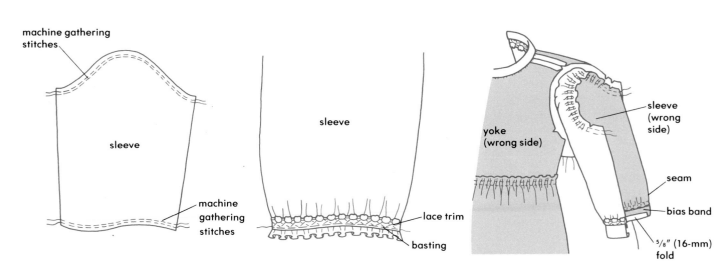

3. The sleeves. Make two rows of machine gathering stitches along the sleeve cap and the wrist edges. Cut two bias strips of corduroy 2½″ (5.7 cm) wide and 1″ (2.5 cm) longer than the measurement of the child's wrist. Cut two pieces of lace the same length.

With right sides up, pin the lace along the seam line of the wrist edge of the sleeve, aligning the ends of the lace with the side edges of the sleeve. Pull up the gathers on the sleeve until it fits the lace. Baste the lace in place.

The bias bands. Press each bias band in half, right side out, then turn under and press a ⅝″ (16-mm) fold along one long side of each strip. Stitch a bias band to the bottom of each sleeve as you did at the neckline, but don't fold the bias bands to the inside yet.

Sew the sleeve cap to the armhole edge, with a double-stitched seam.

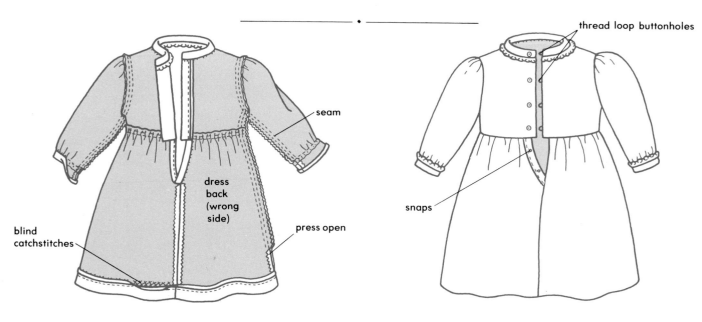

4. Finishing the dress. First pin and stitch the **side and underarm seams,** including the bias cuff seams, in one step. Pink and stitch the seam allowances.

The cuffs. Turn the pressed edge of each cuff to the inside, pin it over the seam, and slipstitch it in place.

The hem. Finish the hem edge with a Hong Kong finish, then turn up the hem and blind-catchstitch it in place.

The yoke facings and closings. Turn in and slipstitch shut the lower edge of the yoke facings and sew two snaps to the placket as for the smocked dress, on page 123. On the right back edge, make four thread loop buttonholes: one on the collar, one just above the lower edge of the yoke, one near the neck edge, and another between them. Lap the right back over the left back, matching the centers. Mark button positions on the left back, opposite the loops, and sew on the buttons.

Embroidered Gingham Dress

Embroidered Gingham Dress

The last member of the yoke quartet is made of baby-checked gingham and boasts a bouquet of flowers embroidered on the yoke. Other grace notes include short, cuffed sleeves and a collar with contrasting piping. Except for the fact that this dress has a lined yoke to cover the back of the embroidery, the construction is basically the same as for the other dresses. Refer to the "Dressmaking Skills" section for any unfamiliar sewing and embroidery techniques.

Materials

2 yards (1.9 m) of 44"-wide (112-cm) small checked gingham

³/₈ yard (.35 m) white fabric for collar and cuffs

¹/₄ yard (.25 m) contrasting colorfast solid-color fabric for piping

1¹/₄ yards (1.2 m) of ¹/₈"-diameter (3-mm) preshrunk cording to coordinate with the dress fabric and embroidery

Six-strand embroidery floss: 1 skein each yellow, white, medium blue, green, red, and brown

Three ³/₈" (9.5-mm) and one ¹/₈" (3-mm) pearl buttons

Two size 4/0 snap fasteners

A commercial pattern with the following features: a deep (below-the-armhole) yoke, short puffed sleeves, and a round collar

Adjusting the pattern and cutting out the fabric

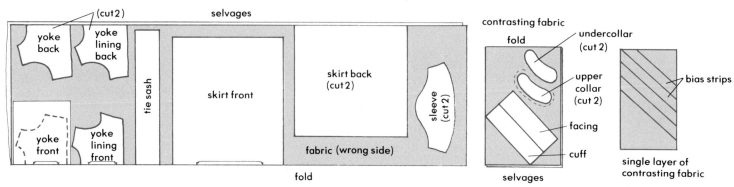

1. Adjusting the pattern pieces. Lengthen the **skirt** front and back, if necessary, to make the hem allowance 4" (10.2 cm).

The bodice back. If you're changing a zipper closing to a button-back closing, follow the instructions given for the smocked dress on page 118, but extend the back opening edges only 1⁵/₈" (4.2 cm).

The collar. Trim away ¹/₈" (3 mm) from the outer edges of the collar to allow for the piped trim; don't trim the neck edge.

2. Cutting the fabric. Fold the gingham in half lengthwise, wrong side out, and lay out the pattern pieces as shown. Note that the yoke front and yoke back pieces are shown twice; that's because the yoke is lined. Cut out all the pieces, except the yoke front, and transfer any relevant pattern markings. Then, with the pattern piece pinned in place, cut out the yoke front, giving it a healthy margin all the way around as shown, to make it easier to handle while embroidering. Save the leftover fabric for cutting the placket later on.

The collar. Fold the white collar fabric the same as for the gingham and, using the altered collar pattern, cut the two undercollar pieces. Then cut the upper collar ¹/₁₆" (1.5 mm) larger than the undercollar, along the outer edge only. Do not alter the neck edge.

The sleeve cuffs and facings. Measure the child's upper arm around the fullest part and add 2³/₄" (4.5 cm) for ease and seam allowances. Then cut four 2¹/₄"-wide (3.2-cm) bias strips this length for the cuffs and facings.

Bias strips for piping. From a single layer of the contrasting fabric, cut four 1¹/₂"-wide (3.8-cm) bias strips the width of the fabric, as shown.

Assembling the dress

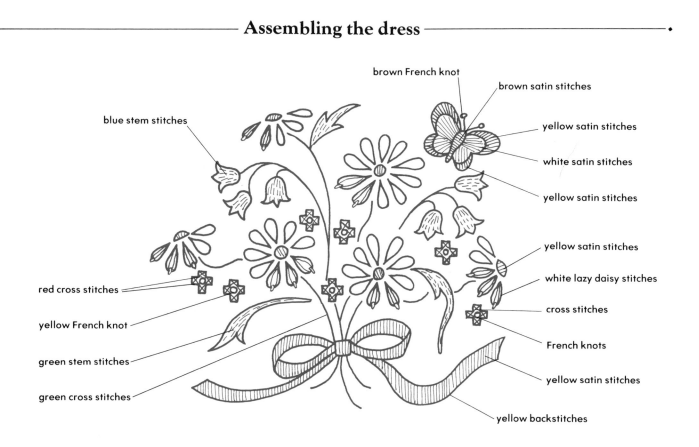

brown French knot

brown satin stitches

blue stem stitches

yellow satin stitches

white satin stitches

yellow satin stitches

yellow satin stitches

white lazy daisy stitches

red cross stitches

cross stitches

yellow French knot

French knots

green stem stitches

yellow satin stitches

green cross stitches

yellow backstitches

1. The embroidery. Trace the yoke front, along the cutting line, onto the fabric while the pattern is still pinned in place; then remove the pattern. Trace the embroidery design and transfer it to the center of the yoke front, following the directions on page 175. Stretch the fabric in a hoop and work the embroidery as follows, sewing the stitches in the direction indicated on the illustration. The thread can be carried across the back of the fabric from flower to flower, but not more than about 1/2" (13 mm).

Daisies. Using three strands of yellow floss, work the centers from one side to the other in satin stitches. Using six strands of white floss, work the petals in lazy daisy stitches.

Bluebells. Using two strands of blue floss, fill in the outlines with parallel rows of stem stitches. Starting at the round end of the bell, work along the outline along one side of the flower and back. Vary the length of each row to fit the outline as you work to the other side of the flower.

Leaves. Using two strands of green embroidery floss, fill in the leaf shapes with parallel rows of stem stitches running lengthwise.

Stems. Using two strands of green floss, work the stems in small cross stitches the size of the gingham squares. Work the stitches in adjoining squares, straight up or down, at a diagonal or to the side, whichever direction conforms best to the shape of the stem.

Bow. Using three strands of yellow, first outline the bow with backstitches. Then work satin stitches perpendicular to and over the backstitches from side to side.

Small flowers. Using two strands of red, work four tiny cross stitches about 1/16" (1.5 mm) across for each flower in adjoining squares of gingham, like a cross, leaving the center square open, as shown. Then sew a yellow French knot in the center square of each flower.

Butterfly. Using three strands of brown, work the body from side to side in satin stitches. Outline the wings and antennae with backstitches. Make a brown French knot at the end of each antenna. Using three strands of floss and satin stitches, fill in the inner parts of the wings in white, and the outer parts in yellow.

Cutting the yoke. Remove the embroidery from the hoop, and steam-press it on the wrong side over a terry towel, using light pressure. Center the yoke front pattern over the embroidery, pin it in place, and cut out the yoke.

2. The yoke, skirt, and shoulder seams. Prepare and stitch the yoke and skirt front, the placket, the yoke and skirt back, and the shoulder seams exactly as for the corduroy dress, on page 131. Save the yoke linings for later.

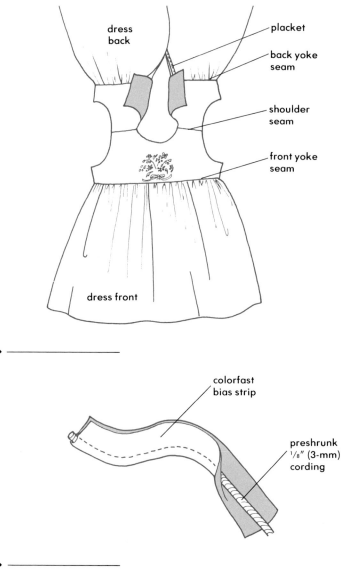

3. The collar. First make the piping as follows: Cut two pieces of cording 1″ (2.5 cm) longer than the outer edge of the upper collar. Trim two of the contrasting bias strips to the same length. Fold one bias strip, right side out, around one piece of cording to enclose it, aligning the raw edges. Then, using a zipper foot, stitch the bias strip next to the cording, without stretching or pulling the strip as you sew. Repeat with the other bias strip and cording. If the seam allowances on the piping are wider than ⅝″ (16 mm), trim them to that width.

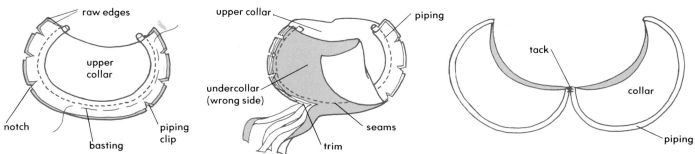

Assembling the collar. Press the piping to conform to the outer edge of the upper collar. With right sides together and raw edges matching, pin a strip of piping to each upper collar section, clipping the seam allowances of the piping as necessary around the curves. Baste the piping in place. With right sides together, pin and then baste the undercollar to the upper collar around the outer edges, working from the ends to the center and easing the larger upper collar in place as you work. Using a zipper foot, seam both sections of the upper collar, undercollar, and piping. Grade the seam allowances (trim each seam allowance to a different width); notch them at the curves, and turn the collar sections right side out. Press, being careful not to flatten the piping. Place the two collar sections right side up, with their center front edges touching. Tack the sections together loosely at that point.

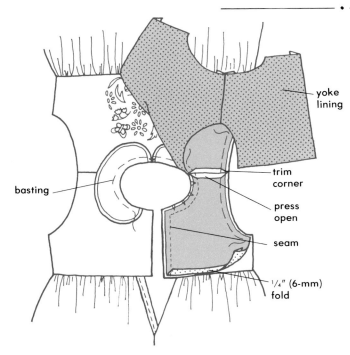

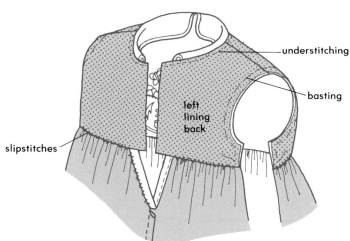

4. Joining the collar and lining to the dress. With right sides up, pin the collar to the dress, matching the center fronts. The back edges of the collar should match the center back of the yoke. Baste the collar in place.

The yoke lining. Join the front and back yoke linings at the shoulders and press the seam allowances open. Leave the lining wrong side out. At the lower edges of the lining, press the seam allowances under. With right sides together, pin the yoke lining to the dress along the neck and back opening edges, and stitch them together. Don't stitch the side, armhole, or lower edges. Grade the seam allowances around the neck, making that of the dress the widest, and clip them at the curves. Turn the lining to the inside and press the neckline edge. With the collar pulled out of the way, understitch 1/4″ (6 mm) away from the neckline seam, through the yoke and lining, from the lining side. Pin the lower edge of the lining over the yoke/skirt seam, and then slipstitch the lining in place. Baste the layers of fabric together at the side and armhole edges.

5. The sleeves. Gather the sleeve cap and lower edges as for the corduroy dress, on page 132.

The cuffs. Make piping for the cuffs as you did for the collar. Now turn to page 155 and follow the instructions for making the sleeve cuffs on the dress shirt, substituting the piping for the pleated trim, and gathering the lower edge of the sleeve to fit the cuff. Sew in the sleeves, following the directions for the corduroy dress, on page 132.

6. Finishing the dress. Make the **sash,** and baste it to the yoke back, following the directions for the Alice in Wonderland style pinafore, on page 108.

The side and sleeve seams. Matching the ends of the facing/cuff, cuff/sleeve, and yoke/skirt seams, pin and stitch the side and underarm seams in one step with French seams. Then finish the sleeve cuffs by turning them up as for the dress shirt, page 155.

The hem and buttonholes. Sew the hem, make buttonholes, and sew on the buttons as for the smocked yoke dress, on page 123.

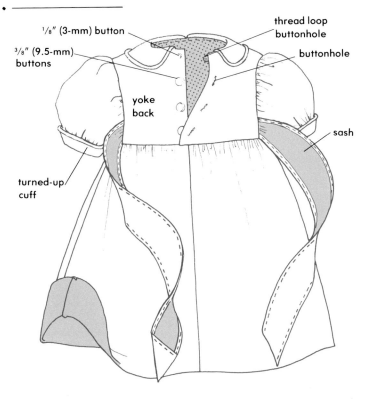

Velvets

"Some in rags, some in tags, and some in velvet gowns," goes the nursery rhyme. Indeed, the mere mention of *velvet* conjures up visions of elegance and refinement: kings and queens in opulent robes, princes of the church in flowing vestments. Only the high and mighty could afford velvet in centuries past, since it used to be made exclusively of silk. The skilled techniques of hand-weaving velvet's threads apparently developed simultaneously in China and Persia in the fourteenth century and then spread quickly throughout Europe; these techniques, along with the expensive and rare dyes used to create the luxurious garments' rich hues, contributed to the high cost of velvet garments. Purple, the color reserved for imperial personages in ancient Rome and for royalty thereafter, was obtained from a rare mollusk. Lesser nobility had to be content with red, wine, scarlet, or crimson dyes derived from certain insects, or with blue, especially rich indigo blue, which comes from a plant of the same name.

Nowadays, velvet is machine-woven from silk, cotton, rayon, and other synthetic fibers and dyed with colors from the chemist's artificial rainbow, but velvet is still unbeatable as a dress-up fabric. Who doesn't remember that long-ago birthday party at which one boy wore a *velvet* suit, much to the envy of his friends, or that holiday when a treasured red velvet dress appeared at a party. Beginning overleaf are detailed instructions for making such a classic dress, much like the one shown opposite, and for a dapper suit and ruffled shirt.

Lace, a traditional decoration for dress-up clothes, is also a centuries-old way to display wealth. The cost of the linen thread and the time required to hand-make intricate lace patterns has made lace very costly indeed. At the height of the lace craze in the eighteenth century, lace was used to trim every imaginable part of a garment, even the inside tops of gentlemen's boots. At that time, lace from Flanders was so valuable that men risked imprisonment and even death for the enormous profits that could be made smuggling it into England. Most lace available today is machine-made, of course, but old-lace collecting is popular and a Hand-made Lace Society flourishes in this country. The lace collar for the velvet dress project is stitched on separately, so if you have a piece of lovely old lace, you might find this the perfect opportunity to use it.

———————— • ————————

Around 1835, an anonymous American School artist created this enchanting portrait of a little Miss in a classic, lace-trimmed velvet gown. Entitled "Little Girl with Flower Basket," it exemplifies the way velvet clothing enchances a child's natural loveliness.

Working with velvet

Velvet, that most regal of all fabrics, is not difficult to sew, as long as you know the rules and follow them.

Determining pile direction. Velvet, like other pile fabrics, is woven by forming loops that are trapped in the weave. The loops are then sheared off, creating the soft, raised surface known as the pile. Because the threads forming the pile all face in the same direction, the effect of light on the pile differs depending on which way it hits the pile. When the pile faces down, the fabric appears lighter because the threads reflect the light. When the pile faces up, the threads catch and absorb the light, making the fabric appear darker and richer.

To determine the direction of the pile (if you can't tell by looking at it), run your finger lightly over the surface of the fabric along the lengthwise grain. If the fabric feels smooth, the pile is running down. If the fabric feels rough and releases little threads, the pile is running up.

You may cut the velvet *with the pile* (down) or *against the pile* (up), whichever you prefer, as long as all the pieces of your pattern face in the same direction. A garment with the nap running down will wear better because it resists crushing and matting. However, you might prefer the deeper color of the nap running up. Hold the fabric up to the light both ways, then choose the look you prefer.

Marking the fabric. Using chalk, mark an arrow near one corner, on the wrong side of the fabric, pointing in the pile direction you plan to use in cutting. Place a pin in the selvage, near the arrow, pointing in the same direction, as another reminder.

Cutting and marking the fabric. Fold the fabric lengthwise (never crosswise), with the pile side out, to prevent the pile from rubbing together and locking. Lay out all the pattern pieces with their tops facing in the same direction, so they'll all reflect the light in the same way when they're sewed together. Check your arrow and pin markings to be sure you've placed the pieces as you intended. Using fine silk pins, pin the pattern pieces in place, picking up the fabric only within the seam allowances; otherwise, you may leave permanent pin marks. Transfer pattern markings, using dressmaker's chalk or tailor's tacks.

Stitching velvet. Do some testing to determine the machine settings that will give you the best stitch quality in sewing velvet. Use a double layer of velvet scraps to simulate actual sewing conditions.

Loosen the upper tension of the machine slightly and reduce the pressure, if possible; check the manual for instructions on how to do this. Use a size 11 (U.S.) or size 70 to 80 (European) needle, and set the stitch length to about ten stitches per inch (2.5 cm). As you stitch, pull the fabric slightly taut behind the presser foot, checking to see that both layers feed evenly and that the upper layer doesn't

"creep." If you have an even-feed attachment, try using it. Keep experimenting until you have a smooth seam.

Seam finishes for velvet. A garment made of velvet deserves fine seam finishes. Here are three to choose from.

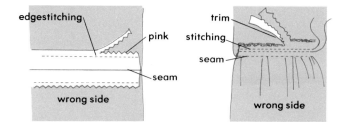

Stitched and pinked finish. Stitch 1/4" to 3/8" (6 to 9.5 mm) away from the edge of the seam allowance. Then pink the edge just outside the stitching.

Double-stitched finish. Finger press the seam allowances to one side, and stitch them together 1/4" (6 mm) away from the seam line, inside the seam allowance. Repeat 1/8" (3 mm) away, if desired. Then trim the seam allowances close to the outer stitching.

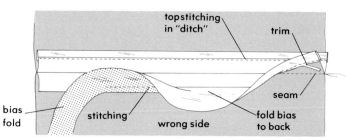

Hong Kong finish. This is a beautiful finish, well worth the extra time it takes. Buy 1"-wide (2.5-cm) polyester/cotton bias tape in a color to match your fabric. Avoid silklike acetate types—they're hard to handle.

Cut a length of tape equal to the seam to be finished. Then cut it in half lengthwise—one half is for each seam allowance. Open out the fold and, with right sides together, stitch the tape edge nearest the fold to the seam allowance along the opened fold line. Turn the tape to the wrong side of the seam allowance. On the right side, topstitch in the "ditch" along the folded edge of the tape, catching the free edge of the tape underneath the seam allowance. On the wrong side of the seam allowance, trim the excess tape close to the stitching.

Pressing velvet. A needle board consists of a firm but flexible backing embedded with tiny needles that prevents deep-pile fabrics from becoming matted. To press velvet, you need lots of steam and minimal pressure. If your iron doesn't have an extra-steam feature, use a damp press cloth between it and the fabric to generate more steam. Place the fabric pile side down over the needle board. Rest the iron *very lightly* on the fabric or hold it just above the surface and let it steam. Use your fingers to open seams and flatten edges. If you don't have a needle board, tightly roll up a large terry cloth towel. Fasten the ends with rubber bands. Cover the towel with a piece of velvet, pile side up. Then press just as if you were using a needle board.

Velvet Party Dress

All little girls, even tomboys, love party dresses. For festive occasions, the velvet dress with lace trim is an outfit that has been around for centuries and still remains a favorite. Pick a rich, dark velvet, such as deep burgundy, to set off the lace to best advantage. And, before you start and as you sew, read and heed the preceding advice on working with velvet.

Materials

A commercial dress pattern with a fitted bodice, a round neckline (with or without a collar), a seam at the waist or above it, a gathered skirt, short puffed sleeves, and a back zipper

2 to 2½ yards (1.9 to 2.3 m) of 42"- to 45"-wide (106 - to 114 -cm) velvet, depending on pattern size and pattern adjustments (see below)

Sewing thread to match fabrics

A back zipper to match dress fabric

A small white shank button

1 package 1"-wide (2.5-cm) bias tape to match dress fabric

1¼ yards (1.2 m) white or off-white soft lace, at least 2½" (6.4 cm) wide

Adjusting the pattern and cutting the fabric

1. Pattern adjustments. Check the back of the pattern envelope for the finished width at the lower edge of the dress. If it is over 72" (183 cm), the gathers at the waist will be too bulky, so the width of both the skirt front and skirt back pieces will have to be reduced equally, as follows: Mark one-quarter of the amount to be reduced along the center top of the front and back pattern pieces. Draw parallel lines from the markings to the bottom of the pattern pieces. Fold the pattern along one of the lines and bring it to meet the second line. Tape the fold in place.

The hem allowance. Check the hem allowance on the skirt front or back pattern piece; it will probably be about 3" (7.6 cm). To get an extra year of wear out of the dress, plan on a deeper hem that can be let down halfway after a year. For size 3 and under, allow 4" (10.2 cm); for size 4 and up, allow 6" (15.2 cm).

When buying fabric, allow an extra amount for the deeper hems, plus another ¼ yard (.25 m) for cutting bias strips.

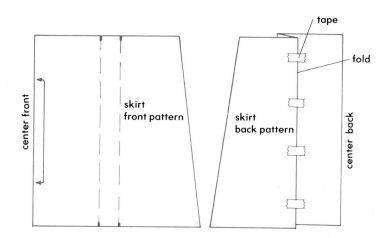

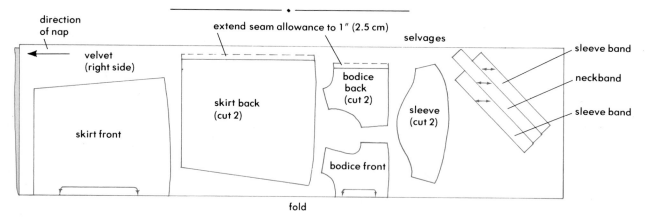

2. Cutting the fabric. Fold the velvet in half lengthwise, right side out. Lay out the pattern pieces for the skirt front and back, bodice front and back, and sleeve, as shown, with the tops of all the pattern pieces placed in the same direction and the nap of the velvet running toward the tops of each piece. Do not use any collar, facing, or cuff pieces. Extend the center back seam allowance of the bodice and skirt back to 1" (2.5 cm), to make zipper insertion easier. Cut out the pattern pieces and transfer any pattern markings.

From the remaining fabric, cut 2"-wide (5-cm) bias strips for the neck and sleeve bands as follows:

1. Measure along the neck seam line of the bodice front and back pattern pieces, multiply by two to get the total measurement of the neckline, and add 1" (2.5 cm) for turning the ends under. Cut a neckband this length.

2. Measure the child's upper arm at its fullest part, and add 2½" (6.4 cm) for ease and seams. Cut two sleeve bands this length.

Assembling the dress

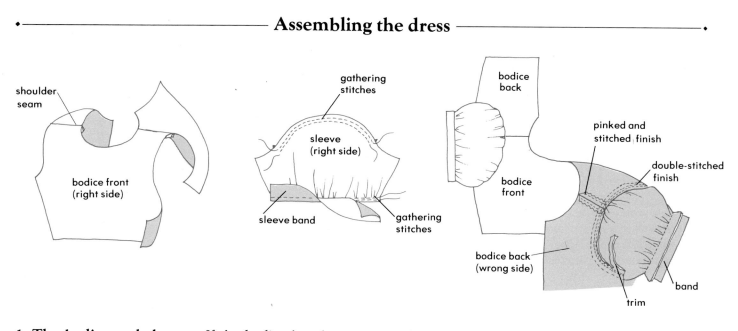

1. The bodice and sleeves. If the **bodice** has darts, stitch them and press them toward the center. Align the bodice front and back pieces, right sides together, at the shoulders, and stitch them together. Press open the seam allowances, then stitch and pink the edges.

Preparing the sleeves. Loosen the tension of the sewing machine and set the stitch length to ten per inch (2.5 cm). Gather the lower edge of each sleeve by making one row of gathering stitches just inside the seam line and another row of gathering stitches 1/4″ (6 mm) outside the first, in the seam allowance. Gather the cap of the sleeve between the notches in the same fashion. Return the machine to its normal setting.

Attaching the sleeve bands. With right sides together, pin a sleeve band to the lower edge of each sleeve, aligning the edges and ends. Pull up the bobbin threads to gather each sleeve until it fits the band, distributing the fullness evenly. Join them with a 5/8″ (16-mm) seam. Trim the seam allowances to 3/8″ (9.5 mm), and press them toward the band.

Attaching the sleeves. With right sides together, pin a sleeve to each bodice armhole edge, matching the notches and other pattern markings. Pull up the easestitching until the sleeve fits the armhole edge, again equalizing the fullness. Stitch the seam and give the seam allowances a double-stitched finish. Do not press the armhole seam allowances, but coax them toward the sleeve.

2. Joining the bodice and skirt. Make two rows of gathering stitches along the top edges of the skirt front and back sections, as you did on the sleeves. Do not seam the skirt sections yet.

With right sides together, pin the skirt front to the bodice front. Draw up the gathering threads on the skirt until it fits the bodice, then pin the skirt to the bodice, right sides together. Pin and fit the skirt backs to the bodice backs in the same way, then stitch the seams and finish them as you did for the armholes. Press the seam allowances up.

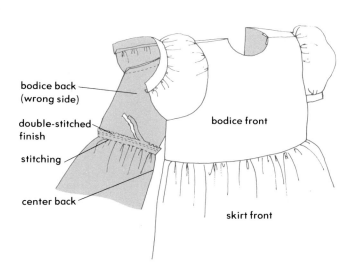

3. Inserting the zipper. To prevent the seam from pulling, clip the center back edges of the skirt in the seam allowance area where the bottom stop of the zipper will go. Pin the center back edges of the skirt and bodice right sides together and, starting at the lower edge, stitch a 1″ (2.5-cm) seam up to the snipped mark for the zipper. Backstitch to reinforce this point, then continue to the top of the seam with hand basting. Press the seam allowances open, and give them a stitched and pinked finish.

With the dress wrong side out, extend one center back seam allowance away from the rest of the dress. Open the zipper and place it face down on the seam allowance, with the bottom stop of the zipper at the clip mark, the coil right next to the seam line, and the top of the zipper tape at the neck edge. Using a zipper foot, start at the bottom and machine-baste the zipper tape to the seam allowance along the woven guideline of the zipper tape.

Close the zipper and turn it face up, keeping the seam allowance free of the rest of the garment; this will form a narrow fold of velvet in the seam allowance next to the zipper. Starting at the bottom, stitch through the fold of the seam allowance to the top of the zipper.

Still working on the wrong side, spread the dress out flat. Pin the unstitched side of the zipper tape to the other seam allowance only—not to the dress.

Turn the dress right side out. Using a single strand of matching thread, start at the neck edge and sew the zipper in place through all layers, making tiny backstitches about

½″ (13 mm) apart and ½″ (13 mm) away from the center back seam. Don't pull the stitches tight or you'll get puckers. When you get near the bottom of the zipper, stitch at a diagonal to the bottom stop of the zipper. Fasten the thread on the wrong side of the dress. Remove the pins and the basting.

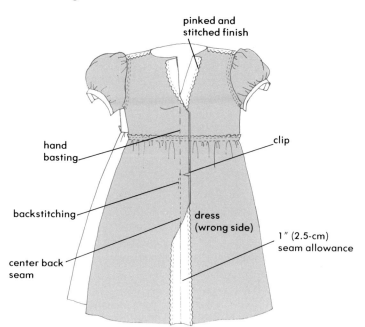

pinked and stitched finish

hand basting

clip

backstitching

dress (wrong side)

center back seam

1″ (2.5-cm) seam allowance

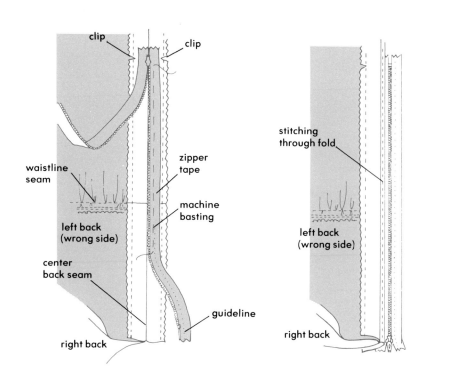

clip

clip

waistline seam

zipper tape

left back (wrong side)

machine basting

center back seam

guideline

right back

stitching through fold

left back (wrong side)

right back

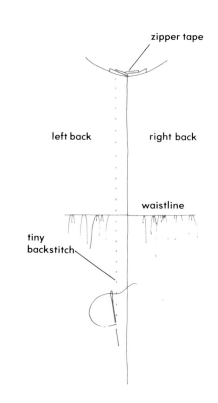

zipper tape

left back

right back

waistline

tiny backstitch

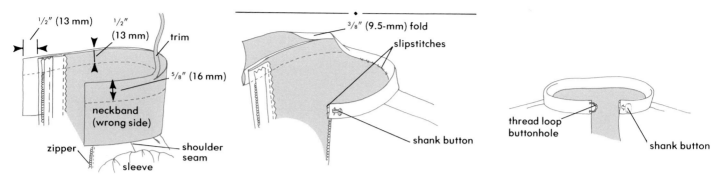

4. Binding the neckline. Center the neckband on the neckline, right sides together, so the ends extend 1/2" (13 mm) beyond the dress at the center back and the raw edges are aligned. Pin, and then stitch them together. Trim the seam allowances to 1/2" (13 mm), but do not clip them. Turn the ends of the neckband under 1/2" (13 mm). Fold the

neckband to the inside, turn the raw edge under 3/8" (9.5 mm), and slipstitch it in place. Keep the stitches fairly loose to avoid diagonal wrinkles. Close the ends of the neckband with slipstitches.

Sew the button near the right back end of the neckband. Make a thread loop near the left edge to correspond.

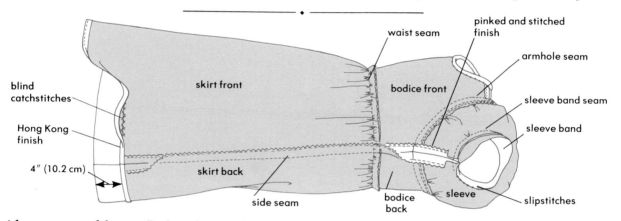

5. The side seams and hem. Right sides together and matching sleeve band, underarm, and waistline seams, pin the side and sleeve edges together and stitch. Press the seam allowances open, and finish the edges by pinking and stitching them. Trim the ends of the sleeve bands to 1/4" (6

mm) to reduce bulk, then finish them as you did the neckband.

Finish the raw edge of the hem with a Hong Kong finish, then turn up the hem, and sew it in place with blind catchstitches.

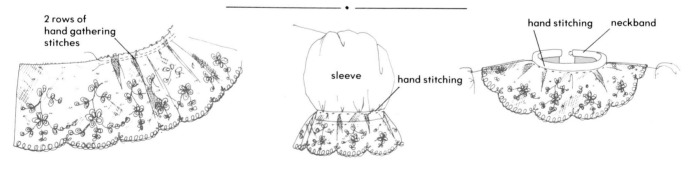

6. The lace trim. Cut a piece of lace twice the length of the neckline measurement (around the base of the neckband), and two pieces each twice the measurement of the sleeve band plus 1" (2.5 cm).

Trimming the neckline. Finish the raw ends of the neckline lace strip with a narrow hem, using hand running stitches. Gather the straight edge of the lace by hand to fit the base of the neckband. Using thread to match the dress,

sew the lace around the base of the band, concealing the stitches as much as possible.

Trimming the sleeves. Seam the ends of each strip of lace for the sleeves, right sides together. Turn the lace right side out, then gather and sew a strip to each sleeve along the edge of the sleeve band as you did at the neck. The lace will cover the sleeve bands.

Boy's Velvet Suit and Dress Shirt

Bearing in mind the adage that clothes make the man, every mother of a little boy must nurse the fond hope that clothes will make *her* little man into a little angel, at least for a while. Perhaps that's why the classic velvet suit, worn with a lace-trimmed dress shirt, has such appeal. But, even if the hoped-for good behavior doesn't materialize, the son-and-heir will still look adorable. And that's what counts, isn't it?

Deep navy is the traditional color choice for a velvet suit, but black or dark green would be equally elegant. All go well with a white shirt. If this is your first experience with velvet (or even if it isn't), be sure to review carefully the information on working with velvet at the beginning of this section.

A word about procedure. Since the jacket and pants are made from the same fabrics, it makes sense to cut them out at the same time. However, once you've done that, put the pants aside and concentrate solely on the jacket. And don't even think about the shirt until the pants are finished.

Materials

The jacket

1 yard (.95 m) of 42"- to 45"-wide (107- to 114-cm) velvet

1 yard (.95 m) lining fabric

1/2 yard (.5 m) iron-on interfacing

Sewing thread to match the fabric

Two spools of machine-embroidery cotton to match the fabric (see page 191 for mail-order sources)

Three 3/4"-diameter (19-mm) sew-through buttons

A commercial pattern: look for a pattern with a collarless V-neck jacket. If the jacket has a round neckline, you can convert it to a V neck by following the instructions given here.

The pants

1/2 yard (.5 m) velvet

1/2 yard (.5 m) lining fabric

Four 5/8"-diameter (16-mm) buttons

Sewing thread to match the fabric

Machine-embroidery cotton to match the fabric

A commercial pattern: chances are that your pattern will have pull-on pants with an elasticized waist. By all means, make these if you like; lining is optional. However, the true classic style has pants that button onto the shirt. To make this style, you will probably need to adapt the pattern you buy.

The dress shirt

3/4 yard (.7 m) of 45"-wide (114-cm) white cotton broadcloth

3 yards (2.9 m) of 1"-wide (2.5-cm) sheer prepleated ruffle trim

Nine 5/8"-diameter (16-mm) buttons

One package 1/2"-wide (13-mm) bias tape

A commercial pattern: use any button-front style with a round collar and short sleeves.

Adjusting the suit pattern and cutting the fabric

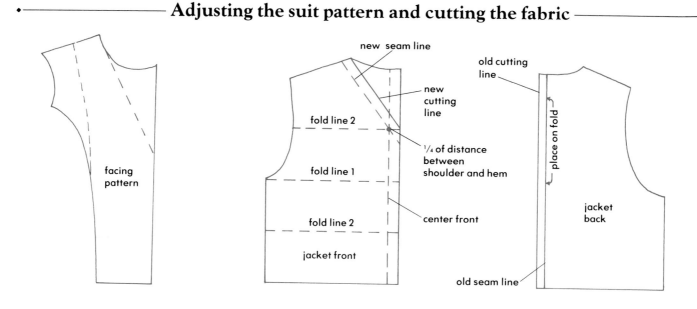

1. Adjusting the jacket pattern. To create a V neck from a round one, fold the jacket front pattern in half crosswise, aligning the shoulder point with the lower edge; then fold it in half crosswise again. Unfold the pattern. At the point where the uppermost fold meets the center front line, mark a dot. Using a ruler and pencil, connect the dot to the point where the shoulder and neck seam lines intersect, extending the line to the pattern edges. Mark a new cutting line ⅝" (16 mm) outside the first line. Respace the buttonhole markings, if necessary.

The front facing. If you've changed the jacket front neck to a V shape, lay the facing pattern over the jacket pattern, matching the pattern markings, and trace the change onto the front facing piece. Cut away the part of the facing pattern beyond the line marked "cut here for facing" and cut along the center front line; use the remaining portion for both the facing and interfacing.

The jacket back. If there is a center back seam, eliminate it by marking "place on fold" along the seam line. First straighten the seam line, if necessary.

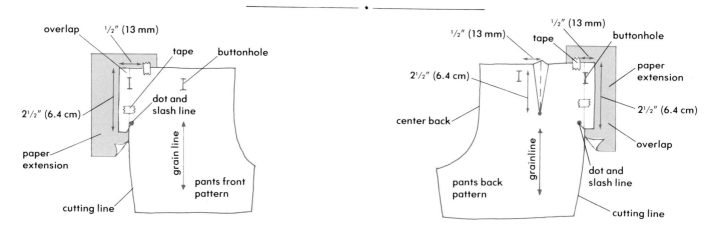

2. The pants. As most commercial patterns have pants with elasticized waistbands, you can simply omit the elastic and add buttonholes by making a few simple changes on the pattern.

To make the overlap for the buttonholes on the back and front pattern pieces, tape a paper extension to the patterns, then measure out ½" (13 mm) and down 2½" (6.4 cm) from the cutting lines as shown. Add a dot ⅝" (16 mm) in from the lower corner joining the extension and the pants,

and draw a diagonal line to it. Trim the excess paper along the lines for the extension.

For the correct fit on the back of the pants, make a dart by folding the pattern in half lengthwise, matching the center back seam line to the side seam line. Measure and mark a point 2½" (6.4 cm) down from the top along the fold; then mark ½" (13 mm) on either side of the fold line at the top of the pattern and join them to the first point with straight lines to form the dart, as shown.

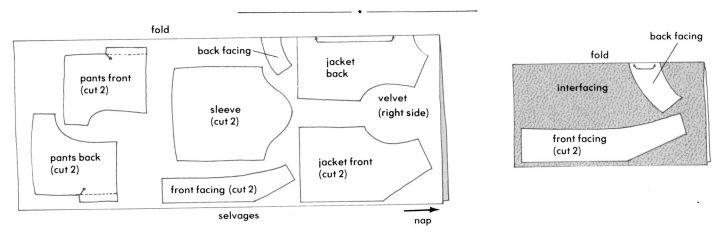

3. Cutting the velvet. Fold the velvet in half lengthwise, right side out. Lay out the pieces so their tops are all facing in the same direction, as shown; pin, and then cut them out. Transfer the pattern markings.

Cutting the lining. Fold the lining fabric in half lengthwise, wrong side out, and, using all the pattern pieces except for the front and back facings, lay out and cut the lining. Use the same cutting lines for the lining that you used on the jacket front and back. Then trim $1/16''$ (1.5 mm) from all the edges of the lining pieces; this will help the lining fit

nicely into the jacket by compensating for the bulk of the velvet. Transfer the pattern markings to the jacket and pants pieces.

Cutting the interfacing. Fold the interfacing fabric in half lengthwise, and cut the interfacing pieces, using the front and back facing patterns, as shown. On the back interfacing, trim $1/2''$ (13 mm) from all the edges. On the front, trim away the hem allowance at the lower edge, then trim $1/2''$ (13 mm) from the three remaining edges.

Assembling the jacket

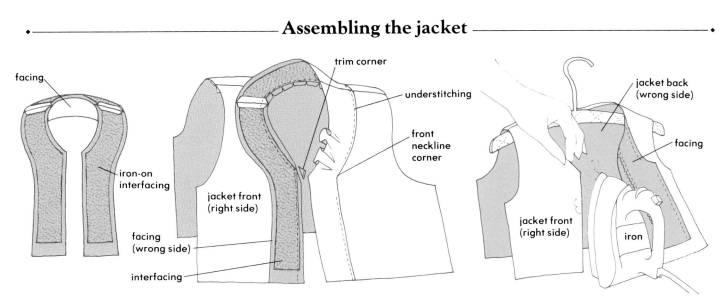

1. The shoulder seams and facings. Align the jacket back and front pieces at the shoulder seams, right sides together, and stitch. Press open the seam allowances.

Fuse the interfacing to the wrong side of the front and back facings, following the manufacturer's recommendations for iron settings. Also make sure to follow the instructions for pressing velvet (see page 140) to avoid flattening the pile of the fabric. Stitch the facing pieces, right sides together, at the shoulder seams, and press open the seam allowances.

With right sides together, pin and then stitch the facing to

the jacket. Grade the seam allowances, clipping along the neckline curve and trimming the corners. Turn the facing right side up and understitch it to the seam allowances, to within an inch (2.5 cm) of the front neckline corner. Steam-press the edges as shown, holding the iron slightly away from the fabric and shaping the edge with your fingers; be careful not to pull on the fabric, because it is cut on the bias and will stretch easily. Finish the outer edge of the facing with staystitching and pinking, then turn the facing to the inside of the jacket.

149

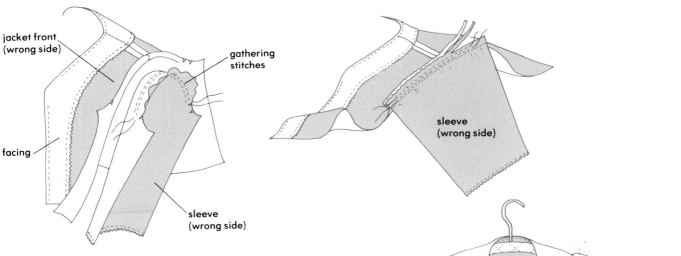

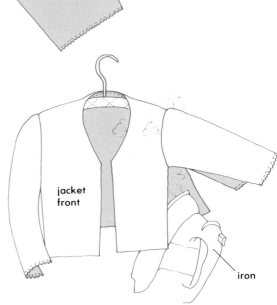

2. The sleeves. Gather each sleeve cap following your pattern instructions. Staystitch and pink the lower edge. With right sides together, pin the sleeve cap to the armhole edge of the jacket, matching notches and symbols. Pull the bobbin threads of the gathering stitches to draw up the sleeve cap slightly until it fits the armhole, distributing the fullness evenly. Baste the seams, being careful to avoid any puckers. Put the garment on a child-size hanger and hold it up to check the way the sleeve hangs. The cap should look smoothly rounded and the sleeve should curve slightly toward the front. If you are satisfied, stitch the seam, again being careful to avoid puckers.

Trim the seam allowance of the sleeve only to ¼″ (6 mm) along the gathered section. Trim both seam allowances below the notches to ¼″ (6 mm). Hang the garment on the hanger again, coaxing the armhole seam allowances toward the sleeve. Holding the iron (or a steamer if you have one) away from the fabric, steam the armhole seams.

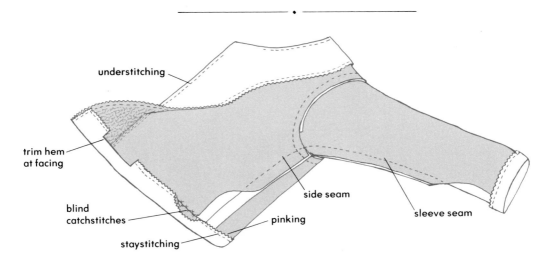

3. The underarm seams. Now pin the side and sleeve edges together and stitch, first the sleeves, from the underarm to the lower edge, and then the sides from the underarm to the lower edge of the jacket. Press the seam allowances open.

Staystitch and pink the lower edge of the jacket.

The hems. Turn up the hems at the lower edges of the sleeves and jacket, trimming the jacket hem allowance in the facing area as shown, to reduce bulk. Blind-catchstitch the hems in place.

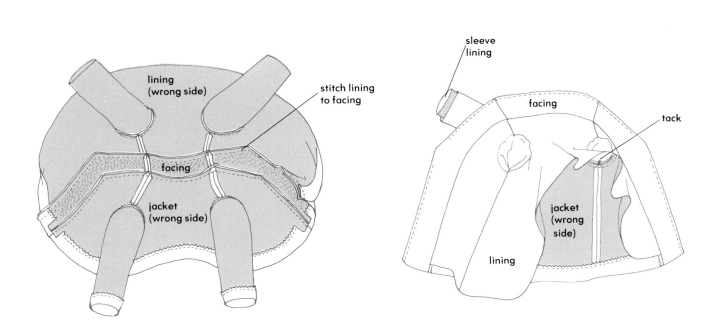

4. The lining. Staystitch the front opening and neck edges of the lining front and back pieces. Assemble the lining the same way as you did the jacket, omitting facings, but do not finish the bottom and sleeve edges.

Inserting the lining. Turn the jacket facing back to expose the raw edges. With right sides together and raw edges matching, pin the lining to the facing. At the lower edges, turn the lining hem so the lining is ¹/₂″ (13 mm) shorter than the jacket. Stitch the lining to the facing. Trim the seam allowances to ³/₈″ (9.5 mm), clipping the curves. Press the seam allowances toward the lining. Turn the lining to the inside of the jacket, pushing the sleeves into the sleeves of the jacket. At the underarm, tack the lining and jacket seam allowances together.

The lining hems. Turn up the lining at the lower edge of each sleeve so that it is ¹/₂″ (13 mm) shorter than the sleeve, and slipstitch it in place. Turn and sew the lining hem at the lower edge of the jacket in the same way, easing in the fullness. The raw edge of the facing will show a little below the lining. You can cover this edge with several closely spaced cross stitches.

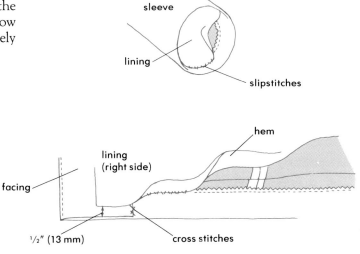

5. Finishing the jacket. Your pattern will probably call for **topstitching** around the neck, front opening, and lower sleeve edges—a nice finishing touch. Do some practice topstitching first on a double layer of velvet scraps, not only to perfect your technique, but also to be sure your machine settings produce acceptable stitching.

Thread the machine with embroidery cotton (the bobbin as well as the upper thread) and use two strands of thread in the needle. If your machine has two spool pins, use two spools, drawing both strands of thread through the needle. Otherwise use two bobbins on one spool pin, or place a straw over the pin you have and stack two spools on it. Set the machine to make its longest stitch, and loosen the tension and pressure slightly (you have already done this to some extent for stitching on velvet). Then practice until your topstitching is smooth, straight, and wrinkle-free. Now topstitch the jacket as your pattern directs.

The buttonholes. Leave the machine threaded with one spool of embroidery cotton, as for topstitching. Make a few practice buttonholes on scraps by whatever method your

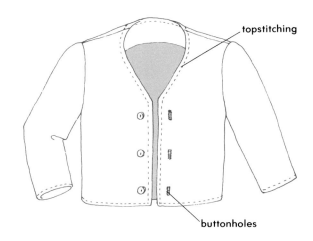

machine offers. Then mark the buttonholes on the jacket front and stitch them. (If you prefer, you may do both the topstitching and buttonholes by hand.) Sew on the buttons.

The pants

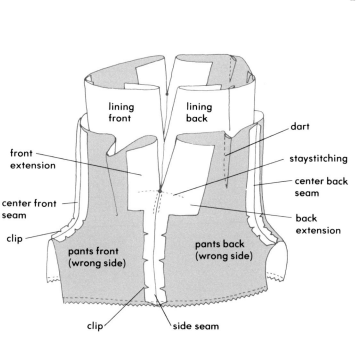

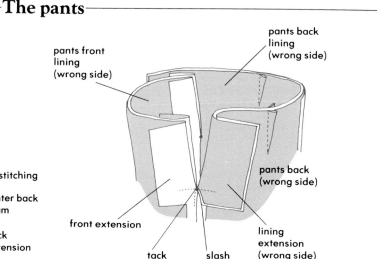

The seams. Stitch the center front and center back seams, then stitch the side seams from the dot markings on the extensions to the lower edge, reinforcing the ends of the seams with backstitching. Clip the curves on the center seams, and clip the side seams to the dots as indicated on the pattern. Press all the seam allowances open. Staystitch and pink the lower edges. Leave the pants wrong side out.

1. Assembling the pants and lining. To reinforce the inner corners of the front and back pants extensions, staystitch on the seam line for 1″ (2.5 cm) on each side of the dot, pivoting at the dot.

The darts. Stitch the back darts and press them toward the center.

The lining. Assemble the lining exactly as you did the pants, but don't finish the edges. Turn the lining right side out. Slip it inside the pants, matching the upper edges, darts, and seams. Tack the lining to the pants at the tops of the side seams. Slash into the corners of the extensions on both the pants and the lining as indicated on the pattern, all the way to, but not through, the stitching.

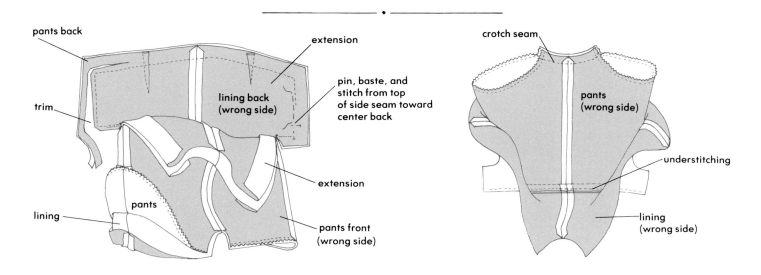

2. Joining the pants and lining.
First sew the extensions and upper edges of the pants together. Bring the lining back extensions out over the pants back extensions. Match the extension and upper back edges, and pin. Stitch, starting and ending at the reinforced points. Be careful to keep the rest of the fabric out of the way; you may have to work at this. Stitch the front extensions and upper edges in the same way. Trim the seams and corners, and turn the pants right side out.

The understitching. At the waist edge, pull the pants away from the lining. Starting and ending about 2″ (5 cm) from the ends of the extensions, understitch the lining to the seam allowances around the back and front of the pants. Press the edges.

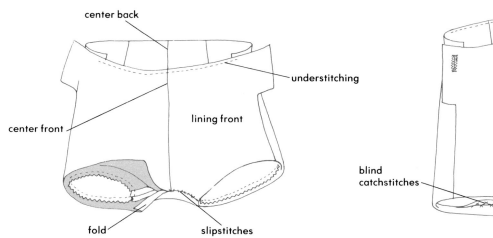

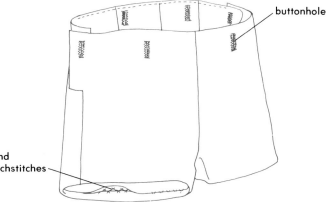

3. Finishing the pants.
To stitch the **crotch seam**, turn the pants wrong side out, pull the lining out of the way, and pin the front and back of the pants right sides together between the legs. Stitch the crotch seam, and press the seam allowances open.

Fold the lining back down over the pants. Turn under the crotch seam allowance of the back section, and pin it over the front lining. Slipstitch the lining together at the crotch, taking care not to catch it in the pants seam allowances.

The hems. Turn the pants hems up along the hemline and blind-catchstitch them in place. Turn the lining hems up so the lining is ¹⁄₂″ (13 mm) shorter than the pants. Slipstitch the lining to the pants.

The buttonholes. Mark vertical buttonholes on the pants front halfway between the center front and side seams and ³⁄₈″ (9.5 mm) down from the waistline. The buttonholes on the pants back are placed 1″ (2.5 cm) away from the darts, toward the center, and ³⁄₈″ (9.5 mm) down from the waistline. Mark the buttonholes on the back and front extensions to coincide, since they take the same button.

Dress Shirt

Adjusting the pattern and cutting the fabric

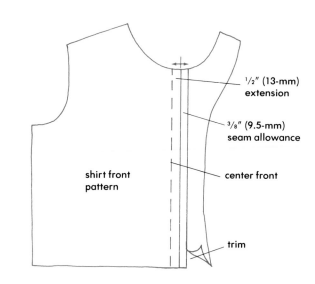

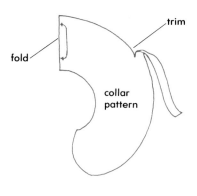

1. Pattern adjustments. To make an extension on the **shirt front,** mark a line on the front extension that is ¹/₂″ (13 mm) outside the center front line. Mark a second line ³/₈″ (9.5 mm) outside the first for the seam allowance. Cut off and discard the rest of the front extension.

The collar. Measure the width of your trim. Cut that amount away from the outer edge of the collar pattern.

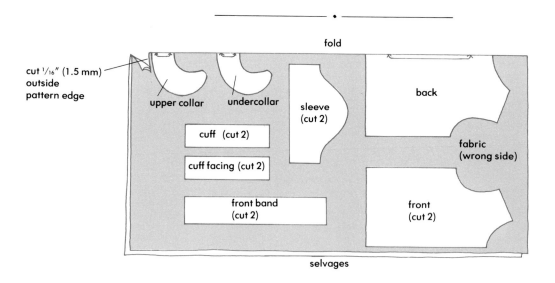

2. Cutting the fabric. Fold the fabric in half lengthwise, wrong side out, and cut the pieces as shown, in the following manner:

The button band. For the front band, cut two lengthwise strips 1³/₄″ (4.4 cm) wide and as long as the center front line on the shirt front pattern. Mark ³/₈″ (9.5 mm) seam allowances on the long edges.

The cuffs and cuff facings. Cut four strips the width of the sleeve hem allowance plus 1¹/₄″ (3.2 cm) and as long as the lower edge of the sleeve.

The undercollar. Cut the undercollar, using the adjusted collar pattern.

The upper collar. Cut the upper collar, using the adjusted collar pattern, but adding ¹/₁₆″ (1.5 mm) around the outer edge.

Assembling the shirt

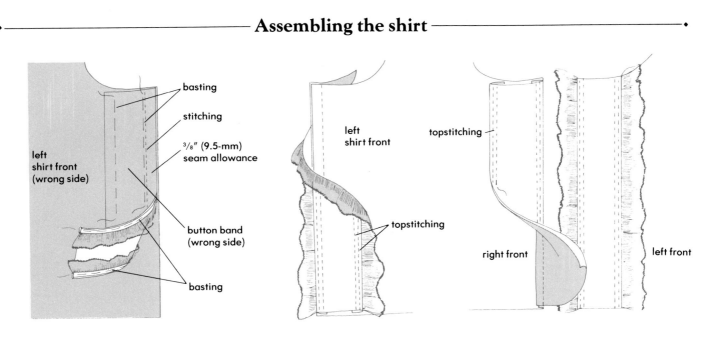

1. The button bands. Cut two pieces of trim the same length as the button bands. With right sides together, pin a strip of trim to each side of one band, aligning the bound edges of the trim with the marked seam lines. Baste the trim in place through its bound edges.

Matching the edges, pin the button band right side down to the wrong side of the left shirt front, and stitch them together along the basting in the outermost edge of the trim. Turn the band to the right side of the left front, and turn the trim so it extends away from the band on each side. Press carefully, protecting the trim so as not to flatten the pleats. Turn under the seam allowance on the free edge of the band so the trim extends beyond it. Pin, and then top-stitch the band in place close to each edge. Sew another row of stitching 1/4" (6 mm) inside the first.

Pin the remaining band right side down to the wrong side of the right shirt front, aligning the edges, and stitch them together along the seam line. Press the seam allowances toward the band. Press the opposite edge of the band under along the seam line. Turn the band to the right side of the right shirt front and finish it just as you did the left shirt front, disregarding references to the trim.

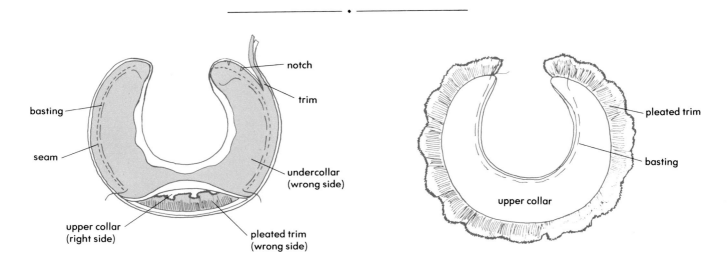

2. Assembling the collar. Cut a length of trim to fit the outer edge of the upper collar. With right sides together, pin and baste the bound edge of the trim to the upper collar along the seam line.

With right sides together, pin the undercollar to the upper collar around the outer edge, easing in the little bit of fullness as you go. Stitch along the previous basting. Trim and notch the seam allowances.

Turn the collar right side out and press, being careful not to flatten the pleats. Align and baste the neck edges of the upper and undercollars together, smoothing any fullness in the upper collar away from the neck edge.

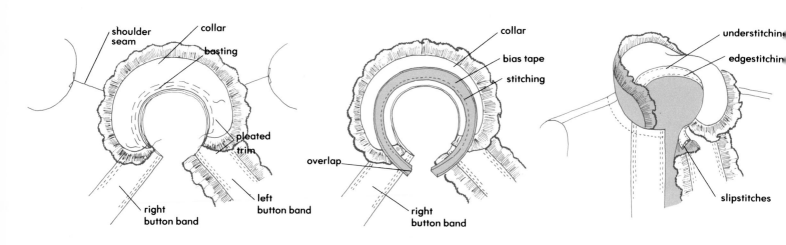

3. Attaching the collar. First stitch the shoulder seams of the shirt, using French seams or any other finish you prefer for these and all seams.

With right sides up, pin the collar to the neck edge of the shirt, aligning the edges of the trim on the collar at the center front with the centers of the front bands. Baste the collar in place.

Measure the distance around the neck edge, including the ends of the front bands. Cut a strip of bias tape 1″ (2.5 cm) longer than this measurement. Steam-press the tape, without stretching it, into a curve to match the neck edge.

Open out one fold of the bias tape and, centering and aligning the edge of the fold with the collar seam line so the other side of the tape extends toward the collar, pin the tape in place. The ends of the tape should extend evenly beyond the neckline. Stitch the tape to the collar along the fold. Trim and clip the seam allowances; then understitch the tape to the seam allowances. Turn the raw ends of the bias tape under even with the edges of the button bands, and then turn the free side of the tape to the inside of the shirt, and pin it in place. Edgestitch the tape to the shirt, and slipstitch the ends of the tape closed.

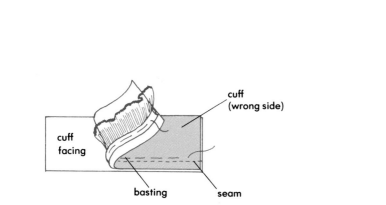

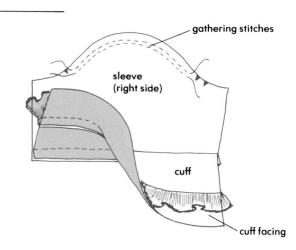

4. The sleeves. Cut two pieces of trim the length of the cuffs. Pin and baste a length of the trim to each of the cuffs as you did on the button band and upper collar, leaving 5/8″ (16-mm) seam allowances.

With right sides together, pin each sleeve to its corresponding facing, sandwiching the trim between them. Stitch the seam along the previous basting stitches. Trim the seam allowances, and then press them toward the facing.

With right sides together, pin and then stitch the untrimmed edge of a cuff to the lower edge of each sleeve. Trim the seam allowances, and press them toward the cuff. Stitch the sleeve cap with two rows of gathering stitches and then sew it to the armhole edge just as you did on the jacket. Trim the seam allowances, and finish as desired.

The side and sleeve seams. Pin the side and sleeve edges together, matching the ends of the cuff-sleeve and cuff-facing seams. Stitch each seam in one step, pivoting the fabric at the underarm.

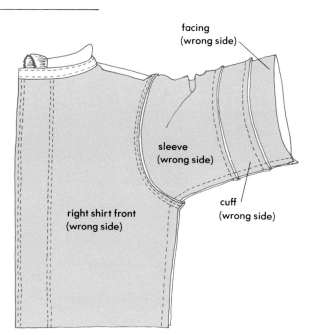

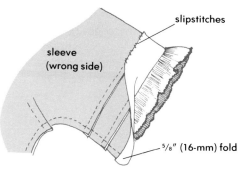

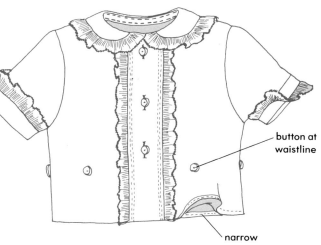

5. Finishing the shirt. At the top of the cuff facing, turn the raw edge under ⁵/₈″ (16 mm). Pin, then slipstitch this edge to the cuff sleeve seam. On the right side, fold the cuff up, covering the seam.

Along the bottom edge of the shirt, make a narrow top-stitched hem.

Mark the left front band for buttonholes. Use your pattern as a guide for placement, but make the buttonholes vertical rather than horizontal. Sew the buttonholes. Sew the buttons to the right front band so they correspond with the buttonholes. Try the shirt and pants on the child to mark the position of the waistline buttons. Sew the buttons to the shirt.

International Outfits

he perennial kilt and sailor suit enjoy a popularity in children's fashion that transcends national boundaries. And it's easy to see why: both designs are trim, distinctive, and becoming to almost any child who wears them.

The earliest type of kilt, worn by Scottish Highlanders since the beginning of the sixteenth century, was donned by spreading a large bolt of plaid cloth, measuring about sixteen by six feet, over a belt laid on the ground. The wearer would lie across the fabric with his knees on one edge of it, tie the belt, and then get up and set the pleats in place around his waist. Excess fabric above the waist was then draped over the shoulders as a cloak. This fashion prevailed for more than 200 years, until 1730, to be exact, when an English blacksmith named Rawlinson, no doubt tired of dressing in this cumbersome manner and being weighed down by so much fabric, cut his tartan in half and stitched the pleats in place. His feelings were obviously shared by his fellow men, for his style has prevailed to this day.

It was not until the mid-nineteenth century, however, that the kilt became an acceptable garment for anyone but a Highlander, let alone a child. Following her passion for things Scottish, Queen Victoria took to dressing her sons in kilts, and the fashion was established once and for all.

Curiously, the popularity of the sailor suit had a similar origin. Prince Albert had the happy inspiration to dress the Prince of Wales as a little Jolly Jack Tar when the Royal Family went cruising on the royal yacht *Victoria and Albert* in the summer of 1846. Of course, the five-year-old Prince's costume was authentic from his wide-brimmed sailor hat down to his bell-bottomed trousers, which had been run up by a Bond Street tailor. The outfit proved so fetching that Albert then had the Prince's portrait done in his sailor suit by the fashionable painter Henry Winterhalter, thus launching a worldwide fashion in children's clothes. During the Edwardian decade, royal children from London to St. Petersburg, princes and princesses alike, stood for their photographs in sailor suits. And commoners from that day to this have followed the royal lead.

Whenever the Royal Family stayed at Balmoral Castle, Scotland, Queen Victoria invariably dressed the young Princes in Highlander kilts. The Queen's royal innovation, immortalized in this painting by John Philips in 1864, not only pleased the Scots immensely but started an enduring fashion in children's clothes.

The Kilt

There is, of course, more than one way to construct a traditional garment such as a kilt, and some clothing firms have been known to guard their secret kilt-making techniques closely. Today, almost any pleated plaid skirt with the following characteristics passes for a kilt: the pleats usually lie in one direction, and the skirt wraps around the waist; the unpleated front overlap is often fringed, and the plaids are meticulously aligned. In addition, plaid ribbon rosettes (as shown here), leather closures, and kilt pins are attractive embellishments that can be used at the fringed opening.

The amount of wool fabric used for a kilt can vary greatly. In fact, when the pattern of a plaid is maintained throughout the pleating, a man's kilt can use up to nine yards of fabric. Although this is fine for a robust adult, it is a bit much for a small child. It can also be a bit much for the pocketbook, so simply purchase the finest wool you can afford. The kilt shown is a mixture of traditional styling coupled with practical modern dressmaking techniques. Refer to the "Dressmaking Skills" section for information on any unfamiliar sewing techniques.

Materials

2 to 4 yards (1.9 to 3.8 m), depending on the size of the child, of a pure wool plaid (see "Measuring and cutting," below)

Sewing thread to match the fabric

1 package seam tape

1/4 yard (.25 m) medium-weight iron-on interfacing

1 yard (.95 m) of 1½"-wide (3.8-cm) plaid ribbon

3 sets of ¾"-long (19-mm) skirt hooks and eyes

A 4" (10.2-cm) length of 1"-wide (2.5-cm) elastic (optional)

Measuring and cutting

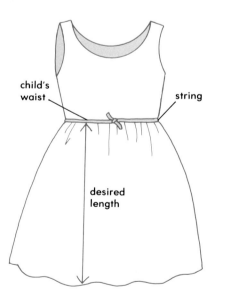

1. Taking accurate skirt measurements. Tie a string around the child's waist and measure down from the string to the desired length of the skirt. Cut the string (do not untie it), and then measure the length of the string to obtain an accurate figure for the waist.

2. Determining yardage. Take one-third of the waist measurement and double this number. Multiply the remaining two-thirds by four. To obtain necessary yardage, add both the resulting numbers plus an extra 9" (23 cm) for safety. For example, if a child's waist measures 21" (53.3 cm): (53.3 cm):

$$\frac{1}{3} \text{ of } 21'' \text{ (53.3 cm)} = 7'' \text{ (17.8 cm)}$$

$$7'' \text{ (17.8 cm)} \times 2 = 14'' \text{ (35.6 cm)}$$

$$\frac{2}{3} \text{ of } 21'' \text{ (53.3 cm)} = 14'' \text{ (35.6 cm)}$$

$$14'' \text{ (35.6 cm)} \times 4 = 56'' \text{ (142 cm)}$$

$$56'' + 14'' = 70'' \text{ (178 cm)}$$
$$\text{(142 cm} + 35.6 \text{ cm)}$$

$$70'' + 9'' = 79'' \text{ (200 cm), or approximately}$$
$$\text{(178 cm} + 23 \text{ cm)} \quad 2\frac{1}{4} \text{ yards (2.2 m)}$$

Cutting

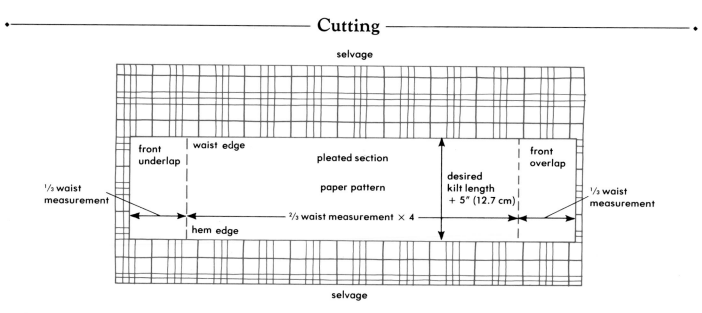

3. Cutting the fabric. The kilt is cut in one continuous piece with the top parallel to the selvage. The cut width of the kilt should equal one-third of the waist measurement, doubled (for the overlap and underlap), plus two-thirds of the waist measurement multiplied by four (for the pleats). Do not be concerned with odd fractions; simply round them off to the next highest 1/4″ (6-mm) increment. (Any slight excess can be taken up by the adjusting elastic in the back.) The cut length of the kilt should equal the desired length plus 5″ (12.7 cm) for hem and seam allowances.

You may mark the measurements of the kilt directly on the fabric using pins or chalk, or cut a length of shelf paper to the same measurements and use it as a pattern.

Study the plaid design of the fabric and position the kilt dimensions over it so that an attractive portion of the plaid falls evenly on the front overlap and the dominant horizontal plaid lines fall between the hem and waistline seams. This is especially important if the plaid is a bold one. Reserve a length of fabric for the waistband to be cut out after the kilt is pleated.

Sewing the kilt

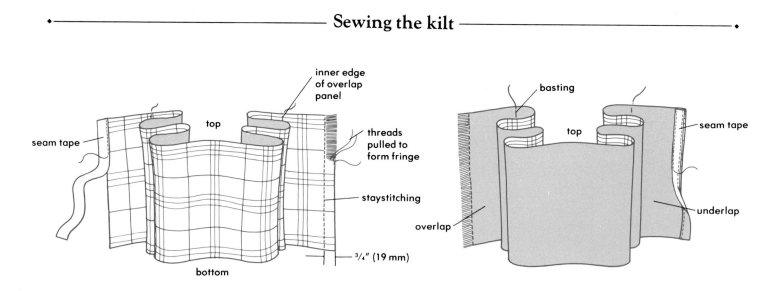

1. Fringing the front overlap. Mark the inner edge of the overlap panel with a row of basting stitches, then sew a row of machine staystitching 3/4″ (19 mm) from the outer raw edge. To create the fringe, pull out all the vertical threads of the fabric weave from the raw edge up to the staystitching line.

2. Facing the underlap edge. Mark the inner edge of the underlap panel with a row of basting stitches. Lay seam tape on the right side of the underlap so it overlaps the raw edge by 1/2″ (13 mm). Edgestitch the seam tape in place. Press the seam tape to the underside of the fabric to form a facing, then edgestitch the free side to the underlap.

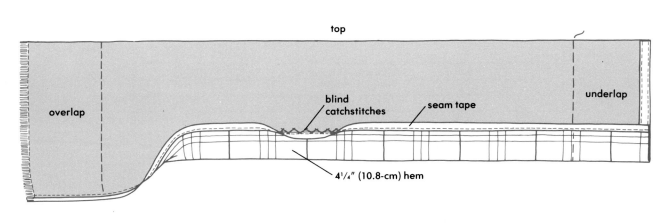

3. Hemming the kilt. Lay seam tape along the right side of the bottom edge, overlapping the edge by ¼″ (6 mm), and edgestitch it in place. Turn up a 4¼″ (10.8-cm) hem allowance and blind-catchstitch the tape in place. Press the hemline carefully.

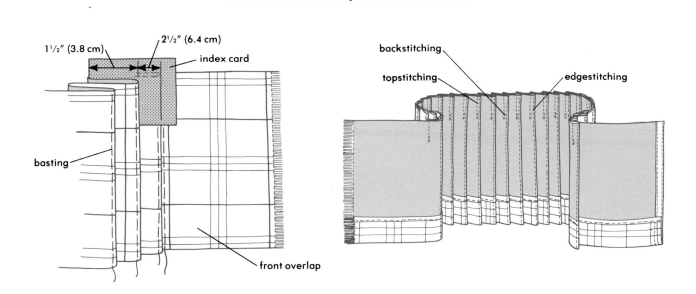

4. Pleating the kilt. The pleats will be 1½″ (3.8 cm) deep and spaced 1″ (2.5 cm) apart. Each set of pleats will overlap at the back. To save measuring time, mark off 1½″ (3.8 cm) on an index card for the first pleat and 2½″ (6.4 cm) for subsequent pleats and use it to mark off the depth of each pleat as you work across the kilt. All the pleats should fall in one direction toward the front overlap.

The fold of the first pleat should fall on the basting line of the overlap. Pin each pleat in place from the right side, along the top of the kilt and down 2½″ (6.4 cm); use the plaid lines as a guide to help keep the pleat folds absolutely straight. Baste each pleat in place all the way down the kilt from top to bottom.

Since the overlap and underlap together equal one-third the waist measurement, make as many pleats as necessary to obtain the remaining two-thirds.

Topstitch along the fold of each pleat through all three layers, starting from the top and stitching down 2½″ (6.4 cm). Be sure to backstitch at the end of each stitching line.

5. Stitching the pleats from the underside. Turn the kilt to the wrong side, and edgestitch along each pleat fold, through two layers only, from the top to the hemline. Again, use the plaid lines as a guide to help keep the pleat folds absolutely straight. This stitching keeps the pleats crisp and sharp, but cannot be seen from the right side.

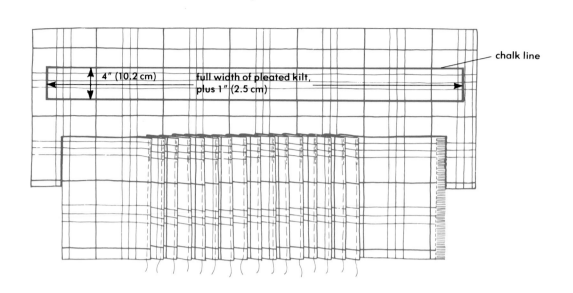

chalk line

4" (10.2 cm) full width of pleated kilt,
plus 1" (2.5 cm)

6. Cutting the waistband. For a finished waistband width of 1¼" (3.2 cm), cut a strip of plaid fabric that measures 4" (10.2 cm) wide (the finished width doubled, plus 1½", or 3.8 cm, for seam allowances) by a length equal to the full pleated width of the kilt, plus 1" (2.5 cm) for seam allowances. Position the pleated kilt on the fabric so that the plaid of the waistband lines up with the plaid of the kilt in the most attractive way. Cut the waistband so that the plaid of the kilt's overlap section will match that portion of the waistband. Mark this overlap end of the waistband with a pin.

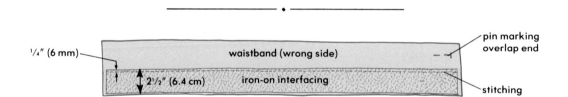

¼" (6 mm)

waistband (wrong side)

2½" (6.4 cm) iron-on interfacing

pin marking
overlap end

stitching

7. The waistband interfacing. Cut a strip of iron-on interfacing that is 2" (5 cm) wide and the same length as the waistband. Lay the waistband down, wrong side up, with the overlap end to the right. Iron the interfacing onto the lower portion of the waistband, centering it and placing it ½" (13 mm) above the lower edge of the waistband. To reinforce the interfacing, sew a row of machine stitching ¼" (6 mm) from the inside edge of the interfacing.

Pressing the waistband. Fold the waistband in half lengthwise, wrong sides together, and press. Press up a ¾" (19-mm) fold along the free edge of the waistband and a ⅝" (16-mm) fold along the interfaced edge. The back of the waistband should then extend ⅛" (3 mm) beyond the front.

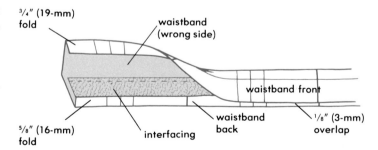

¾" (19-mm)
fold

waistband
(wrong side)

waistband front

⅝" (16-mm)
fold

interfacing

waistband
back

⅛" (3-mm)
overlap

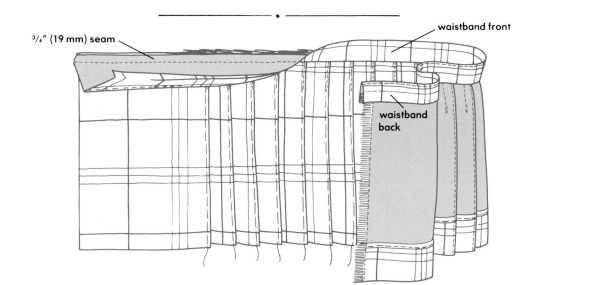

3/4" (19 mm) seam

waistband front

waistband back

8. Attaching the waistband. Unfold the 3/4" (19-mm) fold of the waistband, and align the edge, right sides together, with the top of the kilt, making sure that the plaid lines of the kilt's overlap section match those on the overlap end of the waistband; pin. Stitch the waistband to the kilt along the fold line of the waistband, 3/4" (19 mm) from the edge. Turn the waistband to the inside of the kilt and turn in both ends even with the edges of the kilt. Baste the unstitched edge of the waistband over the seam line. Remember, this back edge will extend 1/8" (3 mm) below the seam line. Turn the kilt right side up, and using both hands, spread the seam line apart and carefully "stitch in the ditch," or right on the seam line. When finished, the stitching will sink right into the seam line to become invisible.

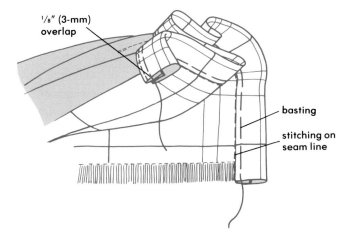

1/8" (3-mm) overlap

basting

stitching on seam line

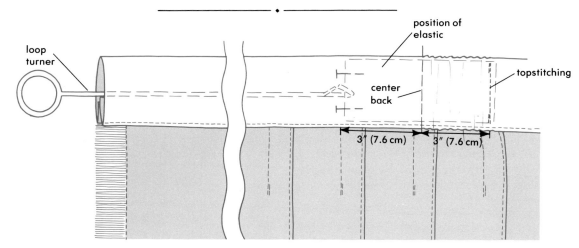

loop turner

position of elastic

center back

topstitching

3" (7.6 cm)   3" (7.6 cm)

9. Inserting the elastic. For a snug fit, a small piece of elastic may be inserted through a portion of the waistband if desired. Although this method is slightly unorthodox, it really does do the trick. Cut a 4" (10.2-cm) length of 1"-wide (2.5-cm) elastic. Attach one end of the elastic to a loop turner and pull the elastic through the waistband. Position the elastic so that one end extends 3" (7.6 cm) to one side of the center back, and pin it in place. Topstitch this end of the elastic through the waistband. Now, using the loop turner, pull and stretch the opposite end of the elastic until it is extended 3" (7.6 cm) to the other side of the center back. Pin this end firmly in place, remove the loop turner, and topstitch the end through the waistband. The elastic will contract, forcing the back of the kilt to gather slightly.

165

Finishing the waistband. Turn in the raw edges at the ends of the waistband, and slipstitch them closed. Sew three sets of skirt hooks and eyes on the waistband, one at the end of the overlap, one about 5½″ (14 cm) back from the first, and the other about 1″ (2.5 cm) below and slightly forward of the second set.

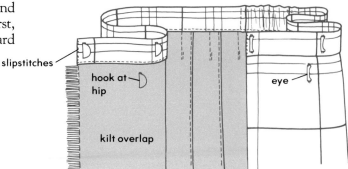

slipstitches

hook at hip

eye

kilt overlap

Ribbon rosettes

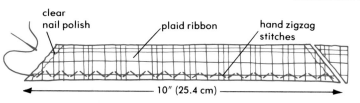

clear nail polish

plaid ribbon

hand zigzag stitches

10″ (25.4 cm)

10. Making rosettes. For each rosette, cut a 10″ (25.4-cm) length of 1½″-wide (3.8-cm) plaid ribbon. Trim the ends diagonally; then, to prevent them from fraying, dab the cut edges with clear nail polish. Along one long edge of each ribbon, sew a row of hand zigzag stitches, as shown. Draw up the thread, forming the gathers of the rosette, and knot it. Tack the ends of the ribbon together to hold the rosette intact. Position and sew one rosette just below the waistband on the overlap to hide the stitching from the hooks. Sew a second rosette 4″ (10.2 cm) above the bottom edge of the skirt.

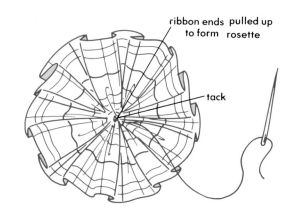

ribbon ends pulled up to form rosette

tack

11. Setting the pleats. Lay the kilt out flat and baste the pleats in place along the hemline, using large diagonal basting stitches as shown. Carefully press the kilt, using a dampened pressing cloth between the iron and the fabric. If convenient, take the kilt to a commercial dry cleaner and let him do the pressing; the pleats will probably be set far more accurately and permanently.

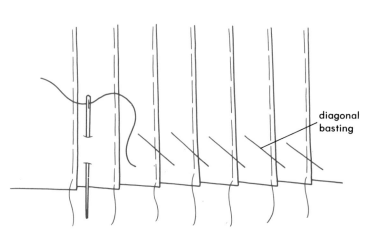

diagonal basting

The Middy

The Middy

What child's garment could possibly be more classic than the sailor suit? Now you can make this timeless style for your little one, either in the traditional navy-and-white color scheme or another color combination. For a little boy, make short pants with an elasticized waist. For a little girl, use the directions for the kilt on page 160 to make a pleated skirt. And, to ensure a crisp, fresh-looking middy bouse—even after much washing and wearing—choose a sturdy, closely woven cotton or cotton-blend fabric, such as poplin or broadcloth.

Materials

1 yard (.95 m) of 45″-wide (114-cm) white or navy fabric

1 package ³/₁₆″-wide (5-mm) contrasting white or navy middy braid

2 small snaps

Purchased appliqué (an anchor or other nautical motif)

¼ yard (.25 m) contrasting fabric for tie

A commercial pattern: Any pattern, so long as it has a middy collar and an outside pocket, will do. Don't be concerned if the blouse has a button front; directions for converting it to the more classic pullover style follow.

Pattern adjustments and cutting the fabric

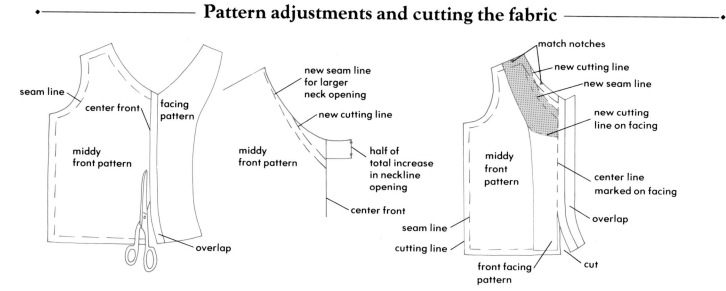

1. Converting a front opening to a pullover. If your pattern is for a button-front blouse, convert it to a pullover style as follows. Cut off the front extension (which forms the overlap and facing) along the center front line of the middy front pattern piece. Keep the cut-off part.

Adjusting the front pattern. To determine if the **neck opening** will be large enough to slip over the child's head, measure around the neck seam line of the front and back pattern pieces. Add those figures together and double the

measurement. Loop the end of the tape measure to that dimension and fasten it with a paper clip. Slip the loop over the child's head. Adjust the loop if necessary.

Adjusting the middy front pattern. Divide the amount of the necessary adjustment in half, and drop the end of the cutting line at the center front by that amount. Taper a line from that point into the old cutting line. Drop the seam line by the same amount in the same fashion.

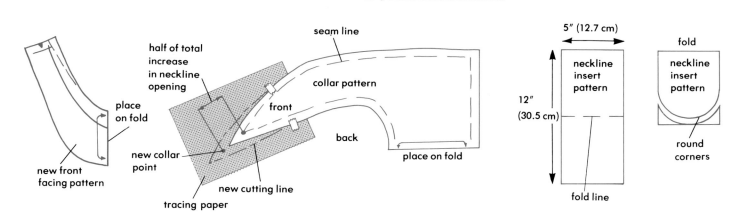

Adjusting the facing pattern for the neckline change. To use the cut-off front extension as a facing pattern, turn it over and place it over the middy front pattern, matching notches and original cutting lines. Trace the center front line and the new neckline onto the facing pattern. Mark the new center front line on the front extension with the words "place on fold." Trim the facing pattern along the new cutting line at the neck and down the center front for 2″ to 3″ (5 to 7.6 cm). Draw a curving line upward from that point to the outer edge of the facing, and trim along that line.

If the neckline of the pattern was not altered, follow the same procedure for the facing pattern, but trace along the original neck seam line.

Adjusting the collar pattern for a neckline change. Place the collar pattern over the middy front pattern, matching the old necklines and notches, just as for the facing. Tape a piece of tracing paper to the center front edge to allow for making the change. Trace the new seam line onto the collar, then draw a new corresponding outer cutting line, tapering it gradually into the old one as shown.

Making a neckline insert pattern. Cut a 5″ × 12″ (12.7 × 30.5-cm) rectangle of paper. Fold it in half crosswise and round off the corners opposite the fold. Open the pattern to cut it out.

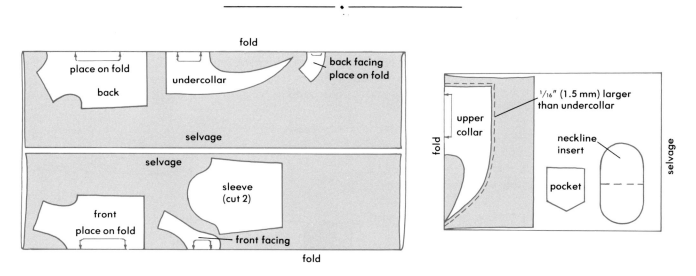

2. Cutting the fabric. Place the fabric wrong side down, and fold both long edges evenly to the center. Lay out and cut the middy front, back, undercollar, and front and back facings along a fold, as indicated, and cut the sleeve pieces on the doubled fabric as well.

Refold the remaining fabric as shown, and cut out the upper collar (cutting it ¹/₁₆″—1.5 mm—larger along the outer edges only, as shown), the pocket, and the neckline insert. Transfer all pattern markings. Mark the center of the middy front with a line of basting.

Assembling the middy

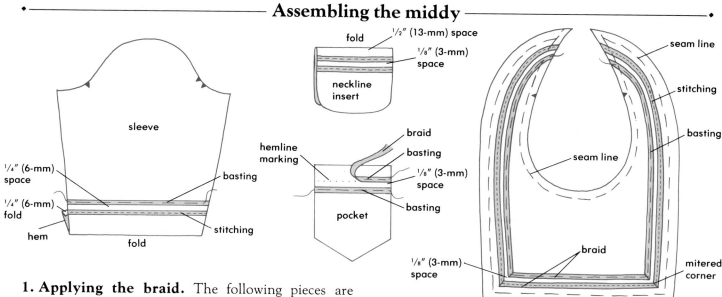

1. Applying the braid. The following pieces are trimmed with navy braid: the upper collar, the pocket, the neckline insert, and the sleeves. To avoid having to change the thread and bobbin frequently, apply braid to all these pieces at one time. But before you start, test-stitch a sample of the braid to a scrap of the fabric to determine whether you'll need to take any anti-pucker measures.

Using thread to match, hand-baste the braid to the fabric, keeping the braid fairly slack. Then slightly loosen the upper tension of your machine and stitch down the center of the braid, gripping the fabric to keep it taut. If the fabric puckers, try placing paper (such as adding-machine tape) under the fabric. Tear the paper away after stitching.

Trimming the sleeves. Press the hem up along the hemline and turn under 1/4" (6 mm) along the edge. Pin the hem in place. Then baste the first row of braid in line with the top of the hem so it will hold the hem in place when stitched. Baste the second row of braid 1/4" (6 mm) above

the first row. Stitch. *Note:* If your pattern has sleeves gathered into cuffs, apply the braid to the cuffs as your pattern directs.

Trimming the neckline insert. With right sides out, fold the insert in half crosswise. Baste the first row of braid 1/2" (13 mm) away from the fold and the second row 1/8" (3 mm) below the first one. Stitch.

Trimming the pocket. Mark the hemline across the top of the pocket on the right side of the fabric. Baste a row of braid below the hemline on the right side of the pocket so it will catch the hem when stitched. Baste a second row of braid 1/8" (3 mm) below the first.

Trimming the collar. Baste two rows of braid to the upper collar, the first 1/4" (6 mm) inside the seam line, the second 1/8" (3 mm) inside the first row, mitering the corners.

Mitering the braid. To miter the braid at the corners, fold the braid back on itself, then fold the upper end at a diagonal to the corner, making a sharp, clean turn, and continue.

Stitch both rows of braid in place and remove the basting.

2. Preparing the pocket. Press the top edge of the **pocket** under 1/4" (6 mm). Then turn the top of the pocket to the right side along the hemline.

Using matching thread, stitch along the seam line from one top corner down around the bottom and up to the other. Trim all corners diagonally. Turn the hem to the inside, push the corners out, and press. Turn the raw edge under just inside the stitching, and press. With matching thread, stitch the basted braid in place.

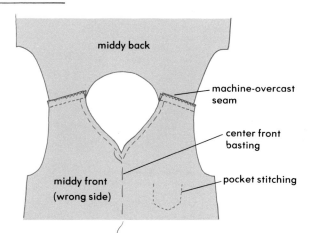

3. Attaching the pocket and stitching the shoulder seams. Pin the pocket to the middy front along the marked placement lines. Slipstitch the pocket in place, or, if you prefer, edgestitch it, reinforcing the upper corners with backstitching.

The shoulder seams. Seam the middy front and back at the shoulders. You may use flat-felled, French, or machine-overcast seams. Then staystitch around the neckline, just inside the seam line.

4. Preparing the collar. If you are using a sturdy, closely woven fabric, interfacing is really unnecessary. However, if you feel that you must use interfacing, choose a lightweight, iron-on type and apply it to the wrong side of the undercollar.

With right sides together, pin the collar pieces around the outer edges. The upper collar will be slightly larger than the undercollar. Stitch them together, easing the upper collar to fit. Grade the seam allowances by trimming them to different widths. Trim the corners diagonally, and turn the collar right side out. Then understitch the collar to the seam allowances from the back, starting and ending 1½″ (3.8 cm) from the corners and points. Press the collar.

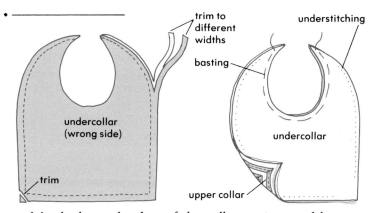

Match the neck edges of the collar sections and baste them together. Press the collar, braid side up, over a seam roll or tightly rolled-up terry cloth towel, to set its shape.

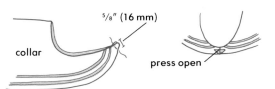

5. Attaching the collar. To facilitate the stitching of a precise point at the bottom of the neck opening on the middy, fold the collar in half lengthwise, right side out, so the front points meet and the rows of braid match exactly. Pin. Determine the spot at which a line drawn across the points will be ⅝″ (16 mm) long, and lightly mark it. Baste along the line. The points should fall inside the seam allowances when they are pressed open, as shown. Press. If the seam allowances don't look like the picture, try again!

With right sides up, pin the collar to the middy around the neck edge, matching the center markings. Baste the collar in place just inside the seam line. Check the basted seam to be sure it has no puckers, and correct it, if necessary.

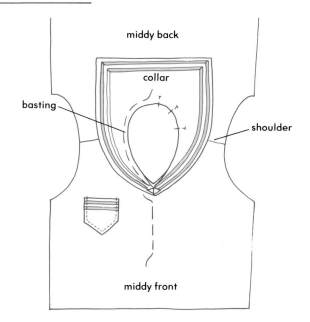

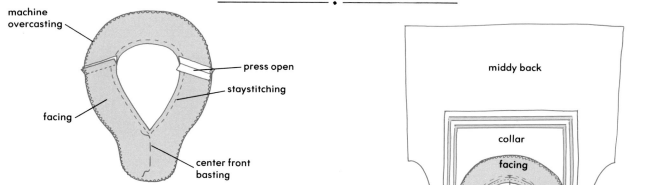

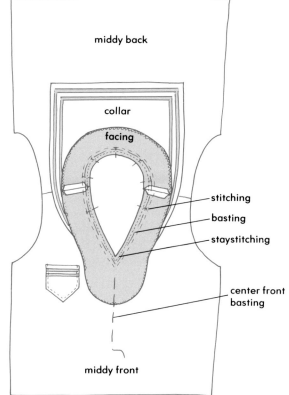

6. Attaching the facing. Seam the front and back facings at shoulders; press the seam allowances open. Staystitch the neck edge as you did on the middy. Then finish the outer edge of the facing by machine-overcasting, or by turning and stitching.

Fold the facing in half down the center, and mark the center front with a line of basting stitches.

With right sides together, pin the facing over the collar, matching all center markings. Baste around the neckline edge, then check again for unwanted puckers and make sure that the little points of the collar don't show at the bottom of the "V." Stitch the middy collar and facing together, pivoting at the point of the neckline as follows: Leave the needle in the fabric at the end of the point, raise the presser foot, turning the fabric on the needle to keep it on the seam line, and then lower the presser foot again and continue stitching.

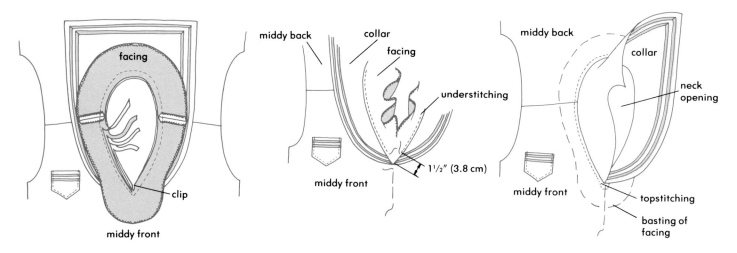

7. Finishing the neckline. Grade the seam allowances, and clip into the front point of the neckline, almost to the stitching, and around the neckline curve.

Understitching the facing. Pull the facing and the seam allowances toward the neck opening and understitch them together, being careful to keep the collar out of the way and ending 1½" (3.8 cm) away from the front point of the neckline.

Topstitching the neck edge. Turn the facing to the inside of the middy and press, keeping the collar clear. Pin the facing to the middy, near the outer edges, then hand-baste and remove pins. Turn the middy right side out, pull the collar out of the way, and topstitch through all remaining layers, ³/₈" (9.5 mm) away from the neck seam; square off the point of the neckline opening, as shown, making the line about ½" (13 mm) across.

Finishing the middy

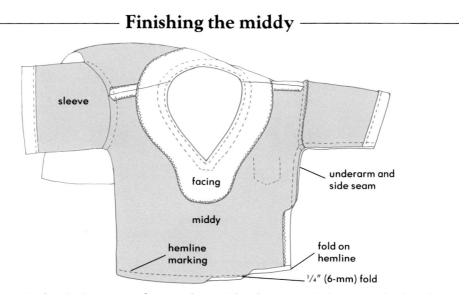

1. The seams and hem. To finish the **seams,** first stitch a sleeve to each armhole, right sides together. Press seam allowances toward the sleeves, trim them to ¼" (6 mm), and machine-overcast the edges.

With right sides together, pin and then join the middy sides and underarm edges of the sleeves, making a continuous seam on each side. Finish the seams as you did the armholes.

The hem. Lightly mark the hemline with dressmaker's chalk on the wrong side of the fabric. Press the raw edge under ¼" (6 mm), then press the hem along the marked line and pin it in place. Secure the hem by hand or with topstitching.

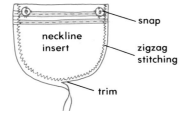

2. Final touches. To finish the neckline insert, overcast the raw edges together by machine, ½" (13 mm) from the edge. Trim close to the stitching. Sew the ball half of a snap in place at each end of the upper row of braid. Place the neckline insert inside the neck opening in the desired position, and mark the placement for the other half of the snaps on the inside of the facing. Sew the snaps in place, and snap in the insert.

The appliqué. Sew the appliqué to the center top of the left sleeve, just above the rows of braid.

The tie. From the contrasting fabric, cut a 4½" × 38" (11.4 × 96.5-cm) strip. Fold the strip in half lengthwise, right sides together, and pin the edges. Starting 1" (2.5 cm) from the center of the long side, stitch a ⅜"-wide (9.5-mm) seam to within 2½" (6.4 cm) of the end; then stitch a diagonal to the bottom corner. Repeat on the other end, leaving an opening at the center for turning. Trim the excess fabric at the ends outside the stitching, trim the corners, and turn the tie right side out. Press the edges and slipstitch the opening closed.

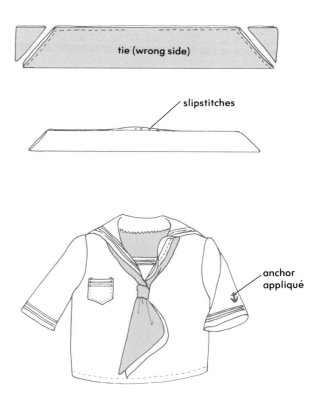

Dressmaking Skills

"Smocktop" Pattern for Child's Dress

New Combination Smocking and Dress Pattern
Requires no other Pattern to Cut out the Dress

1610

8605

8605
Front View.

8605
Back View.

8605

8605
Front View.

8605
Back View.

SET OF CHILD'S
SHORT CLOTHES, COM-
PRISING A DRESS,
CAMBRIC SKIRT AND
FLANNEL SKIRT.
(COPYRIGHT.)

(For Description **see**
this Page.)

Sewing Techniques

Just as certain clothing styles have become classics, so certain sewing techniques have become traditional through years of universal use. It is these techniques, used throughout the book, that you will find explained and illustrated here. Many of them—particularly the hand stitches—have been kept intact for over 200 years. Others, thanks to the inventiveness of enthusiastic and dedicated dressmakers, have been simplified and updated to make use of the sewing machine. In either case, the results are entirely compatible, and the overall effect will be one that suggests the finest handwork.

Transferring patterns, designs, and markings

To transfer pattern markings onto fabric for sewing, use dressmaker's carbon and a tracing wheel, and follow the directions that come with the carbon.

To transfer a design for embroidery or appliqué, first trace the design from the pattern or source you are using on tracing or tissue paper. Place dressmaker's carbon between the design and the wrong side of the fabric, and trace over the design with a pencil or tracing wheel. This method can be used on any fabric and should be used for all deep-pile fabrics such as velvet. To make lighter markings on a closely woven fabric, use the paper and pencil method that follows.

Paper and pencil. For symmetric designs to be used on a smooth fabric, trace the design from the pattern on tracing or tissue paper with a soft pencil. Turn the paper over and retrace the design, transferring it to the fabric. If the design is asymmetric, go over the lines with the same pencil on the underside of the tracing or tissue paper and do not turn the paper before placing it on the fabric. For dark fabrics, use a light-colored pencil.

Window. Trace the design with a heavy pencil or pen on tracing or tissue paper. Place the fabric over the paper against a window during daylight hours. Using an embroidery pen with dissoluble ink or a pencil, trace the design on the fabric.

Enlarging patterns

Several methods used for enlarging patterns are described below. Choose the one that best suits your needs.

Creating an enlarged grid. Use a piece of tracing or wrapping paper large enough to accommodate the final design. Starting with a perfect right angle of the paper at one corner, duplicate the number of squares indicated on the original pattern grid, spacing the lines 1/2" (13 cm), 1" (2.5 cm), 2" (5 cm), etc., apart according to the scale indicated on the original. Copy the pattern square by square, first marking dots on the grid where the pattern lines intersect it. Then sketch in the lines between the dots, and include any other pattern markings. Cut out the enlarged patterns.

Using grid paper. Instead of drawing a grid, you can save time by using a sheet of blue graph (quadrille) paper, which is available in several forms. One type has ten squares to the inch (2.5 cm) with a heavier line marking every inch. Another has 1/4" (6-mm) squares; draw a heavy line where necessary to mark the dimensions you need. Sewing supply stores sometimes carry special grid paper for enlarging patterns or dressmaker's pattern paper with marks an inch (2.5 cm) apart that can be connected to form a grid.

Photostat. The patterns in this book can be Photostated to the scale given with the pattern. However, this process is somewhat expensive. Check the classified directory of your telephone book for a Photostat service in your area.

Straightening the grain of fabric

When buying fabric, check the weave to be sure that the crosswise threads are perpendicular to the selvage, and that the lengthwise and crosswise threads cross each other at right angles. If the threads do not cross properly, the fabric is "off-grain" and must be straightened.

To find out whether the fabric is on or off grain, cut through the selvage near one end. Pull one crosswise thread, gently easing the fabric in the opposite direction. If the thread breaks, pull it out to create an empty space in the weave. Cut along this space until you reach the point where the thread broke. Carefully pick up a new thread and continue pulling and cutting until you reach the other selvage. Align a corner of the fabric with the corner of a table top or an L-square. If the corners do not match the 90-degree angle, you'll have to straighten the fabric. Make 1/4" (6-mm) horizontal snips through the selvages down the length of the fabric to ease the tighter weave found in the selvages, and free the crosswise threads. Tug the fabric diagonally in the direction opposite from the slant, along the entire length of the fabric. Don't be afraid to pull hard! Press the fabric along the lengthwise grain. Check the angle, repeating the tugging and pressing until the corners form 90-degree angles.

Some synthetic or blended fabrics are treated with finishes that make straightening impossible, and some prints and printed plaids are actually printed off-grain. If you happen to have fabric of this kind, cut it along the lines of the design instead of along the grain.

Bias strips

Cutting bias strips. To find the true bias of a fabric, fold it diagonally so the crosswise grain is parallel to the lengthwise grain. Press along the fold. Open out the fabric and use the crease as a guide to mark and cut parallel strips of the desired width.

Joining bias strips. Mark $1/4''$ (6-mm) seam lines along the short diagonal ends of the bias strips. With the right sides together, match the seam lines (not the cut edges) so the strips form a V as shown. Stitch the strips together, and press the seam allowances open. Cut off the protruding ends of the seam allowances.

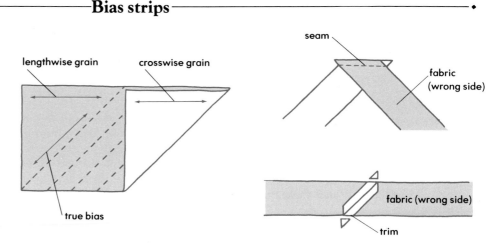

Hand stitches

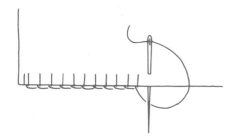

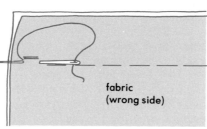

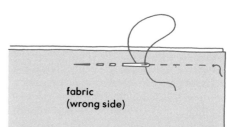

Blanket stitch. Used for bar tacks, button loops, and as a decorative finish on the edge of fabric. Working from left to right, secure the thread at the edge. For the first and each succeeding stitch, insert the needle just above the edge of the fabric from the right side, keeping the thread under the tip of the needle as shown. For bar tacks and button loops, make the stitches close together.

Fastening stitch. Used to secure an end of thread in any hand stitching. Make one or two short backstitches on top of one another to end off a thread. Insert the needle through all the layers of fabric one stitch length behind the point where the thread emerged and bring it up in the same spot again. Make another stitch over the first one.

Running stitch. Used for fine hand seaming, gathering, and basting. Working from right to left, weave the needle evenly in and out through the fabric. Pick up as many stitches as possible on the needle before pulling the thread through. Make small stitches for fine seams and gathering, and longer stitches for basting.

Slipstitch. Used to join a folded edge almost invisibly to a flat layer of fabric. Knot the end of the thread and bring the needle and thread out through the fold of the fabric. Pick up one or two threads of the garment close to the fold. Insert the needle back into the underside of the fold close to the previous stitch. Slide the needle along the fold for about $1/4''$ (6 mm); draw the needle and thread through the fold, then continue to alternate the stitches between the garment and the folded edge.

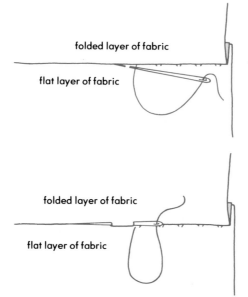

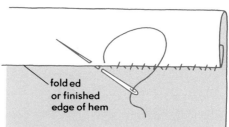

Slanted hemming stitch. Used for all types of hems. Knot the end of the thread and bring the needle and thread out through the fold of the hem. Working from right to left, pick up one or two threads of the garment. Insert the needle diagonally into the fold or finished edge of the hem, then pick up a thread or two of the garment. Continue to alternate stitches between the hem and garment, spacing them about $1/4''$ (6 mm) apart.

Seams

Unless otherwise indicated, seams called for in this book are ⅝" (16 mm).

French seam. A French seam is also called an enclosed seam (and the French call it an English seam). This seam gives a fine finish to children's wear because it encloses the raw edges of the seam allowances. With wrong sides together, align and pin the fabric edges to be seamed. Stitch ⅜" (9.5 mm) from the edge. Press the seam allowances to one side and trim them to a scant ⅛" (3 mm). Fold the fabric so the right sides are together and the raw edges are enclosed. Press the fold. Stitch ¼" (6 mm) from the fold.

To make a **narrow French seam,** sew the seam ½" (13 mm) from the fabric edges, and trim the seam allowances to ¹⁄₁₆" (1.5 mm). Fold the fabric, right sides together, to encase the seam allowances, press the fold, and stitch ⅛" (3 mm) from the fold.

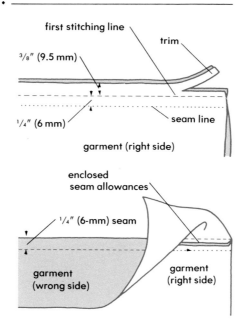

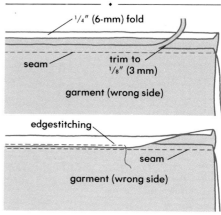

Self-bound (mock French) seam. With right sides together, align the edges of fabric to be seamed and stitch along the seam line. Press the seam allowances to one side. Trim the underneath seam allowance to ⅛" (3 mm). Fold the upper seam allowance under ¼" (6 mm), then fold it again to meet the seam line. Edgestitch along the second fold.

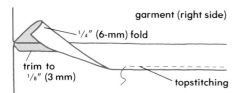

Flat-felled seam. This seam is durable as well as decorative. With wrong sides of the fabric together, stitch along the seam line. Press the seam allowances to one side. Trim the underneath seam allowance to ⅛" (3 mm). Turn the upper seam allowance under ¼" (6 mm), and pin it over the trimmed edge of the other seam allowance. Topstitch close to the turned edge.

Double-stitched seam. This seam finish is good for seams that join gathered sections together since it is fairly flat and easy to handle. With right sides together, stitch along the seam line. Stitch the seam allowance ¼" (6 mm) away, outside the seam line. Trim close to the second row of stitching. If your fabric frays easily, make two rows of stitching inside the seam allowance.

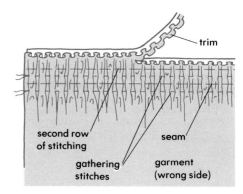

Seam finishes

Machine-overcast finish. This is a quick, easy way to finish edges on heavier fabrics. Using a medium-width zigzag, stitch ¼" (6 mm) from the raw edges of each seam allowance. Trim close to the stitching.

Turned and edgestitched finish. This finish is most suitable for light- to medium-weight fabrics. Turn under the edge of each seam allowance ⅛" (3 mm), and press. Stitch close to the folded edge.

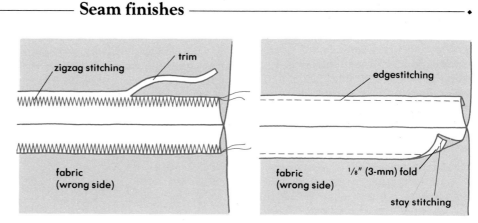

Construction techniques

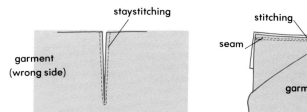

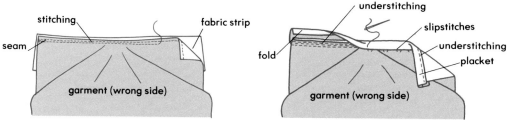

Continuous bound placket. A simple way of finishing the raw edges of a slit opening, using a separate strip of fabric. Cut a strip of fabric on the straight grain twice the length of the slash, or placket, and 1½" (3.8 cm) wide.

Mark the placket line on the fabric, then staystitch along both sides of the line as follows to reinforce the placket. Starting ¼" (6 mm) from one side of the

top of the placket line, stitch down to the bottom of the line at a diagonal. Leaving the needle in the fabric, lift the presser foot of the machine, pivot the work, set the presser foot down again, and stitch to a point ¼" (6 mm) from the top of the placket line on the other side. Slash to the point, cutting up to, but not through, the stitching.

Spread the slash open and, with right

sides together, place the stitching line of the garment ¼" (6 mm) from one long edge of the placket strip, and pin it in right place. Stitch the two pieces of fabric together just outside the staystitching. Understitch the placket strip to the seam allowances. Fold the strip over the seam allowances, turn the raw edge of the strip under ¼" (6 mm), and slipstitch it in place along the seam line.

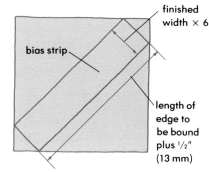

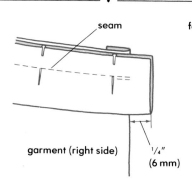

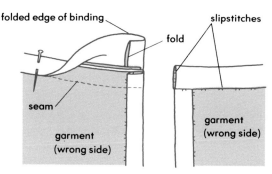

French binding. An attractive and easy finish for necklines and sleeves. Cut a bias strip ½" (13 mm) longer than the area to be bound and six times the desired finished width. For example, if the finished binding is to be 10" × ⅜" (25.4 cm × 9.5 mm), cut the bias strip 10½" × 2¼" (26.7 × 5.7 cm). Trim the seam allowances to be bound to the same

width as the finished binding. Fold the binding in half lengthwise, right side out. With raw edges matching and the ends extending ¼" (6 mm) beyond the garment edges, pin the binding to the right side of the garment. Stitch them together, leaving seam allowances equal to the width of the finished binding. Turn the ends of the binding under so they are

even with the edge of the garment. Trim the corners of the seam allowances. Fold the binding up over the seam allowances to the inside of the garment. Do not trim or clip the seam allowances, since they support the binding and prevent diagonal wrinkles. Pin, then slipstitch the folded edge to the seam line on the inside. Slipstitch the ends of the binding closed.

Machine gathering. Loosen the upper tension slightly and set the stitch length to 12 to 14 stitches per inch (2.5 cm) for regular fabric, or 14 to 16 stitches for fine fabric. With the right side up, stitch the seam allowance just outside the seam line. If you are joining a heavily gathered section to another section, stitch the fabric just inside the seam line for better control of the gathers. Sew a second row of stitching a generous ⅛" (3 mm) away from the first, inside the seam allowance. With right sides together, pin the edge to be gathered to the shorter edge,

matching the seams and any notches or other symbols. Pull the bobbin threads at each end, sliding the fabric along the threads until the gathered edge fits the shorter one. Secure the threads at both ends by winding them around a pin in a figure eight. Adjust the gathers evenly. With the gathered side up, stitch along the seam line just inside the first row of gathering stitches.

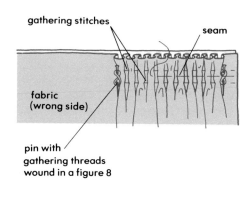

Hems

Blind catchstitched hem: Turn the hem edge under ¼″ (6 mm) and edgestitch close to the fold. Turn up the desired hem allowance and pin it in place about 1″ (2.5 cm) from the top of the hem.

Fold the garment away from the hem so the hem edge extends about ⅛″ (3 mm) above the garment. Knot the thread and secure it in the hem. Make the first stitch through the edgestitching on the hem. Move the needle ¼″ (6 mm) to the right and, with the needle pointing left, pick up a thread or two on the

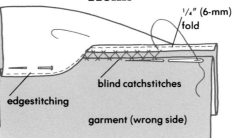

garment fold. Move the needle ¼″ (6 mm) to the right again and, with needle still pointing left, make a stitch through the edgestitching on the hem.

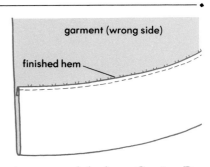

Continue around the hem. *Caution:* Do not pull the thread too tight. The stitches will hold securely and will be almost invisible.

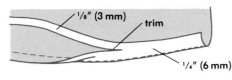

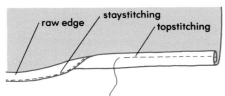

Narrow topstitched hem. Staystitch ¼″ (6 mm) away from the raw edge of the fabric. Turn the fabric under along the stitching and press. Then trim ⅛″ (3 mm) from the raw edge. Turn the folded edge under so the remaining raw edge meets the second fold. Topstitch close to the first fold, pulling the fabric gently to keep it somewhat taut. Each time you stop to get a new grip, be sure that the needle is in the fabric.

Machine-whipped hem. This method quickly produces a hem similar to the hand-rolled hem found on expensive scarves and sheer fabrics. First staystitch ⅛″ (3 mm) from the raw edge of the fabric. Set the machine for a medium-width zigzag and about 16 to 18 stitches per inch (2.5 cm). Position the fabric, wrong side up, so that one side of the zigzag stitching falls just over the raw edge and the other side over the staystitching. As you sew, the edge of fabric will be rolled up by the stitching.

To finish the edge of fabric and attach lace edging at the same time, first staystitch the fabric as described above. Then, with right sides together and raw edges aligned, pin the lace to the fabric. Zigzag-stitch as for a machine-whipped hem through both layers, then turn the lace right side up over the stitched edge and press.

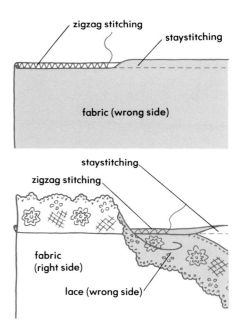

Finishing

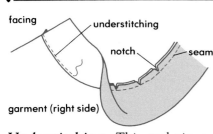

Understitching. This technique is used for holding facings in place. Stitch the facing to the garment, then trim and clip the seam allowances along the inside curves or notch them on outside curves. Press the seam allowances toward the facing. Pull the facing away from the garment and stitch through the facing and seam allowances close to the seam line.

Thread loop buttonholes and belt carriers. Mark the loop placement along the edge of the garment. For belt carriers, mark the placement above and below the waistline seam. Using a double strand of regular thread or a single strand of buttonhole twist, make two or three stitches connecting the marks; secure the stitches with a few fastening stitches. Make sure the button or belt slips easily through the loop before securing the first stitch.

Make closely spaced blanket stitches over the strands of thread. When the strands are completely covered, bring the thread to the wrong side of the fabric and finish with a fastening stitch.

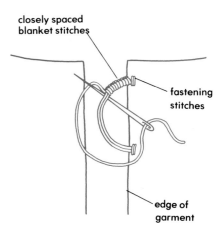

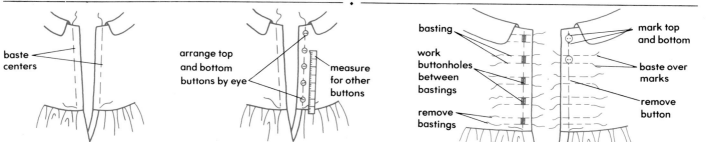

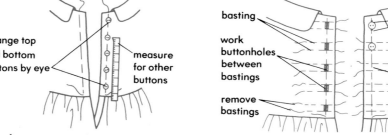

Marking for buttonholes. Mark both center fronts or backs of the garment with basting stitches along which the centers of the buttons and buttonholes will be placed. If you are using a commercial pattern, transfer the buttonhole markings from it to the garment. If not, arrange the top and bottom buttons by

eye, on the right front for girls, on the left front for boys. On the back, the buttonholes fall on the left for girls and on the right for boys. Measure the distance between the centers of the buttons, and mark the midpoints. Place a button at each point.

With chalk or a marking pencil, mark

the edges of the buttons with two dots along the basting line. Remove the buttons. Make two horizontal rows of basting stitches to mark the outer edges of each button. Work the buttonholes by hand or machine on the center line between the horizontal bastings. Remove the basting stitches.

Hand-stitched buttonholes. Mark the buttonholes with an embroidery pen, chalk, or a pencil. Using regular sewing thread, outline the buttonhole with a row of small running stitches a scant 1/8″ (3 mm) from the marking. Slash carefully along the buttonhole marking, and overcast the edges as shown. Using two strands of embroidery floss or silk buttonhole twist, run the end of the needle under the overcasting stitches, and, working from right to left, bring the needle up just outside the running stitches. With the thread looping around

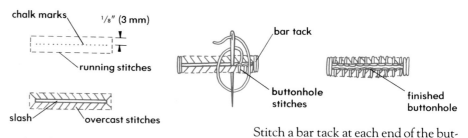

and under the needle to the left, pass the needle under the cut edge of the buttonhole and bring it up through the fabric. Pull the needle through the fabric, then toward the cut edge.

Stitch a bar tack at each end of the buttonhole by bringing the needle out just below the last stitch on the outer edge of the buttonhole. Then take several stitches across the full width of the buttonhole.

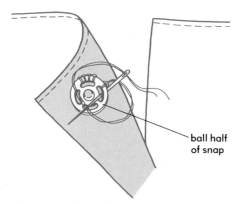

Snaps. These fasteners are used on overlapping edges where there is very little strain. Sew the ball half of the snap to the overlap section on the inside of the garment about 1/8″ (3 mm) from the edge. Secure the thread under the snap and bring the needle up to the left of the first hole. Allow the thread to form a loop to the right of the needle. Bring the needle through the hole; then pull the thread taut to form a knot on the outside of the

snap. Make four stitches in each hole.

To mark the position for the socket half, close the garment and stick a pin through the center of the ball section. Sew the socket half the same way you did the ball half.

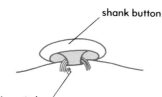

Shank buttons. Position the shank of the button parallel to the buttonhole. Using a double strand of thread, make several fastening stitches at the button marking. Then sew through the shank and the fabric several times to attach the button. Finish with one or two fastening stitches.

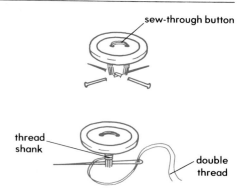

Sew-through buttons. Sew-through buttons will close without pulling if they are sewn on with a thread shank. To make the shank, secure the thread with one or two fastening stitches at the button marking. Place two crossed pins at the button marking. Center the button over the pins, and sew through the holes several times. Remove the pins; then wind the thread around the stitches to form the shank. Make several fastening stitches in the shank to secure the thread.

Embroidery Stitches

Embroidery has been used for centuries to adorn and embellish clothing. There are scores of embroidery stitches, and it seems as though new ones—or variations of old ones—are always turning up. The ones shown here, however, are fairly basic and simple. Some are used primarily to outline, others to fill in an area, still others to create texture. Using even this limited assortment of stitches, it is possible to create almost any decorative effect.

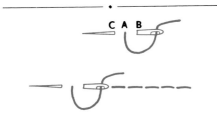

Backstitch. Work from right to left. Bring the needle up at A. Insert it at B, a little to the right of A, then bring it up at C, the same distance to the left of A. Insert the needle again at A and bring it up to the left of C. Continue across the row, always inserting the needle at the beginning of the previous stitch.

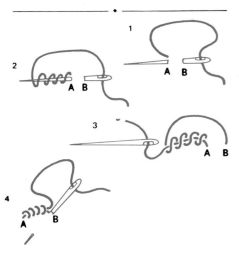

Bullion stitch. Bring the needle up at A. Insert it at B and bring it back out next to A. Wrap the thread snugly around the needle from back to front until you have enough thread loops to fill the space between A and B. Pull the needle through the loops and back toward B until the coil lies flat against the fabric. Insert the needle to the wrong side at B to hold coil in place; then fasten off or start a new stitch.

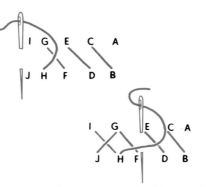

Cross stitch. Row 1 (worked from right to left): Bring the needle out at B and insert it at C. Bring the needle out at D and insert it at E. Continue in this manner to the end of the row. Row 2 (worked from left to right): Work as for Row 1, but in reverse, to cross each stitch in the first row. End by inserting the needle at A.

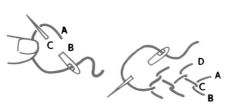

Featherstitch. Bring the needle out at A. Loop the thread to the left, holding it with your thumb. Insert the needle at B, 1/8″ (3 mm) below A, and bring it out at C, 1/8″ (3 mm) to the left of A. Now loop the thread to the left again and insert the needle at D, 1/8″ (3 mm) above and to the left of C. Bring it out at E, 1/8″ (3 mm) to the left of C. Continue in this manner, alternating stitches from side to side.

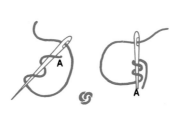

French knot. Bring the thread out at A. Wrap the thread two or three times around the needle from front to back. Hold the wrapped threads loosely against the needle with your thumb, reinsert the needle at A, and pull the thread through. Repeat or end off.

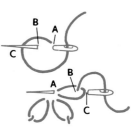

Lazy daisy. Bring the thread out at A. Loop the thread to the left and hold the loop with your thumb. Reinsert the needle near A, then bring it out at B. Insert the needle at C. Bring it out again at A to start a new stitch. To end off, knot behind C.

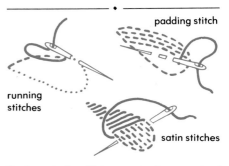

Satin stitch. Using a single strand of embroidery floss, first outline the design with tiny running stitches. Then, using two or three strands of floss, fill in the design with parallel satin stitches made from one side of the design to the other. Pull the satin stitches only tight enough to lie flat, but not so tight that fabric puckers. For **padded satin stitches,** first outline, then fill in the design with lengthwise rows of tiny running stitches. Finish with satin stitches made perpendicular to the running stitches.

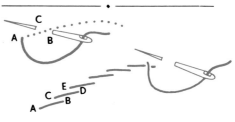

Stem, or outline, stitch. Bring the needle up at A. Working from left to right, and with the thread below the needle, insert the needle at B, about 1/8″ (3 mm) to the right of A. Bring the needle up at C, a little above A and B and about halfway between them. Keeping the thread below the needle, insert it at D, 1/8″ (3 mm) to the right of B, then bring it up at E, above and between B and D. Continue in this way across the row.

Appliqué

A French word, "appliqué" means "applied," a very apt description of this decorative technique, in which fabric shapes are stitched to a background to form a design. Here are some guidelines and how-to's for successful appliqué.

Fabrics. Choose fabrics with care and an eye to compatibility. Background and appliqué fabrics should be similar in weight and texture. The appliqué fabric can be lighter in weight than the background, but not vice versa. For the appliqué fabric, choose a firm weave that doesn't fray easily; raveling can drive you crazy. Avoid knits; they're wonderful for many things, but appliqué isn't one of them. Both fabrics should have the same care requirements; and if they're washable, both must be colorfast.

Color. If the suggested color combinations for a commercial appliqué design don't suit you, or if you're designing your own appliqué, experiment first by trying swatches of several colors on your background fabric. Colors must harmonize and offset each other as well as the background, and they must contribute to the overall design.

Shape and proportion. Keep one key word in mind when making an appliqué: simplicity. Avoid shapes with lots of angles and curves and fussy details. They'll be difficult to work with and won't convey your message as well as simpler ones.

The size and shape of the background area will indicate the correct proportion and position of the appliqué design.

Creating your own design. Don't be afraid to take inspiration from sources all around you—books, magazines, nature guides, fine art, photographs, Mother Nature herself. Or combine two or more ready-made designs to create a new one all your own.

Start by making a rough freehand sketch of your idea. Don't worry about size at this point; a large drawing is easier to work with than a small one. Once you've arrived at your basic concept, you can refine your drawing on graph paper.

Use scrap fabric or shelf paper to cut an actual-size replica of the area to be appliquéd. Enlarge or reduce your design in proportion. Then make a paper pattern for each appliqué shape, or cut the pieces from construction paper, adding 1/2" (13 mm) all around for the seam allowances. (If you prefer, you can cut the pattern to finished size and add the seam allowance when cutting the fabric. This method lets you visualize the design without changing its proportion.) Color the pieces with felt-tip markers. Arrange the patterns on the background, numbering them in the order in which they'll be sewn.

Using a ready-made design. If you're using a design that must be enlarged or reduced from a book or magazine, follow the instructions on page 175 for making the patterns.

Cutting the appliqués. Pin the patterns to the right side of the fabric, and cut them out. (Add 1/2"—13-mm—seam allowances around the patterns, if they have not already been included.) If you need several pieces of one shape, make the pattern from lightweight cardboard. Fold the fabric to make two or three layers, then trace around the cardboard as many times as needed. Cut through all the layers at the same time.

Staystitching. To keep the appliqués from stretching, staystitch each shape along the seam line, slightly loosening the tension of your machine. Or, if you prefer, staystitch by hand. Then, depending on which sewing method you use, prepare the shapes as directed below.

Positioning the appliqués. Arrange the appliqués on the background. Pin and baste the pieces in place, or iron them on with bits of fusible web.

Sewing the appliqués. Appliqué can be attached by machine or by hand, using a variety of stitches. Some of the variations follow.

1. Machine satin stitching. Trim the seam allowances to 1/16" (1.5 mm). Baste or fuse the shapes in place. Thread your machine with embroidery cotton or silk, both of which look more delicate than regular sewing thread. Loosen the upper tension slightly and set the stitch controls to make a medium-width satin stitch. Then stitch around the edges of the appliqué, covering the raw edges and the staystitching.

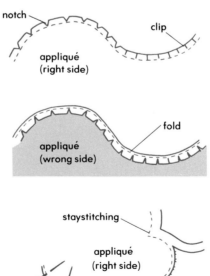

2. Slipstitches or hemming stitches. Trim the seam allowances to 1/4" (6 mm). Notch the outside curves and clip the inside curves and corners, to help the appliqué lie flat. Press the raw edges under just outside the seam line or turn them under with your fingers as you sew, so the staystitching will be hidden. Then baste or fuse the appliqués to the background and slipstitch the edges in place or use vertical hemming stitches.

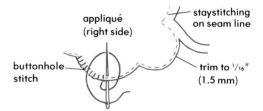

3. Buttonhole stitches. Trim the seam allowances to 1/16" (1.5 mm), and stitch around the edges of the appliqué with buttonhole stitches.

Smocking

Although smocking is an art of infinite variety and complexity, the basics are easily learned. The stitches that follow will enable you to tackle any project in the book. They will also give you such a good foundation in smocking techniques that you will be able to pursue the art on your own. Many beautiful color plates of smocking designs are available from mail-order smocking sources, and most are based on the stitches taught here.

Smocking is always done before a garment is assembled. Allow 3″ to 4″ (7.6 to 10.2 cm) in the width of the fabric to be smocked for every finished inch of smocking.

English smocking. The smocking taught here, known as English smocking, calls for pregathering the fabric into neat rows of pleats before the smocking is started. It is the best smocking technique to use when a number of smocking stitches are combined, and it results in beautifully symmetrical and elastic work.

Gathering fabric for smocking. There are a number of ways to gather fabric for smocking. One relies on sheets of hot-iron transfer dots that are ironed onto the wrong side of the fabric. (Such dots are supposed to wash out, but don't always, so test them on a swatch of fabric first.) The fabric is gathered by stitching from dot to dot with short, widely spaced stitches, and then pulling the threads to make even pleats. See the Appendix for mail-order sources if you have difficulty finding such transfers.

A second method relies on a small pleating machine that feeds the fabric through rollers and can pleat up to sixteen rows at one time. In addition, many needlework and smocking supply stores offer a pleating service.

The instructions for any given design will indicate the number of gathering rows needed, which includes the number of rows to be smocked; for large areas of smocking, two auxiliary rows are needed: one above and one below the smocking

section to stabilize the pleats until the garment or project is finished. In addition, many smocking patterns use outline, stem, or cable stitches at the top and bottom, because they help to control gathers and keep them even. The space between smocking dots is usually 1/4″ to 3/8″ (6 to 9.5 mm), and the space between the rows is usually 3/8″ to 1/2″ (9.5 to 13 mm). For these projects, dots spaced about 3/16″ (5 mm) apart and rows spaced 5/16″ to 3/8″ (8 to 9.5 mm) apart were used. Dot grids close to these dimensions will work for any of the projects, as will a pleater machine. A pleater machine makes pleats that are 1/8″ (3 mm) in depth and rows that are spaced 3/8″ (9.5 mm) apart. Eight rows of pleater gathers will measure 1/4″ (6 mm) wider than dot gathers, but will not seriously affect the measurements of the projects in this book. Avoid very tiny and very large dot transfers that are suitable for very sheer or heavy fabrics, respectively.

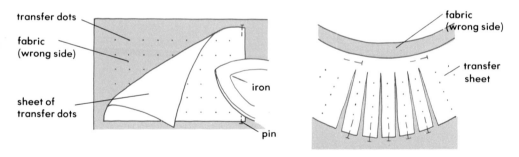

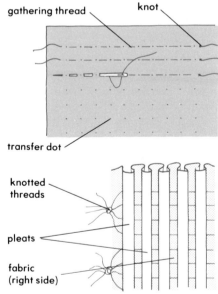

Transfer dots. To transfer the dots to fabric, lay the fabric, wrong side up, on an ironing board. Place a sheet of dots, ink side down, on the area of the fabric to be smocked. Heat an iron to medium, and make a test on a scrap of the fabric. Pin the dots and fabric to the ironing board, as shown. Press the iron on a section of the dots for ten seconds. Lift the iron, and check to see if the dots have been transferred to the cloth. If not, press them longer.

Lift the iron each time you move it; do not rub the iron back and forth, or the dots will smudge. Continue pressing in a similar fashion until all the dots have been transferred. Once some of the dots have been pressed, they will cling to the fabric, helping to hold the transfer sheet in place; you may then remove the pins to finish pressing.

Marking dots on a curved area. Slash between the rows of dots on the grid up to the top row. Align the top edge of the grid with the curved edge of the fabric, such as along a neckline, then pin the dots in place and transfer them as usual.

Sew the rows of dots with gathering stitches and pull the gathering threads until the finished width measures the amount indicated in your instructions.

Gathering the fabric. To gather the fabric, thread a needle with enough heavy-duty cotton sewing thread to complete a row of stitching across the entire width of the fabric. Knot one end of the thread. Pick up each dot across the row with a 1/16″-long (1.5-mm) stitch. By aligning the stitches from row to row in this fashion, the resulting even gathers will provide a uniform foundation for the

smocking. The rows of gathering stitches also help to serve as a guide for the smocking pattern, although they will be pulled out after the smocking is completed.

When all the rows of dots have been stitched, pull up the gathering threads so the fabric is 1″ (2.5 cm) narrower than the desired finished width of the smocking. Tie the gathering threads in groups of four or less, as shown.

Learning the stitches

A sampler. The best way to learn smocking is to make a small sampler using the basic stitches. Cut a piece of white broadcloth that measures 10″ × 20″ (25.4 × 50.8 cm). Using a sheet of transfer dots or a pleater, make 18 rows of at least 50 pleats (dots) each. Each row is identified in the accompanying illustrations with letters of the alphabet, starting from the top down. Pleats are numbered from left to right. Count the pleats in your sampler. You must have an even number to find the center. If you have an uneven number, simply omit the last pleat when counting and stitching. The center of the sampler should fall in the "valley" between the two center pleats. Mark the center with a vertical line of basting.

Thread. Cut a 20″ (50.8-cm) strand of six-strand embroidery floss. Three or four strands are usually used for smocking, depending on personal preference. Four strands give a slightly richer look, but try both on your sampler to see which you prefer. Separate the strands, and thread them through a crewel needle with an eye large enough to accommodate them. Knot one end of the strands securely.

Smocking rules

1. Smocking is always worked from left to right. The needle moves from right to left and is held parallel to the gathering row. Each stitch picks up one new pleat to the right.

2. The placement of the thread above (up) or below (down) the needle governs the appearance of a stitch.

3. Secure the thread with a figure-eight knot at the beginning of each row, and fasten the thread with a snail knot at the end of each row of smocking. Then trim off the thread ends.

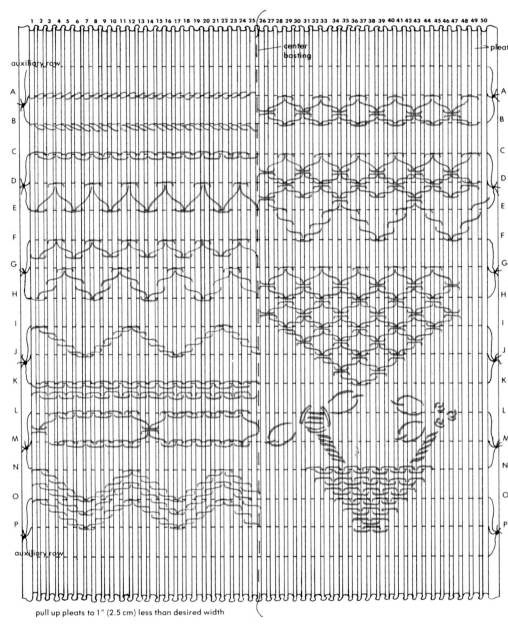

pull up pleats to 1″ (2.5 cm) less than desired width

Figure-eight knot. Make a loop in the end of the thread as shown. Wrap the free end around the thread and back down through the loop. Pull tight. Cut off the free end close to the knot.

Snail knot. This knot is used to tie all threads securely in smocking. Make a backstitch loop of thread in the fabric, as shown. Weave the needle through the loop and leave it loose to form a second loop. Weave the needle back through the second loop and pull it tight. Cut the thread end close to the knot. Work the sampler in two parts: the left side first, up to the center, and then the right side.

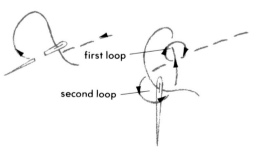

Basic Stitches
Left side

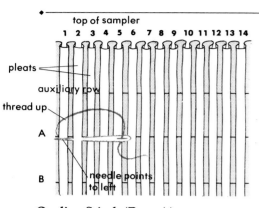

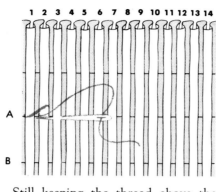

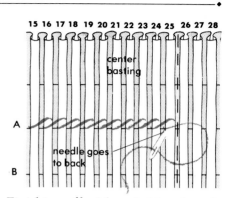

Outline Stitch (Row A)

Bring the needle up from the wrong side to the left of Pleat 1, just above the gathering thread in Row A.

Holding it parallel to the gathering thread, insert the needle through the top of Pleat 2 from right to left, keeping the thread *above* it. Pull the stitch up firmly, but not too tight.

Still keeping the thread above the needle and the needle parallel to the gathering threads, insert the needle through the top of Pleat 3, from right to left. Continue working toward the center of the sampler, picking up one new pleat at a time with each stitch, until you have stitched 25 pleats.

Finishing off. After stitching through the top of Pleat 25, the thread will be between Pleats 24 and 25. Push the needle to the back of the fabric, next to where the thread just came out on the front. Turn the work over. End off with a snail knot on the pleat where the thread comes out. (See page 184 for the snail knot.)

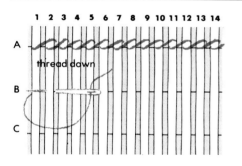

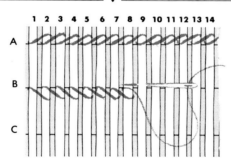

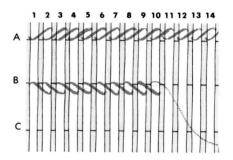

Stem stitch (Row B)

Bring the needle up from the wrong side of the fabric to the left of Pleat 1, just above gathering Row B. Keeping the thread *below* the needle, insert the needle through the top of Pleat 2, from right to

left, so it emerges between Pleats 1 and 2.

Continue working across the row, from pleat to pleat, keeping the thread below the needle at all times. Stitch Pleat 25 and end off the thread with a snail knot as in Row A.

Note: See how the position of the thread above or below the needle when making a stitch affects the final appearance of the stitch.

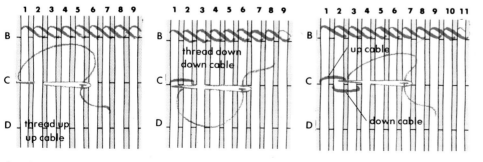

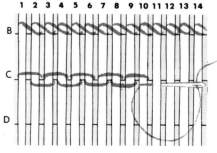

Cable stitch (Row C)

Stitch 1: Bring the needle up to the left of Pleat 1 on Row C. With the thread *above* the needle, pick up Pleat 2. This is called an "up" cable.

Stitch 2: With the thread *below* the needle, pick up Pleat 3. This is called a "down" cable.

Stitch 3: Pick up Pleat 4, with an up cable.

Stitch 4: Pick up Pleat 5, with a down cable.

Continue across the row to Pleat 25, alternating up and down cables.

185

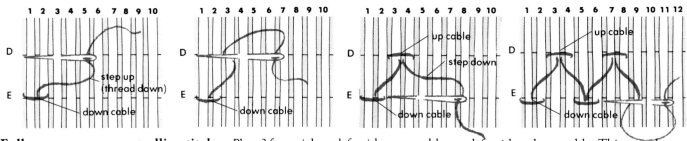

Full-space wave, or trellis stitch (Rows D and E)

Stitch 1: Bring the needle up to the left of Pleat 1 just above Row E. Work a down cable through Pleat 2, bringing the thread up between Pleats 1 and 2.

Stitch 2: Move the needle up to Row D, keeping it parallel to the row, with the thread below the needle, and pick up

Pleat 3 from right to left with an up cable. This completes an up wave.

Stitch 3: Work another up cable through Pleat 4 at the same level (Row D).

Stitch 4: Move the needle back down to Row E, keeping the thread above the needle, and pick up Pleat 5 from right to

left with a down cable. This completes a down wave.

Repeat the sequence from Stitch 1 through Stitch 4 across the sampler through Pleat 25, keeping in mind that *the thread is down when waving up, and up when waving down.*

Baby wave (Rows F and G)

This stitch is exactly the same as a full-space wave, but only covers half a space.

Stitch 1: Bring the needle up to the left of Pleat 1, midway between Rows F and G. Make a down cable through Pleat 2.

Stitch 2: Wave up through Pleat 3 on Row F, keeping the thread down.

Stitch 3: Stitch an up cable through Pleat 4 on Row F.

Stitch 4: Wave down to Pleat 5, at the starting level (midway between Rows F and G), keeping the thread up.

Repeat the sequence from Stitch 1 through Stitch 4 across the sampler through Pleat 25.

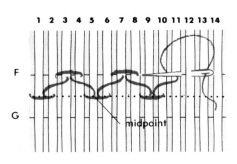

Two-step wave (Rows G and H)

Stitch 1: Bring the needle up to the left of Pleat 1 on Row H. Make a down cable through Pleat 2 on Row H.

Stitch 2: Keeping the thread down, wave halfway up to Row G through Pleat 3.

Stitch 3: Thread down, wave the rest of the way up to Row G through Pleat 4.

Stitch 4: Thread up, make an up cable through Pleat 5 on Row G.

Stitch 5: Thread up, wave halfway down to Row H through Pleat 6.

Stitch 6: Thread up, wave the rest of the way down to Row H through Pleat 7.

Repeat the two-step wave sequence across the sampler through Pleat 25.

Note: The up cables at the top and down cables at the bottom are not counted as part of the wave. *A two-step wave means two wave stitches between the top and bottom cables.*

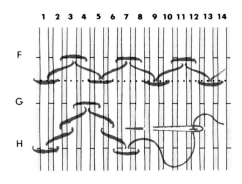

Four-step wave or quarter wave (Rows I and J)

Stitch 1: Bring the needle up to the left of Pleat 1 on Row I. Keeping the thread up, work an up cable through Pleat 2.

Stitch 2: Keeping the thread up, wave one-quarter of the way down to Row J through Pleat 3.

Stitch 3: Wave one-half of the way down to Row J through Pleat 4.

Stitch 4: Wave three-quarters of the way down to Row J through Pleat 5.

Stitch 5: Wave the rest of the way down to Row J through Pleat 6.

Stitch 6: With the thread below the needle, work a down cable through Pleat 7.

Keeping the thread below the needle, wave back up to Row I in four similar steps. Continue the wave pattern to Pleat 25.

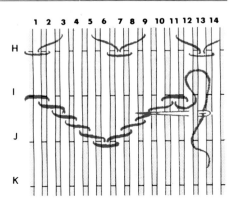

Combination stitches

Combination stitches require two or more rows of smocking to complete a pattern.

Double cable (Row K)

Row 1: Bring the needle up to the left of Pleat 1, just above Row K, and, keeping the thread down, work a down cable through Pleat 2.

With the thread above the needle, work an up cable through Pleat 3. Continue alternating down and up cables just above Row K through Pleat 25.

Row 2: Make a second row of cables just below the first row; start with an up cable, so the up cables in the second row will be back to back with down cables in the row above.

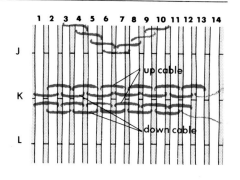

Cable link (Rows L and M)

Row 1: Beginning halfway between Rows L and M, bring the thread up to the left of Pleat 1. Keeping the thread below the needle, work a down cable through Pleat 2. Still keeping the thread below the needle, wave up to Row L through Pleat 3. Work 9 cables across Row L, starting and ending with up cables. With the thread above the needle, wave down halfway to Row M, through Pleat 13.

With the thread below the needle, make a down cable through Pleat 14. Continue this pattern of waves and cables to Pleat 25.

Row 2: Bring the needle up to the left of Pleat 1, just below the beginning of the first cable in the row above. With the thread above the needle, work an up cable through Pleat 2 back to back with the first down cable in the row above. Keeping the thread above the needle, wave down to Row M through Pleat 3. Work 9 cables across Row M, starting and ending with down cables.

With the thread below the needle, wave up halfway to Row L through Pleat 13. With the thread above the needle, work an up cable through Pleat 14 back to back with the down cable in the row

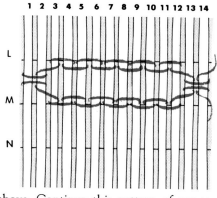
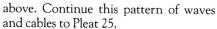

above. Continue this pattern of waves and cables to Pleat 25.

Chevron or "echo" outline stitch (Rows N through P)

Row 1: Bring the needle up to the left of Pleat 1 on Row N and work an up cable through Pleat 2. Work quarter waves between Rows N and O to Pleat 25.

Row 2: Starting with an up cable midway between Rows N and O, work

an identical row of quarter waves a half space below the first row.

Row 3: Work a third row of quarter waves starting at Row O. This stitch looks particularly beautiful with darker and lighter shades of one color. (See the pink and white dress on page 118 and the smocked pillow sham on page 40.)

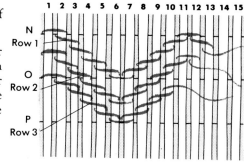

Right side of sampler: start all rows to the left of Pleat 26

Baby diamonds (Rows A and B)

Row 1: Starting halfway between Rows A and B, work a row of baby waves up to Row A across the sampler to Pleat 50. Make sure to start with a down cable.

Row 2: Starting halfway between Rows A and B, make an up cable back to back with the down cable in the row above. Then work a row of baby waves down to Row B across the sampler to Pleat 50.

Note: Two rows of waves in opposite directions form diamonds; diamonds can be made from any type of wave.

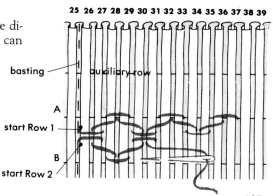

187

Diamonds and hearts (Rows C through F)

Row 1: Work a row of baby waves across the sampler between Rows C and D, starting halfway between the rows and waving up to Row C.

Row 2: Starting halfway between Rows C and D, work a row of baby waves down to Row D, starting with an up cable back to back with the first cable in the row above.

Row 3 (shaded): Starting halfway between Rows D and E, repeat the first row of baby waves to form a second row of baby diamonds.

Row 4: Make hearts by starting with a back-to-back cable, as if to work another row of diamonds. Wave down 3 half steps to Row F. Stitch a down cable, then wave 3 half steps back up to the starting level, completing one heart. Repeat the three-step wave pattern across the sampler to complete the row of hearts.

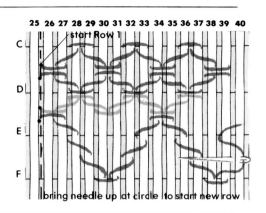

Geometrics

Interlocking diamonds (Rows G through I)

Row 1: Start with a down cable halfway between Rows G and H, and wave up to Row G. Continue making baby waves until you have 5 up cables on Row G. Wave down and end the row with a down cable.

Row 2 (shaded): Start the second row with an up cable back to back with the first down cable in the row above, and wave down to Row H. Complete 5 down cables to make the first row of 5 diamonds.

Rows 3 and 4: Repeat Rows 1 and 2 between Rows H and I to make 3 rows of interlocking diamonds.

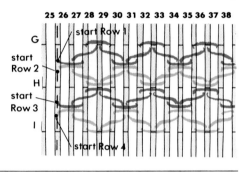

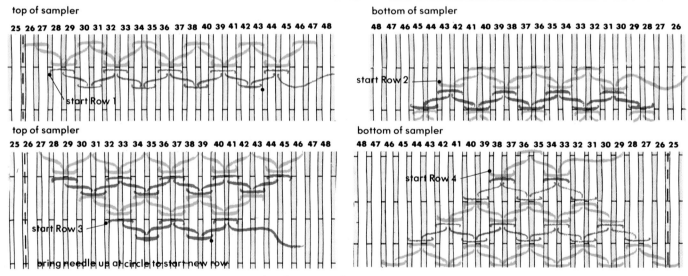

Diamond points (Rows I through K)

Diamond points are generally worked below interlocking diamonds.

Row 1: Start the first row with an up cable back to back with the first down cable in the preceding row of stitches (the bottom of the diamonds on Row I). Complete 4 diamonds by working a row of baby waves down along Row I. End with an up cable back to back with the last down cable in the preceding row. Push the needle to the back of the sampler as if to knot the thread, and rotate the sampler 180 degrees. After turning the

sampler, Row 2 will be worked above Row 1.

Row 2 (shaded): Bring the needle up to the left of Pleat 43, and work a down cable back to back with the first cable that now makes the top of a diamond in the preceding row. Wave up and continue making baby waves until 3 complete diamonds are formed. Push needle to the back of the fabric.

Row 3: Turn the sampler 180 degrees so the top is up again. Work an up cable back to back with the first down cable in the row above. Make a baby wave down

and complete 2 diamonds with 3 more complete baby waves. Push the needle to the back of the fabric.

Row 4: Turn the work again. Complete the last diamond with 2 complete baby waves. Push the needle to the back of the fabric and knot the thread.

Turned patterns. When the overall pattern of a smocking design has a graduated shape, such as Diamond Points, it is easiest to turn the work and continue stitching another row from left to right rather than to cut the thread to begin each new row of smocking.

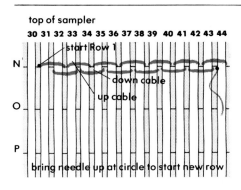

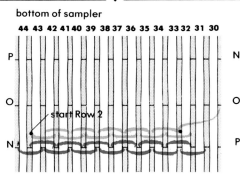

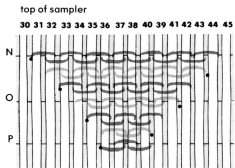

Stacked cables (Rows N through P)

This stitch is the basis of all "picture" smocking, and it is used to work the vase in the smocked pillow sham, page 40.

Row 1: Starting and ending with an up cable, work 13 cables on Row N; begin by bringing the needle to the left of Pleat 31. Push the needle to the back of the fabric, and turn the work around 180 degrees.

Row 2: (shaded): After turning the sampler, Row 2 will be worked above Row 1. Bring the needle up to the left of

Pleat 43 (marked by a circle in the drawing). Make a down cable back to back with the second cable of Row 1. Work 11 cables, ending with a down cable back to back with the next to last cable of the preceding row. Push the needle to the back of the fabric, and turn the work 180 degrees so that the top is up.

Row 3: Start with an up cable back to back with the second cable of the preceding row. Work 9 cables, ending with

an up cable back to back with the next to last cable of the preceding row.

Rows 4 through 6: Continue turning the work and decreasing 2 cables in each row. The odd rows are worked right side up and start with up cables. Even rows are worked upside down and start with down cables.

Row 7: The seventh row, which comes to a point with the center cable, is the last row, and it is worked with 3 cables.

Flowers (Rows L through N, in the stacked-cable vases)

Leaves. Make leaves of lazy daisy stitches by bringing the needle up on the right of the desired pleat. Loop the thread over the tops of the three pleats to the left. Holding the thread down with your thumb, insert the needle into the right side of the starting pleat and bring it out through the top of the second pleat to the left. Push the needle to the back of the fabric to the left of this last pleat and either knot the thread or continue making more leaves in a similar fashion.

Small flowers. French knots make perfect small blossoms at the ends of

leaves. To make French knots on smocking, bring the needle up in the peak of the desired pleat. Wrap the thread counterclockwise three times around the needle, and push the needle back through the fabric next to where it first came out.

Large flowers. Make large blossoms by working 3 up cables one above the other over the same 2 pleats. Wrap the cables with a triangle of down cables in a contrasting color. Stitch over the triangle twice for greater emphasis.

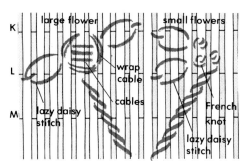

Stems. Attach the flowers, blossoms, and leaves to the vase with tiny outline or stem stitches.

The finishing touches for smocking

When the smocking is completed, remove the gathering threads. Pin the smocked piece to an ironing board, as shown, and steam the pleats with an iron to set them, but do not rest the iron on the smocking, or you will crush it. Hold the iron one or two inches above the work and let the steam set the pleats. Smocking expands slightly when blocked.

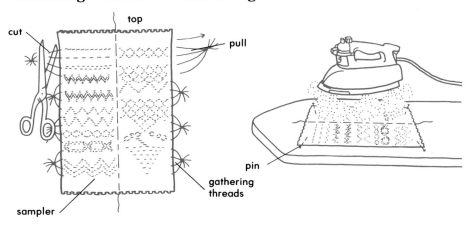

Appendix

Provisions for growth

Measurements in the clothing industry will vary, but, in general, children's sizes are based on an average difference of 2″ to 4″ (5 to 10.2 cm) in height between sizes and a 1″ (2.5-cm) difference in chest or bust measurement. Grading any garment through an entire size range is a precise and sometimes mystical art that is not easily mastered, but in some basic styles a few simple adjustments incorporated into the cutting can eke an additional year out of the clothing.

Vertical growth. The obvious place to allow for a child's growth in height is the **skirt hems.** Plan to increase the hem allowance of a garment to a total of 4″ to 6″ (10.2 to 15.2 cm), depending on its style and the size of the child. Let the hem down exactly halfway the second year and rehem it to the original fold line. The fold will blend in with the stitches, the top of the hem will be barely noticeable, and the depth of the hem will still be attractive. Also, the extra-wide hem the first year is downright luxurious.

Seams of yokes and high-waisted garments. An additional ½″ (13 mm) can be gained above the waist in an outfit that has a high waist or underarm yoke seam. Cut the original bodice or un-

derarm yoke piece with a ⅞″ (22-mm) seam allowance, making sure the back matches the front. A mid-armhole yoke cannot be enlarged without distorting the armhole beyond redemption. Leave the seam allowance on the skirt, which will probably be gathered or smocked, as it is. Seam the skirt to the bodice or yoke along the original seamline, using about 10 stitches to the inch (2.5 cm), so the stitching will be easy to remove later. When the outfit becomes skimpy, open the seam and resew it, leaving only a ⅜″ (9.5-mm) seam allowance on the yoke or bodice section.

Blouse, pants, and long-sleeve hem allowances. Add as much length as you can, although a total hem allowance of more than 2″ (5 cm) will probably distort the shape of the pattern. Rehem the garment later to the original fold line, as for a skirt hem. Don't forget to make corresponding adjustments on all lining pieces if the garment is lined.

Buttons. Add an extra 1″ (2.5 cm) to the length of shoulder straps, and place buttons so they can be moved along the strap as the child grows. Reposition buttons on a blouse to change the waistline for button-on pants and skirt styles.

Horizontal growth. When sewing children's clothes, it is advantageous and even preferable to sew the side and underarm seams in one continuous line of stitching. If you allow extra seam allowances, you may easily provide for horizontal growth as well, particularly in the armhole area. Cut the side seams of skirts, bodices, or yokes and the underarm seams of sleeves and cuffs or bands with ⅞″ (22-mm) seam allowances. Set the stitch length for approximately 10 stitches to the inch (2.5 cm) and sew the seam along the original seam lines. Open the seam when the garment becomes tight for the child, and restitch it with ½″ (13-mm) seam allowances. You will gain ⅜″ (9.5 mm) on the left back, the left front, the right back, and the right front for a total of 1½″ (3.8 cm), or ¾″ (19 mm) on each side. If you are afraid that the bottom of the sleeve will be too big, taper the line of stitching toward the original seam line on the sleeve. A large French seam is usually the best way to finish the seam. If extra fabric bunches up under the arm, release as many stitches as necessary in the underarm portion of the sleeve seam allowance to ease the pull.

Spot removal

The sooner you get to a spot, the better your chances of removing it. No matter what method you choose for removing a spot, saturate a cotton swab with your cleaning agent and dab a little in a small inconspicuous area before plunging ahead. If you decide to proceed, roll up a terrycloth towel and spread the soiled fabric over it. Then soak a terry washcloth or cotton swab with your cleaning agent, and apply it to the spot with light one-way strokes in the direction of the fabric weave.

Always try plain water or club soda first. Then graduate very slowly to more

heroic measures, such as adding detergent and/or bleach to the water, making pastes of detergent, using stronger proportions of bleach, experimenting with dishwasher detergent, or combining all of the above. Proceed with caution lest you find yourself with a hole or a bleached ring where the spot used to be. Old-fashioned methods include stretching the fabric over a bowl and pouring boiling water through the spot. You may also try soaking the spot with lemon juice before pouring the boiling water through it.

Commercial cleaners are available in many stores, and you may have a favorite, which you should use by all means. Ever Blum cleaning fluid is widely used in the garment industry and is available at notion stores. Gartsides Iron Rust remover is an old-fashioned favorite, sold in some drugstores.

Remember, spots always appear darker when wet. If you are battling with a particularly stubborn spot, let it dry from time to time to see if it doesn't just fade from notice. Sometimes you will simply have to give up and embroider a flower or a butterfly over a stain.

Freshening an heirloom. When the next generation comes along, your heirloom may look yellowed and timeworn no matter how carefully you have packed it away. To restore a fresh appearance to clothing that has been stored, first make sure that the garment is washable. Then prepare the following brew: 1 cup Cascade dishwasher detergent, 1 cup Tide, 1 cup liquid Chlorox bleach. Fill your washing machine with enough cool water for a medium load, add the mixture, and agitate until the detergents have dissolved. Add the clothes and agitate just as long as is necessary to thoroughly moisten them. Then let them soak overnight. In the morning, finish the cycle and run through one more complete cycle with clear water.

A white collar on a non-colorfast dress can be soaked by simply moistening it with the diluted mixture and letting it sit overnight. Mix a teaspoon of each ingredient with a pint of water. But be sure to *test it first!*

Storage. Light, dampness, abrasion, soil, and critters that chew are all enemies of heirlooms. Wash and *thoroughly* dry or dry-clean any fabric article before it is stored. Store clothes flat in a dark place that has enough ventilation to keep the atmosphere dry. Use plenty of tissue paper to prevent sharp creases in the fabric; creases may weaken the fabric or become discolored. Unless a hanger is contoured and padded, hanging may distort seams and put undue strain on the shoulders of a garment. Cedar chests, mothballs, and old-fashioned camphor squares help control pests, but, to prevent discoloration, *never* let camphor or moth balls touch the fabric.

—————————— **Mail-order sources for supplies** ——————————

If you have difficulty finding supplies in your locality, the following mail-order sources carry many of the fabrics, patterns, trims, and threads mentioned in the book.

Laura Ashley Mail-order Department
714 Madison Avenue
New York, New York 10021

G Street Fabric Store
805 G Street, N.W.
Washington, D.C. 20001

Ruffles and Flourishes
2776 South Randolph
Arlington, Virginia 22206

Grace Knott Smocking Supplies
86 Larkfield Drive
Don Mills, Ontario M3B2H1

Thimbleweed
2975 College Avenue
Berkeley, California

The World in Stitches
82 South Street
Milford, New Hampshire 03055

For further information about smocking, contact the Smocking Arts Guild of America, Box 75, Knoxville, Tennessee 37919.

Index